P9-DUC-968

DATE DUE

NOV 2 7	DEC 9		
NOV 30 77	MAR 2 '94		
DEC 14 77	OCT 26		
MAR 1 4	SEP 25 '95		
NOV 8			
FEB 14 78			
NOV 17			
NOV 10			
OCT 12			
OCT 12			
MAR 26			
MAR 2			
JUN 1 5 '90			

ECONOMICS OF RACISM U.S.A.

ECONOMICS

119

OF RACISM U.S.A.

Roots of Black Inequality

Victor Perlo

INTERNATIONAL PUBLISHERS New York

Charts and Drawings by Peggy Lipschutz

Printed in the United States of America 209

Library of Congress Cataloging in Publication Data

Perlo, Victor
  Economics of racism U. S. A.

  Includes bibliographical references and index.
  1. Negroes—Economic conditions.   2. Negroes—Employment.
  3. United States—Race question.   I. Title.
E185.8.P418   331.6'3'96073   75-9911
ISBN 0-7178-0418-6
ISBN 7178-0419-4 pbk.

Contents

Charts

Tables

Foreword

This book by Victor Perlo is a most penetrating study of racism in the realm of economics, a key question for the whole course of development of our country in this historic period.

This study responds to the need of achieving a higher level of class consciousness within the labor movement. Such consciousness must lead to a strengthened relationship of white working people with Black people and other oppressed minorities.

The book goes to press at a period of deepening crises, economic and political, afflicting the world of capitalism. So far, big business and the government it controls have been able to place the full burden of these crises on the working people. Living standards are declining as never since the great crash of the 1930s. Inflation and unemployment are both striking blows not felt before by most of this generation.

These blows are hitting Black people with doubled and tripled force. The "first to be fired" rule is being applied without restraint, decimating the employed Black labor force in major industries. Inflation is even more severe for the poor, to which most of the Black population are restricted. Millions of the poor, especially Blacks, are suffering severely in this crisis, from hunger and cold, from loss of means of transportation and utilities, and even of a roof over their heads.

Failures are weeding out the weaker businesses, and with tenfold frequency the all-weak ranks of Black business. The panacea of Black capitalism lies in ruins as bankers, power companies, suppliers, show no mercy to the struggling minority enterprises.

Economic and political events interact. There is an almost desperate

xi

atmosphere as the rulers of the country try to solve their difficulties at the expense of other countries, and, above all, at the expense of the people of the United States. The appeal of the corporate rich to the public to accept greater sacrifices is accompanied by a sharp increase in the use of racism as a weapon of divide and rule.

The Supreme Court, for example, has handed down racist decisions wiping out an important part of the legal-political gains of the past two decades. The substitute-President Gerald Ford has outdone Richard Nixon in overt encouragement to racism. The events in Boston and the increasing bombings of Black homes are most serious signs.

In this critical environment the forces of reaction are advancing new theories to try to justify racist discrimination, while would-be liberators are advocating new diversions from the necessary course of struggle.

The author presents in all its dimensions the realities of economic discrimination against Black people. He demolishes all the main lines by which racist reaction strives to justify it, deny it, or belittle it.

He shows the futility of all programs which aim at separating Black and white workers. On the one hand, says Perlo, Black liberation cannot be won without accomplishing at the same time major victories for the entire working class, white and Black. On the other hand, no prior work has shown so conclusively the cost to white workers, and the profits to monopoly capital, of discrimination against Blacks. And none has proven so forcefully the responsibility of white working people, and their positive stake in participating in the struggle for Black equality.

The volume closely examines the records and policies of capital, of labor unions, and of government in relation to discrimination. The fundamental fact comes through, remorselessly, that discrimination and gross inequality are rooted in capitalism, in state-monopoly capitalism in its period of decay. The point is demonstrated that socialism is the highroad to full national and racial equality, by the very nature of the system, and as realized in practice in the lands where peoples' power has been won and socialism built.

A final chapter explains in detail what is required for equality, and spells out the forces which must unite in order to win it.

The balance of power in the world is more and more rapidly shifting in favor of the working people, against their exploiters and dividers. Great victories are being won on all continents, with a profound influence in our own land.

An important requirement for victories here is the renovation and democratization of the trade union movement. The present major leaders, men like George Meany, I.W. Abel, and Albert Shanker, are pro-capitalist, pro-militarist, and racist. However, newer more progressive forces are gaining ground, with Black workers playing an outstanding part in the process.

This book will help in the struggle to redirect policies in the labor movement, through the building of a mass rank and file center in every shop, in every union. And this must and will have in its program, second to none in importance, the fight to completely eliminate racism from the American industrial scene, achieving factual economic equality as well as statute-book proclamation of the right to equality.

Equally important is the building of an anti-monopoly political formation that can conduct and win a serious struggle for effective people's power. The role of Blacks in such a formation must be very large, as must be the struggle for Black equality in its program.

The Economics of Racism is an excellent addition to Perlo's past works such as *American Imperialism. Empire of High Finance, Militarism and Industry, the Negro in Southern Agriculture,* and *The Unstable Economy.*

It helps light the way to the struggle here and now, to overcome all of the ignorance, and erroneous conceptions, which hold back the forces of anti-monopoly unity. It appeals to all persons of good will, who may differ on other questions, but can agree on their common interest in struggling for the real equality of rights of all persons, regardless of their race or color or nationality.

And in so doing, I am convinced, it moves us closer to the ending of all exploitation of man by man, of all national and racial oppression, towards the abolition of monopoly capitalism and the achievement of socialism.

Henry Winston
National Chairman, Communist Party U.S.A.

ECONOMICS OF RACISM U.S.A.

1. Introduction

The Civil Rights Movement, involving millions of Black people and their white supporters, reached its climax during the mid-1960s. Through laws passed by Congress and the retreat of racist ruling cliques in southern states, some essential goals of that movement were partly won. These were the right to enter public places and to purchase all services offered to the general public without being segregated or otherwise discriminated against; the right to vote and to be elected to office; security from arbitrary arrest, imprisonment, police brutality and killings.

Of course these victories were and remain far from complete. Many eating places evaded the law by establishing themselves as "whites only" private clubs. School desegregation was only fractionally accomplished, and in many northern cities has increased. Gerrymandering and other tricks are used to reduce the effectiveness of Black people's votes. There are still many cities, suburbs, sections of towns, where Blacks are not permitted to live. Police brutality and killings of Blacks continue on a serious scale.

An important gain was the invalidation of all overtly segregationist and discriminatory laws, which existed in many states and cities, and the formal illegalization of segregation and discrimination in all major areas of life.

Yet the most frequent criticism by Blacks of what has been accomplished is expressed in this bitter comment:

"Yes, we've won the right to sit at variety store lunch counters."

The vast majority of Black people cannot afford to exercise most of their civil rights. They cannot afford to eat at good restaurants, sleep at good hotels, reside in choice residential areas, conduct modern political campaigns.

The Black people still lack basic economic rights. The most important of these are essential equality in access to employment at all levels, sufficient income to afford a "normal," "average" U.S. standard of living. Related rights are equality of educational opportunity, equality of access to all housing anywhere, equality of access to health services. These contribute to a person's actual economic status in important ways.

Many battles are still being waged on the traditional civil rights fronts—to consolidate gains, to extend their scope, to defeat the continuous efforts of racists to nibble away at them—to eliminate the many de facto violations of Black people's civil rights.

But the main efforts of activist movements, of the NAACP and other Black people's organizations, have shifted to economic issues. Dr. Martin Luther King, Jr., and the Southern Christian Leadership Conference, perhaps the most successful to date of all organizations in mobilizing vast numbers of people in the civil rights struggle, by 1967 turned their main attention to the struggle for economic rights. It was while participating in a campaign of Black sanitation workers for decent wages that Dr. King was assassinated in Memphis.

The current priority of economic struggles is quite logical. *Economic equality is a necessary condition for furthering and safeguarding the gains of the Civil Rights movement, for making real the formal political and social equality now inscribed in law.*

Economic struggles of Black people have included attempts by workers in the lowest wage occupations to form unions and win decent conditions. In industries with established unions Black workers have formed their own caucuses, or have actively participated in progressive rank and file groups seeking to win a fairer deal for Black workers. Much effort has gone into waging court cases, arranging hearings and presenting briefs to government agencies and local "Human Rights Commissions" seeking legal redress of discriminatory employment and wage patterns. Some prominent personalities have focused on "Black capitalism" campaigns—attempts to promote Black-owned business enterprises and to win for Blacks places in the executive suites of large corporations. There have been scattered efforts to reestablish a place for Blacks on the land through cooperatives.

However, the economic struggles of Black people have not yet attained the degree of mass participation, nor the extent of centralized leadership and direction, that was achieved during the earlier civil rights phase. Moreover, again in contrast to the earlier phase, there is relatively less participation by white liberals, progressive student youth, white trade unionists.

These economic struggles are certain to grow. They are bound to become central to any new upsurge of activity involving large-scale public participation that aims to deal with the country's economic problems. Objective study of the reality of our economic life leads to that unavoidable conclusion. Forty years ago, Franklin D. Roosevelt, then President of the United States, referred to the South as our nation's number one economic problem. And so it was, largely because the Black population was then concentrated in the South, and their special oppression, economic and otherwise, was most extreme there. Now this oppression has been modified, but not ended. And it has spread geographically, and has to some extent become more uniform geographically in its severity.

Today we have to say that economic discrimination against Blacks is the nation's number one economic problem. No economic problem affecting the majority of the population can be solved or significantly eased unless the solution includes a vast improvement in the economic situation of Black people and substantial reduction of the discrimination against them.

This book aims to contribute to the factual and analytic basis for attempts to solve that number one problem, and to provide ammunition for the mass struggles that must become a major part of such attempts. It is, then, a partisan book. But, to the best of the author's ability, it portrays reality and strives to avoid distortions, one-sidedness, and exaggeration.

Factual data center on income, kinds of employment, wages, and unemployment. Attention is focused on *relative* conditions, that is, the comparative conditions of Blacks and whites, rather than on measures of conditions of Black people dealt with in isolation. There are some references to housing, health services and education, but without attempts to deal with these factors exhaustively. Extensive use is made of the exceptionally rich data of the 1970 Census of Population, together with subsequent annual Census surveys. Analysis relates to the situation in the present decade, and to trends since the end of World War II.

There are fundamental similarities in the economic and social situations of Blacks, Puerto Ricans, Chicanos, Native Americans, and Asian peoples, as well as some differences. Any real improvement in the situation of one of these groups will benefit these other groups that are subject to racist and national discrimination. To some extent the book compares conditions of these different groups. But the focus remains on the Black people, because they are the most numerous, because racist discrimination against them is most persistent and nationwide in scope, and yields the most billions of dollars in extra profits. And the focus remains on Blacks because their struggle for equality and for liberation from all forms of oppression and inequality has been and will continue to be a prime stimulant and guiding factor for all other struggles against discrimination, and because the outcome will be decisive for many other issues, including the struggles of other oppressed peoples.

There is an old saying that Black women are triply oppressed, as workers, as women, and as Blacks. In some ways this is more true than ever. The proportion of Black women who work has increased substantially, and their need compels them to take traditional "women's jobs" at very low pay, when white women are able to leave them for better opportunities. As the Black population has been concentrated in urban ghettoes, Black women have borne the brunt of the rot of capitalist society. Many have been left with the overwhelming burden of heading families, caring for their children, and working to feed them, all at the same time—or of subsisting on the humiliating welfare system without any way out in sight.

The book deals with the special economic problems of Black women, as the key to the unification of the modern movements of Black liberation and women's liberation.

The book examines the question of responsibility. Who causes and perpetuates discrimination? Who organizes resistance to ending it? Who profits from it?

Racism is a complex phenomenon, with a long history. Starting from that, apologists for the status quo tend to end up regarding racist discrimination as something inevitable and ineradicable, like "original sin." To the extent that they identify any culprits, they often place the main blame on the victims, on the alleged "shortcomings" of the Black people themselves. Usually, nowadays, this is done with some subtlety, by reference to the Blacks as "disadvantaged." But the crude form persists. Dr. William Shockley, a Nobel prize-winning physicist, is the latest of a long line of men who abused their scientific reputation to spread the fascist lie of "inferior races." He may be a qualified physicist, but he is no more qualified in genetics than the architect Alfred Rosenberg, the ideologist of Hitler's race theories.

True, along with this there is often the concession that whites are partly to blame, but mainly the white workers, who are pictured as hopelessly prejudiced, while aspirations of sincere brotherhood are attributed to the rich. The contention of this book is that it is precisely the millionaires, those in positions of control over the corporate economy, who inspire and deliberately perpetuate inequality, and especially economic discrimination. The motive is clear—billions of dollars in profits. It is in accord with the traditional imperial doctrine of divide and rule.

Yes, millions of white working people are infected with racist prejudices to varying degrees. But these prejudices are not the cause of discrimination. They derive from discrimination, and from the racist propaganda fostered by those who profit from discrimination. Popular prejudices can be overcome, and the majority of the white working people can be enlisted to participate in the mutually advantageous effort to end all racial and national discrimination.

There are two distorted views of the actual situation concerning economic inequality. There is the apologetic view that everything is rapidly becoming all right, that discrimination will soon be a thing of the past. Thus Tilford Gaines, vice president and chief economist of the Manufacturers Hanover Trust Co.:

"The U.S. has made more rapid progress toward equality of opportunity for all people in the past two decades than during any similar period in its history. Acceptance of the justice and logic of equality of opportunity is now almost universal . . ."[1]

Then there is the defeatist view that nothing gets any better, so what's the use of struggling. The Reverend Theodore M. Hesburgh, president of Notre Dame, taking note of recent setbacks to the cause of equality, writes:

"Even good people are losing heart . . . the more pessimistic say that we face a second abandonment of a promising Reconstruction Period, a new rebirth of apartheid in America."[2]

Hesburgh, it should be added, does not share this view, but stresses the importance of a rededication of the United States to the cause of equality of opportunity. Both the Pollyanna optimists and the unrelieved pessimists end up in the same place, fostering passivity and capitulation to racism.

This book attempts to demonstrate that there have been gains, and that these gains have been connected with mass struggles against discrimination. On the other hand, these gains have been very limited, and reactionary forces are constantly striving to chip away at them.

It is important to define our goals. The phrase "equality of opportunity" used by Reverend Hesburgh and many others, is not enough. It can conceal situations where Blacks, in a formal sense, have "equality of opportunity" to get better jobs and incomes, but never get them in reality. It is like the traditional capitalist slogan "laissez faire," which is a mockery in an epoch of monopoly.

The goal is *equality* in practice. This requires more than a formal equality of opportunity, as in a race where the runners compete from a single starting line at the firing of a gun. It requires special measures to overcome the inequality built into the existing structure, to systematically and deliberately raise the relative economic status of masses of Black people to a level of equality within a short period of time.

The present period is of crucial importance in the struggle for equality, because of the beginnings of recognition of this requirement. In the two years since passage of the Fair Employment Act of 1972, a new set of principles has been getting increasing recognition in court decisions, in agreements between groups and agencies striving for equality, and by private and governmental employers.

These principles include the responsibility of employers for paying monetary compensation on account of losses sustained by Black workers because of past de facto discrimination, for accelerated promotion of Blacks previously held back, and for priority employment of Blacks in better positions. Underlying these approaches are the general principles that major differences in job patterns to the disadvantage of Blacks are convincing evidence of discrimination, and that Blacks are entitled to employment at all levels of pay and skill in approximate proportion to their numbers in the population.

Clearly, such principles are based on the right of Blacks to effective equality, and not mere "equality of opportunity."

Most impressive are the decisions which require that a substantial proportion of all new hires—often one-half or one-third of the total —must be Blacks until Blacks comprise specified percentages of total employees in given occupations.

If these decisions are carried out, if they are generalized, and if they are not reversed by Supreme Court edict or some racist action by Congress and the president, they can lead to a most important and historic breakthrough in the economic status of Black people. However, these are big ifs. Certainly there will be those who will spread wide the word that the promise is already reality. But there have been too many false promises in the past for realistic people to believe this.

Such decisions, to date, directly affect a tiny fraction, probably fewer than one percent, of Black workers. Some of them have negative features, which partly wipe out the gains they decree. And there is no more certainty of enforcement than of past decisions in this area, which have generally been ignored.

Thus, the decisions provide not the solution, but a new and improved base on which the campaign for a solution can be accelerated. The prerequisite for the realization of these approaches is the building of a broad, powerful, labor-backed movement of Black and white people.

This caution is very necessary. The first fruits of the 1972 Act were widely reported throughout the following year, in a series of court orders and consent decrees, providing material recompense to Black workers and women workers for past discrimination, and positive measures to improve their status. Also, 1973 was a peak year in the business cycle, which usually leads to some slight diminution in the relative economic discrimination against Blacks. Frankly, I, and I assume other economists, expected official statistics to show such an improvement. Yet when the figures were published in mid-1974, they showed an unusually sharp *drop* in the ratio of Black to white family incomes for 1973. Other factors proved more powerful (Chapter 4).

What is the trouble? There is by now a comprehensive set of legal guarantees of equality in education, housing, employment. But the enforcement of these laws is in the hands of a social class that profits from inequality, and which throws up an infinite series of roadblocks against making the laws effective.

Already a specific pattern of maneuvers to minimize the impact of the 1972 law has been worked out and applied by the steel corporations, the Justice Department, and the right-wing leadership of the United Steelworkers of America (Chapter 12.)

Moreover, there is a close interconnection between various forms of discrimination. So long as Blacks are discriminated against and segregated in housing and education they will inevitably be discriminated against, at least in some degree, in economics. Housing discrimination is one of the most powerful levers of racial inequality in employment (Chapter 10). And trends in education have set the tone of race relations for decades.

"Landmarks," at ten-year intervals, mark the progress or regress in the struggle for equality since World War II.

The first two of these were expected to usher in a "new era" in race relations. The *Brown vs. Board of Education* decision of the Supreme Court in 1954 forbade segregated schools, and the Civil Rights and Voting Rights legislation of 1964 and 1965 provided for the elimination of virtually all legal discriminatory and segregationist measures. But in each case the gains, while real, have been limited, and largely neutralized in the overall sweep of events which determine the relative economic status of Blacks and whites.

In 1974 came the Supreme Court decision in *"Bradley vs. Milliken"* which, in the words of dissenting Justice Thurgood Marshall, was "a giant step backward . . . guaranteeing that Negro children in Detroit will receive the same separate and inherently unequal education in the future as they have been unconstitutionally afforded in the past."[3]

It is, in the words of Judge J. Skelly Wright of the United States Court of Appeals, a decision which means that "the national trend toward residential, political and educational apartheid will not only be greatly accelerated, it will also be rendered legitimate and virtually irreversible by force of law."[4] And not only that. The newly exposed 5 to 4 segregationist majority on the Supreme Court is an open invitation to all who wish to ignore *all* Civil Rights legislation, in employment, housing, or any other field, as well as education.

The "separate but equal" Supreme Court decision in *"Plessy v. Ferguson,"* handed down in 1896, remained essentially intact, determining the dominance of racism in all aspects of U.S. life for more than a half a century. It was changed under pressure of a burgeoning mass movement. The dwindling of that movement, the decline in the level of mass struggles, created the climate in which this new "separate but *unequal"* decision could be made.

But it will be reversed, and in much less than 50 years. The whole of U.S. history shows that progressive laws are effective only to the extent that they reflect the power of organized mass movements that stand behind them. And that applies fully to the cause of Black equality. The world today is such that the masses will not remain quiescent for 50 years, or for 5 years.

The Nixon majority in the Supreme Court is part of the foul remains of the political corpse of the most ultra-right president in modern history. The blow struck for racism by that majority must and will be overcome, by the combined actions of millions, Black and white.

Racism is a specific product of capitalism and a universal feature of capitalism. Racist and national oppression and discrimination will be completely eliminated only under socialism. But major gains can be made beginning right now, especially in a world environment in which the forces of socialism and national liberation are gaining the upper hand over those of capitalism and national oppression. What is necessary, however, in the hostile environment of capitalism, is massive, persistent, and organized struggle. And in the United States, an absolutely essential requirement is participation in that struggle by millions of whites, but not in the old patronizing style of "do-goodism," handing down benefits to the Blacks. Whites must realize that already, *in fact,* Black leadership has come to the fore in the struggle for Black liberation, and that Black leadership is essential for its success. And this must be a leadership rooted in the working class, which alone can pursue the cause of equality without inner contradictions such as those confronting Black capitalists, who are simultaneously victims of discrimination by white capitalists and exploiters of workers and profiting from low wages.

Gains are possible under capitalism, but not inevitable. Matters can go in the opposite direction, towards a fascist apartheid system. Powerful forces push in that direction. Those who support the racist regimes in South Africa are quite capable of imposing such a regime in the United States, with suitable variations for the specific conditions. Passivity opens the door to apartheid. And if unrestrained racism, all-out fascism, prevailed in such a powerful country as the United States, the danger of nuclear war, with its threat to the existence of humanity would become most acute indeed.

This book is offered to Black readers who, it is hoped, will find material of use in their liberation struggles.

It is offered at least as much to whites, who need the information even more, who are most likely to have illusions, who must be convinced that they have everything to lose by permitting or encouraging the apartheid trend, and much to gain, as well as a *duty,* to participate in the campaign for Black equality.

2. The Black People

The 1970 Census counted 22.7 million Black people, or 11.2% of the total population. The Black population has increased by about 400,000 per year since then, according to official estimates. There is always a serious undercounting of the Black population. Census statisticians estimated that 1.9 million Blacks were not counted in the 1970 Census, up from 1.6 million in 1960, but there is evidence that they were too cautious, and that the undercounting may have been 3 million or more.[1] Thus, as of mid-decade, 1975, there are about 28 million Black people, or one-eighth of the total population of the country.

Similarly, there will be about 16 million Chicanos, Puerto Ricans, Mexicans, and people of other Latin American and "Spanish" nationalties,* and close to 4 million Native Americans, Asians, Eskimos, Hawaiians, and what the Census Bureau calls "other races." That will make a total of 48 million people of minority races and nationalities, more than one-fifth of the total population.

---

* The Census Bureau uses different definitions of "Spanish heritage" people in different parts of the country, which has the effect of failing to count substantial numbers of them, especially in the Northeast. From regional data of the Census, it appears that actually 10,320,000 Chicanos, Puerto Ricans, and other people of Latin American or Spanish origin were counted in the 1970 Census, a million more than the total reported as "persons of Spanish heritage." According to Census estimates, the population "of Spanish Origin" increased 16.6% in the three years 1970-1973, indicating an annual rate of increase of 5.2%, and a five year increase of 29.0%. This would bring the 1975 population of the group up to 13.3 million.[2] In addition to the undercounting of Puerto Ricans and Chicanos, which is certainly of substantial magnitude, it must be assumed that most of the Mexicans, Colombians, and others, in this country without legal visas are not counted. According to the most conservative estimates, the number of these "illegals" runs into the millions. Thus a minimum of 2.5 million must be allowed for non-counting of illegal and legal residents among Mexicans, Colombians, Chicanos, Puerto Ricans, and others.

The undercounting of Blacks is not a technical accident. It is a result of and an expression of racist discrimination against Blacks. It is used as a practical political and economic weapon against Blacks, and is connected with a sinister design to hold down or reduce the Black population.

Owing to their class and racial prejudices, many Census takers omit counting people in some of the poorest areas, especially those inhabited by Blacks. Simultaneously, many of the most oppressed people fear all government representatives in view of their life experience in which government men appear only as persecutors—as policemen to harass and arrest, as bailiffs to evict, as FBI and Immigration agents to deport, as tax and bill collectors, and as welfare investigators to subject a whole family to starvation if a man is found living in the house.

True, it would be difficult to obtain a complete count of Blacks, and to a lesser extent of poor whites, unless decisive steps were taken to end discrimination, segregation, and poverty generally. The problem could be partially overcome by hiring large numbers of Black working people to be exclusively responsible for counting and editing returns from predominantly Black areas.

But even short of that, the practical effects of undercounting could be eliminated, and a realistic figure of the total Black population could be obtained and officially certified, by standard statistical methods. Nowadays most Census totals are "blown-up" from 5%, 15%, or 20% samples. Moreover, totals of most categories are increased, above those counted, to allow for unreported numbers. Thus if only 80% of workers report their occupations, the Census statisticians allocate occupations to the other 20% by correlating other data about these workers.

There are equally valid techniques for estimating the numbers of people in various major categories who are omitted from the formal Census count. Census statisticians have applied these techniques and published the results. Black organizations have requested the Census Bureau to make these results official, and thereby come closer to an officially recognized accurate counting of the Black population. But the Census Bureau chiefs refuse to do so, and thereby collaborate in the practical financial and political discrimination that results from this undercounting.

The actual situation today is that the Census statisticians use figures adjusted upwards to allow for undercounting in their internal calculations, because they regard the adjusted statistics as providing *more* *accurate* distributions of the population by age, sex, and race than the "official" statistics. For example, in estimating the population for non-Census years, say for 1973, the Census takers start with the 1970 Census figures corrected for undercounting, add births and net immigration, and subtract deaths in each age/sex/race group for the next three years in order to get corrected figures for 1973. They then reduce this set of figures by the exact percentages necessary to get the same percentage undercounts which they found in 1970, in order to get a new set of inadequate, inaccurately distributed figures for purposes of publication and all official applications. The technical excuses given for this official use of admittedly inaccurate, distorted, and undercounted figures are not convincing. The real reason is political, and distinctly racist.*

The population count is the basis for allocation of seats in federal and state legislatures, and for a variety of governmental money grants. Undercounting of Black and Puerto Rican people in New York City alone costs the city a whole Congressional district which, logically, would be located in a largely Black and Puerto Rican area. Dr. Robert B. Hill, director of research of the National Urban League, estimated that undercounting cost New York State and California each $15 million in federal revenue sharing funds.[3]

A lawyers' group demanded of the U.S. Secretary of the Treasury, on behalf of Newark Mayor Kenneth Gibson, additional federal funds because of the undercount of Blacks in that city, where they constitute more than half the population. The National League of Cities, representing 15,000 municipalities, made a request for cities in general on the same basis, at the same meeting at which it elected its first Black president, Mayor Thomas Bradley of Los Angeles.[4]

The Black population is increasing much faster than the white population. Between 1950 and 1960 the Black population increased 19.6%, as compared with 11.9% for the white population.[5] However, the white population includes almost all of the Chicanos, Puerto Ricans, and other people of Latin American or Spanish origin, whose population increased approximately 40% during the decade.[6] Thus, the "white-Anglo" population increased approximately 10.5%, or at barely half the rate of increase of the Black population, and at barely one-fourth the rate of increase of the Chicanos, Puerto Ricans, and others. Furthermore, the Census estimated that Blacks were 11.3% of the total popula-

---

* This method of estimating population in intercensal years, called the "Inflation-Deflation Method" is described in P-25, No. 619, pp. 6-7.

tion in July 1973, but 14.3% of the population under 15 years of age, indicating a substantial growth in the proportion of Blacks in the adult population in the decades to come.[7]

The Campaign to Stop Black Population Growth

After World War II, as U.S. power spread to Asia and the Far East, it confronted social upheavals which threatened the stability of regimes that welcomed U.S. investments and military bases. Wealthy U.S. families, headed by the Rockefellers, formed the Population Council, with the aim of persuading the peoples of Asia to curtail their population so that there would be fewer mouths to feed instead of taking radical measures to alleviate poverty, and to increase the supply of goods available to the masses.

Through its propaganda and subsidies, the Population Council boasted of stimulating hundreds of thousands of abortions in Japan at a time when abortions were still illegal in the United States. Later the focus shifted to India, where U.S. private and governmental monies were used to finance large-scale sterilization.

Along with continued global practical application of this Malthusian doctrine, in recent years it has been brought home to the United States, with Blacks the scarcely concealed main targets. Up to a point, the main interest of the ruling Establishment was to increase the number of Blacks available as a cheap urban labor force. But that force has become increasingly political, increasingly explosive, more determinedly demanding full human rights. For the present, then, employers prefer to seek additional workers among immigrants, unskilled workers from Mexico, Central and South America and the Caribbean and among others, including "brain drain" professionals and technicians, from India and the Philippines, and emigres from socialist countries.

These groups lack political power and cohesion. Many are brought in illegally, and lack the most elementary civil rights. Others, enemies of Communist-led governments in their homelands, start out with loyalty to the capitalist status quo in the United States.

Of course, some developing countries have practical population problems, especially where population growth outstrips the increase in food output. Also, all people everywhere should have access to birth control information and supplies without charge, so that they can rationally regulate the size of their own families. But this must go along with basic social and economic reforms, not be used as a substitute. This was the main approach expressed at the United Nations-sponsored international conference on population problems held in Brazzaville, the Congo, in June 1974. The present-day Malthusians have no concern of this sort with the rights and welfare of all people, especially the poor and oppressed. That their motives are different, anti-human, and racist, is made clear by their propaganda and by the practices of government agencies under their influence.

Not long ago the Sunday *New York Times* carried a two-page advertisement signed by 17 key individuals, urging population stabilization. Playing on the popular concern with pollution and the deteriorating environment, it blamed these evils on too many people: "For, let's face it, *people pollute!*" exclaimed the ad. Of course, people pollute, but people also clean up dirt, and can prevent and reverse the worst forms of pollution. Whether they do so depends not on how *many* people there are, but on how well society organizes the disposal of waste, how well it acts to preserve and improve the environment.

The Earth, and the United States, can comfortably support many more people than now live there. The problem of pollution and conservation of the environment will be solved when we have socialism. The Soviet Union is engaged in a comprehensive, planned program of improving the environment, with signal successes already registered, and more than 10 million organized conservationists actively participating in it.

It is private corporate profiteering, and war and preparations for war that mainly destroy the environment and pollute the air and water. But the signers do not address themselves to these factors. The real point has nothing to do with pollution.

To understand the motivation, look at the signers. They include George Champion, retired chairman of the Chase Manhattan Bank, and Frank W. Abrams, retired number one man of Exxon, both leading executives of the Rockefeller corporate empire. Also signers are William F. May and Hugh Moore, present and retired high executives of the American Can Company, associated with the Morgan banking group. Then there is Lammot du Pont Copeland of the billionaire Delaware family, General William H. Draper Jr. of Dillon Read & Co., and Robert S. McNamara, ex-Ford official and now President of the World Bank. As Secretary of Defense, he bore major responsibility for destruction of the Vietnamese environment on a scale never paralleled anywhere.

The advertisers claim that "the flood of people now engulfing the earth is a threat to future peace in the world." They compare the "population bomb" with the "atom bomb" as "twin clouds" threatening mankind's survival. But they do not urge banning the bomb, a real threat to mankind. Indeed, they have usually actively opposed positive disarmament steps. Instead, they urge banning people, calling for congressional endorsement of zero population growth and a step-up in governmental spending to that end.[8]

And that is being done. The federal government plans to spend $284 million on family planning in fiscal year 1975, and to "serve" 7 million people, up from 5 million two years earlier: "Efforts will be concentrated on providing services to low-income persons."[9] The main practical effort has been providing the "service" of sterilization to low-income persons, primarily Black. This has been done to welfare mothers on a large scale, and even to Black children and teenagers who have borne no children. People are induced to sign authorizing papers without adequate explanation, and in some cases even this formality has been avoided,

A National Welfare Rights Organization (NWRO) law suit brought out shocking facts about the mass sterilization activities of the U.S. Department of Health, Education and Welfare, in cooperation with local welfare offices, health clinics and doctors. U.S. District Judge Gerhard A. Gesell found that the government has paid for sterilizing 100,000 to 150,000 persons annually over the last few years. This was sanctioned by the Health, Education and Welfare Department (HEW) rules which effectively coerced people into seeking sterilization by threatening them with the loss of welfare payments. The judge ordered the federal government to stop paying for sterilization operations on mentally incompetent or very young people, and ordered the HEW to redraft rules to protect against coercion.[10]

A white doctor in South Carolina refused to deliver the third child of welfare mothers, almost all Black, until they agreed to a simultaneous sterilization operation.[11] A number of similar reports make it clear that poor Black people are the main victims. As a result of this practice during the 1960s, by 1970 one out of every six married couples between the ages of 20 and 39 included at least one sterilized partner.[12] Certainly the proportion is higher among Blacks, and this is obviously on a scale sufficient to seriously affect population growth.

Eva Clayton, a North Carolina activist against racism, contended:

Whether by accident or design, family planning, as it is now conceived, is directed mainly toward reducing population growth among the poor, and primarily the Black poor. The implication in this direction is genocide.[13]

As yet, this frightening practice only points in the direction of genocide. But there is a sinister parallel with the beginnings of Hitler's policy of reducing the population of "undesirables," which began with 56,000 sterilizations a year, and ended with the mass murder of millions in the gas chambers.[14]*

There are not yet calls for genocide, although an organization calling itself "Negative Population Growth" is already campaigning for cutting the population in half! It should be noted that the campaign to curb the population, spearheaded against Blacks, inevitably has its harmful impact on people of all races. The latest Census calculations show that the fertility rate of all women has fallen below that necessary to maintain the population over the long run, and apparently it is the white population, first, that is threatened with an ultimate significant decline in numbers. Judge Gesell's insistence on new rules moderating government pressure for sterilizations is insufficient. Ample means of contraception are now available, and abortions have been legalized. Taking these facts into account, as well as the racist campaign against the Black population, the irreversible sterilization operations should be limited to cases where they are required for medical reasons.

More fundamentally, it is time to defeat the use of the population control weapon and turn instead to defining and moving to end the severe social and economic discriminations against Blacks. This is the direction of the present volume.

A People of Workers

The principal social sectors in capitalist society are the capitalist class and the working class. The former own the means of production and distribution and derive most of their income from the labor of others. The latter work for wages and salaries and own no means of production. In between are the traditional middle classes, or "petty bourgeoisie," who own small productive property—a neighborhood store, a doctor's

---

* Even more outrageous than the sterilizations has been the forced performance of harmful medical experiments on Blacks, such as the infection of Black men with syphilis. On a scale of millions is the new practice of forcibly drugging school children, especially Black, on the grounds that they are "hyperkinetic."

equipment, a family farm—but who derive much of their income from their own labor.

The Black people are overwhelmingly of the working class, more so than any other national or racial group: 96% of all gainfully employed Black people are wage and salary workers, as compared with 89% of gainfully employed "white-Anglo" people.[15] On the other hand, the Black people include only a handful of capitalists, properly speaking, and have the smallest proportion of petty bourgeoisie of any national or racial group.

Today a real capitalist, as distinct from a petty bourgeois, generally must have assets of at least a million dollars and an income of at least $100,000. The Census reports on families with incomes over $50,000. In 1969 there were 360,048 white families or eight out of a thousand, in this high income group, but only 4,807 Black families, or a mere one out of a thousand. The majority of these had two or more income earners, suggesting that many derived a major share of income from salaries, rather than from exploitation of other people's labor.[16]

Because there are so few real capitalists among them, in classifying Black population we consider statistically only two groups, the petty bourgeoisie and the working class. From amongst the workers, however, we separate out the bulk of the intellectuals, who constitute an upper stratum of the working class (or, in the view of some, a separate social class). The results are shown in Table 1.

TABLE 1

CLASS STRUCTURE OF EMPLOYED BLACKS, 1970

CATEGORY	THOUSANDS	% OF TOTAL
Petty bourgeoisie	238	3.2
Intellectual workers	586	8.0
Working class, except intellectuals	6,537	88.8
Total	7,361	100.0

SOURCE: U.S.-C-91.

The Black petty bourgeoisie, including the few capitalists proper, totalled only 238,000 or 3.2% of those employed. Among them were 170,000 managers and administrators, some salaried and some self-employed; 43,000 farmers; and 25,000 upper-strata professionals —engineers, physicians and dentists. This group has held the leadership in traditional Black people's organizations. Then there were 586,000

Chart 1

CLASS STRUCTURE OF EMPLOYED POPULATION
BLACK AND WHITE, 1970

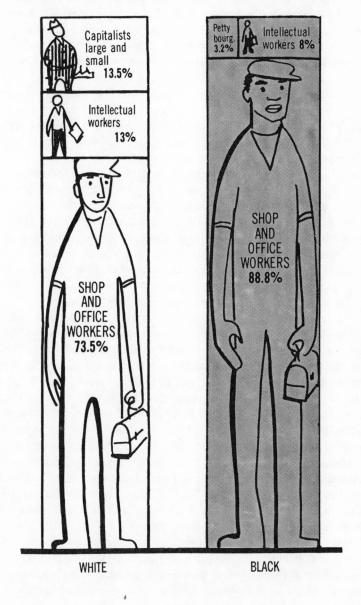

Capitalists large and small **13.5%**

Intellectual workers **13%**

SHOP AND OFFICE WORKERS **73.5%**

Petty bourg. **3.2%**

Intellectual workers **8%**

SHOP AND OFFICE WORKERS **88.8%**

WHITE

BLACK

Black teachers, nurses, clergymen, and other professional and intellectual workers, some of whom have been associated with the dominant petty bourgeoisie in the leadership of Black organizations. But among these, more and more teachers and nurses, for example, tend to orient towards the trade union movement and the working class generally.

More than 6½ million, 88.8% of gainfully employed Blacks, were in the principal sections of the working class. Nearly half of these, close to 3 million, were in the lowest paid and generally most undesirable categories—the laborers and service workers. About 1.8 million were in traditionally better off categories of sales, clerical, and skilled craft workers, although, as will be shown later, their advantages are dwindling, especially for many Black clerical workers.

Among the white population, 13.5% were small and large capitalists, more than four times the proportion among the Blacks. Moreover, a significant number of these were of the capitalist class proper, the real economic and political rulers of the country. Another 13.0% of whites, again a larger proportion than among Blacks, were intellectual workers. The remaining 73.5% of whites, a considerably smaller proportion than among Blacks, were in the working class, other than intellectuals. And among the white workers, a significant majority were in the traditionally better off categories of sales, clerical and crafts workers.[17]

Altogether two-thirds of all gainfully employed whites were either capitalists, in the "middle classes" or in the upper layers of the working class. Not that many of them were so far up. But they are the objects of the most intense propaganda attempting to cultivate among them a pro-capitalist ideology, in which racism is prominently included. In fact, the majority of white working class families do not even earn enough to support the moderate living standard budgets priced by the Labor Department. Whatever short-range advantages they may enjoy by being favored over Blacks, in the long run they lose by the existence and potential competition of a major group subject to discriminatory economic conditions. But despite this objective reality, the influence of racist and divisive propaganda is serious. It must be combatted, and not alone on moral grounds, but also on the grounds of the fundamental interests of all working people, white included.

There is another important feature in the class structure of the Black population, and especially in prevailing trends. Prior to World War II, the majority of Black working people were engaged in small, scattered, low productive agriculture, in small service establishments, and in household work. Only a minority were able to obtain places in the productive industries of the country.

This is changing rapidly. By 1970 about 2.8 million Black workers, or 40% of all gainfully employed Blacks, were engaged in industrial production: mining, construction, manufacturing, transportation, communication and utilities.[18] They comprised 8.8% of the total number of workers in these industries, and 11.3% of the blue collar or production workers in these industries. That exceeded the 9.6% of all employed persons reported as Black.[19]

Considering their age and sex distribution, it seems likely that as many as one-fifth of Black industrial workers were among those not counted in the Census. Thus by 1970 Black workers may have actually comprised 13 to 14% of all industrial blue collar workers, and, considering the increasing trend, by 1975 their share in the total is likely to exceed 15%.

Thus the Black workers by now comprise a very substantial proportion of the industrial proletariat, the most indispensable workers for the entire economy. These workers produce most of the surplus value —over and above their own wages—the surplus which is converted into most of the profits of the capitalist class. Because they are brought together in large numbers by the scale of production, because of the character of their work and the intensity of their exploitation by employers, the industrial proletariat, historically, has proven to be the political core of the working class. It has provided the base for successful socialist revolutions in the USSR and other socialist countries, and for powerful trade union movements and revolutionary parties in France, Italy, Japan, and other capitalist countries. And it was the industrial workers who provided the power which the modern trade union movement has in the United States—strong potentially, if weak as yet in its practical exercise.

Thus the Black workers comprise an important and increasing segment of the core section of the U.S. working class. Because they are subject to special oppression and exploitation, the Black workers have proven to be among the most militant and reliable in struggle against employers. Their role in trade union activity is increasing rapidly, as their consciousness of national, racial and class solidarity increases. Progress of labor in this country is not possible without recognition in practice of the special role that Black workers can and are prepared to play within the working class movement, including in its leadership.

Black Women as Workers

Black women bear an exceptionally heavy proportion of life's burdens: as workers, as homemakers, as heads of family, and as mothers. And their rewards for all of these efforts are exceptionally small.

Three out of five Black women work for wages or salaries, as compared with about half of white women. The Black women as workers are relatively numerous, in relation both to Black men workers and white women workers. (Table 2).

TABLE 2

LABOR FORCE, BY RACE AND SEX, 1973
(Thousands of Persons)

	WHITE	BLACK AND OTHER MINORITIES	BLACK AND OTHER MINORITIES % OF WHITE
Male	50,610	5,868	11.6
Female	30,085	4,476	14.9
Female as a percent of Male	59.4	76.3	

SOURCE: U.S. Dept. of Labor, *Employment and Earnings*, Jan 1974, pp 140-141

Although the statistics here are for "Negro and other races," there is relatively little distortion. Blacks comprise about nine-tenths of the people in this broader group. The proportion of women in the labor force among other minority groups is nearly as large as among Blacks, and the addition of other minority people tends to offset the general undercounting of Blacks.

While the number of white women who work equals three-fifths the number of white men who work, the number of Black women workers exceeds three-fourths the number of Black male workers. And there are many places, as in the New York metropolitan area outside of New York City, where the number of Black women with jobs exceeds the number of Black men with jobs. Moreover, the number of Black and other minority women workers is close to 15% of the number of white women workers, a much higher percentage than the share of minority women in the female population.

The figures on the percentage participation in the labor force in various age groups are also instructive (Table 3).

TABLE 3

PERCENTAGE OF WOMEN IN THE LABOR FORCE
BY AGE GROUPS, BY RACE, 1973

AGE GROUPS	WHITE	BLACK AND OTHER MINORITIES
16-19	50.2	34.5
20-24	61.8	57.7
25-34	48.6	61.1
35-44	52.2	60.7
45-54	53.4	56.4
55-59	47.1	50.3
60-64	33.8	38.3
65 and over	8.7	11.1

SOURCE: *Employment and Earnings,* Jan 1974, p. 141

A considerably higher percentage of whites than Blacks are in the labor force among teenage women, and this continues, to a less marked extent, in the early twenty age group. This, certainly, is not because fewer Black women in these groupings *want* jobs, but because they are more readily available to white youth. However, in the 25-34 year range, the principal child-bearing years, there is a sharp drop in white participation, but an increase in Black participation, which reaches its peak exactly in these years when working is most difficult because of the presence of small children. It is in this age range that the excess of Black over white women in percentage of labor market participation reaches its peak, 61.1% versus 48.6%. At older age ranges, as children become more able to take care of themselves, the percentage of white women working increases, but never reaches the percentage of Black women working in the same age group. And generally, the figures show, Black women are not able to retire as early as white.

Other data show that Black women are more likely than white to be working while simultaneously being heads of households, and more likely to be on full time schedules rather than part time schedules.

In 1970, of Black women with children under 6 years of age, 47.6% were in the labor force, as compared with 28.4% of white women who were in a similar situation.[20]

The proportion of Black women working has been very high through the decades, while prior to World War II, fewer than a third of the white women aged 25 and over worked. However, while the percentage of labor market participation of Black women increased more slowly than that of white women until about 1970, there has been a rapid change in

the types of work Black women do. In 1940 they were primarily household workers, in other service jobs, and working on farms. The number
of Black women household workers has declined steadily, while the
number on farms has become trivial. Simultaneously, there has been an
increase in the number of Black clerical, professional and factory workers, an increase which has become especially rapid in the past 15 years.
Between 1960 and 1970 the number of minority women clerical workers increased from 219,000 to 719,000, or more than three times, the
number of minority women professionals increased from 197,000 to
407,000, or more than doubled while the number of minority female
operative, other than in transport, increased from 316,000 to 526,000,
or by two-thirds. In each case the increase was far more rapid than the
increase in the same category of white women or Black men.[21]

This process has continued. By 1973 there were 976,000 minority
women clerical workers, 480,000 professional workers, and 656,000
operatives, other than transport. These three occupation groups accounted for more than half of all Black women workers, and taken
together, were four times as numerous as the rapidly declining number
of Black private household workers. One fourth of all Black women
workers were employed as service workers in establishments—
hospitals, restaurants, laundries, etc.,—twice as many as in private
households.[22]

Black women, symbolized by Rosa Parks, the private household
worker and active church member in Montgomery, Alabama, played a
leading role in the earlier (Civil Rights) period of struggle. Now Black
women trade unionists from the factories and hospitals, schools and
offices are destined to be among the leaders in the current and future
battles.

City People

In 1970, 81% of the Black people lived in urban areas, as compared
with 72% of white people. A similar, or even greater, degree of urbani-
zation applied to other minority peoples, except for the Native Americans.

What is more significant, however, is the concentration of Blacks in
central cities, as distinct from suburbs. In 1970, 58% of all Blacks lived
in the central cities of large urbanized areas, and only 11% in the urban
fringes of these areas. Among the white population, however, only 28%
lived in central cities, while 29% lived in the urban fringes.[23] Since

these statistics for white people include Chicanos and Puerto Ricans, who are concentrated in the central cities, the predominance of suburbanites over central city dwellers among the "white-Anglo" people is now substantial.

The shift from white to Black and Brown peoples in the central cities has been very rapid. Between 1950 and 1970 the percentage of whites living in central cities declined from 31.1 to 27.9, while the percentage of minorities living there increased from 39.2 to 56.5. The numerical increase in the white central city population between 1960 and 1970 was less than 2 million, probably all accounted for by Chicanos and Puerto Ricans.[24] Hence the "white-Anglo" population of the central cities was stagnant, and during the 1970s will almost surely show a decline nationwide, as it already has in many major cities.

The increasing concentration of Blacks in small central city areas is not voluntary. It results from a combination of those living in rural areas in the South being left without means of livelihood and forced to migrate to the cities, and the effective barring of Black families from most suburban areas, and from the choice areas in cities. The residential concentration of Blacks is an important factor in the economic discrimination against them in terms of income and employment (Chapters 3 and 4).

$3,383
per
capita
income
1969

$1,818
per
capita
income
1969

Chart 2

3. *Real Income Differential*

Personal income is the most meaningful single indicator of living standards. Widely disseminated official publicity aims to convey the impression that Black people have attained virtual parity with whites in incomes, and hence in living standards. The main technique is to emphasize unusual situations of seeming near-equality, a device developed by Daniel Patrick Moynihan, promoter of the policy of "benign neglect," as Urban Affairs Advisor to President Nixon in 1969-1971.

An example is provided by a U.S. Commerce Department press release describing the contents of a regular statistical report on Black social and economic conditions. Under the headline: "Young Blacks Make Impressive Gains, Census Report Shows," the release begins:

Entering the 1970's, young college-trained Black women (25 to 34) were earning about as much nationally as similarly educated white women and, at the same time, well-educated young Black men were coming closer to income parity with their white counterparts . . .

27

The national median* earnings of both Black and white women (35 to 54 who worked year around) with four years of college was about $7,300 in 1969 . . .

In the North and West, the median annual earnings of the comparable group of Black women exceeded that of white women—$8,100 versus $7,600. . . . Outside the South, young Black husband-wife families (with the head under 35) both of whom worked, achieved income parity with whites similarly situated.

Since 1964 . . . the income differentials between Negro and white families have narrowed. The ratio of Negro to white median income was 0.59 in 1972, the same as in 1967, which was higher than the 0.54 in 1964.[1]

This kind of release cruelly deceives the public. The examples of equality represent narrowly defined, better off groups of people, and the proportion of Blacks getting into these favored categories is much smaller than the proportion of whites. Also, contrary to the impression generated by the release, there is nothing new about approximate equality of Blacks and whites in these specially defined categories.

Consider the young husband and wife families in the North and West. As the release admits, they constituted "a relatively small proportion—6 percent—" of all Black families. And analysis shows that the equality was achieved by the Black women in the families working much more than their white counterparts. The detailed data show that while the Black husbands earned, on the average, 12% less than the white husbands, the Black wives earned, on the average, 36% more! But it is clear from supplementary data that this was not because the Black women were paid higher wages or salaries, but simply because most of them worked all-year around and full time, while most of the white women worked only part of the year, and many of them part-time within a given week.[2]

More representative of reality, but much less emphasized in recent

* The median number is that which applies to the person in the middle, if all persons are lined up in order of the size of the characteristic being measured. Thus if there are three families with incomes of $10,000, $5,000, and $3,000 respectively, the median income is $5,000, the income of the middle family. The mean is the arithmetic average of a series of numbers. Thus, in the case of the three families the mean is $6,000 ($18,000 divided by 3). To put it more simply, the median is the income of the middle family, while the mean is the average income of all the families. In this book we sometimes use one and sometimes the other of these "measures of central tendency," usually depending on which is available. The mean is almost always larger than the median in economic statistics of this type. But the ratios of Black to white incomes are about the same, whether medians or means are used. In the case of family incomes, medians are generally used because usually the Census only provides this measure. However, later in this chapter we use statistics of mean per capita incomes, because the data are given in that form. It is simpler to calculate means, and one can make more flexible adjustments than with medians.

official propaganda, is the statement that the median Black family income was 59% of the median white family income in 1972. But even that gives an exaggerated impression of the relative economic status of Black people.

One significant distortion is the inclusion of almost all Chicanos, Puerto Ricans, and other peoples of Latin American origin with whites. Since their incomes are close to those of Blacks, their inclusion with whites lowers the median for whites, and artificially raises the ratio of Black to white incomes. Since these Latin American peoples are subject to oppression and discrimination also, they should not be included with the whites for comparison of Black and white conditions. The proper comparison is between Blacks and whites other than those of Latin American origin. For convenience, we refer to this dominant group as "white-Anglos," although, obviously, far from all are of North European origin. Census statistics show that average incomes of "white-Anglos" are about 2% higher than average incomes of all whites, including Latin American peoples. Adjustment for this results in a corresponding lowering of the Black/white average income ratio. The adjustment to medians would be similar.

Another distortion results from the sampling procedure. As brought out in Chapter 2, a substantial proportion of Blacks are never counted in the Census. It seems reasonable to believe that the median income of those not counted is lower than the median income of those counted. Census year income statistics are based on a sample of 20% of the population, and the annual surveys on samples of less than one-tenth of one percent of the population. Inevitably relatively fewer usable returns are received from low income than from high income people, with a resultant tendency to exaggerate average incomes for whites more than for Blacks.

Then certain kinds of income are not counted. These are capital gains, gifts and inheritances, expense account income, income in kind, that part of self-employment income, farm income, and rental income which is cancelled out for tax purposes as an expense. Whites receive much higher percentages of their gross incomes in these forms than do Blacks. The total income *excluded* in these ways may amount to at least 20% of the income that is counted for people in the upper half of the income distribution. For example, capital gains income, even as indicated incompletely in personal income tax returns, is of the order of $30 billion per year. Expense account income and related loophole tax deductions from reported income certainly total much more than that. These exclusions affect whites several times more than Blacks, in relation to their respective total incomes.

Also, certain types of income are only partly reported to the Census takers. The Bureau estimates that in 1972, while 98.3% of wages and salaries were reported to enumerators, only 45.0% of dividends, interest, net rental income, income from estates and trusts, and net royalties were reported.* [3] Since Blacks receive a larger proportion of their incomes from wages and salaries than whites, but only a trivial proportion of their incomes from ownership of property, it means that Census statistics exclude much more of the incomes of whites than of Blacks.

Adjustment to exclude Latin American families from the totals for whites reduces the ratio of Black to white family incomes by more than one percentage point. Adjustment for disproportionate coverage of different types of income reduces the ratio of Black to white income by about 2 percentage points. Adjustment for exclusion of capital gains accounts for another 2 percentage points. Thus a ratio of 59% reported Black to white median incomes becomes less than 54%, and this does not cover all of the appropriate adjustments.

So far we have been discussing family incomes. This involves another distortion, since the average Black family is larger than the average white family. Obviously, the economic status of a family of 5 with an income of $8,000 is lower than that of a family of three with an income of $8,000. This difficulty can be overcome, approximately, by comparing per capita incomes of Blacks and whites, covering people in families as well as those living as single individuals.

The average size of the "white-Anglo" economic unit, as used for Census calculations of per capita income, is 2.710 persons, and of the Black economic unit, 3.087 persons.**

---

* Includes amounts allocated by type of income by Census editors on the basis of correlation with otherwise similar returns reporting distribution of income by type.

**There is a slight distortion in the opposite direction here, as the money required for a given standard of living decreases with each additional family member. Thus, a given per capita income for a family of 3 represents a higher living standard than the same per capita income for a family of 2. This distortion tends to minimize the ratio of Black to white per capita incomes. However, the distortion is trivial in this case, and fully counterbalanced by opposite distortions, such as expense account income accruing to whites more than to Blacks, for which we are unable to make a correction.

Real Income for Black People Half That of Whites

The 1970 Census, for the first time, provided figures of per capita income by race. These figures showed that in 1969 the per capita income of Blacks was $1,818, or 54% of the $3,383 per capita income of "white-Anglo" people.*[4]

Allowing for distortions resulting from noncounting or undercounting of property income and capital gains, as indicated above, reduces the effective ratio by four percentage points, to 50%. Allowing further for the inferior quality and higher prices of commodities which most Black people have to purchase reduces the real effective per capita income of Blacks to less than one-half that of whites, as of 1969.

This is by no means a minor factor. Consider the example of housing. Henry J. Aaron, in a Brookings Institution study, provides massive evidence of gross economic discrimination against Blacks in housing. For example, among renters paying rent of $61-$75 per month in 1966, the median group, 86.0% of the whites but only 65.3% of the nonwhites had sound units to live in. Whites paying $31-$40 rent had a higher percentage of sound units, and a lower percentage of dilapidated units, than Blacks paying twice as much. Similar statistics are provided for homeowners' units.

A whole series of city studies are cited, each showing higher payment by Blacks for housing of equivalent quality, such as a median excess of $2,555 paid by Blacks in St. Louis.

A much larger proportion of whites than Blacks are homeowners. Homeowners in general, and especially white homeowners, receive billions in direct and indirect federal subsidies, including, as of 1966, about $7 billion in tax benefits. About one-third of all non-farm housing starts have been financed by FHA or VA guaranteed mortgages, with certain advantages, and these have been available primarily to whites. Federal subsidies to tenants of public housing have been trivial in comparison.[4a]

The program of federal interest-subsidy applied during the early

* The per capita income figure for all white people was $3,314. However, this includes the much lower per capita incomes of the Chicano, Puerto Rican and other peoples of Latin American origin. The per capita income for white Anglo people was calculated by subtracting out from the totals of population and incomes of all whites the corresponding totals for "persons of Spanish heritage," as reported in the Census, and then recomputing per capita income for the remainder. A very small proportion of "persons of Spanish heritage" are classified as non-Anglo, but not enough to affect this adjustment significantly.

1970s to reduce the rents of lower and middle income tenants also operated to discriminate against Blacks. Allan R. Talbot, executive director of the Citizens Housing and Planning Council, explained that the program required that tenants must pay fully 25% of their incomes for rent, regardless of the real value of the apartment. With few exceptions, only Black people had such a desperate need for housing as to pay such rents. On the other, whites in New York were able to rent state-subsidized Mitchell-Lama housing where only one-seventh of the income was required for rent. [4b]   Thus it often worked out that Blacks were forced to pay nearly twice as much as whites for equivalent housing. Of course, there were Black families in the Mitchell-Lama housing and whites in the federally-subsidized housing, but the racial division applied to the majority of tenants or cooperators in both.

Banks and savings and loan associations use the savings of city dwellers, including Black workers, to finance the housing of suburbanites. Central city dwellers, especially Black, find it impossible to get mortgage loans for buying or improving houses, because of "redlining." Banks systematically refuse "to sink money into neighborhoods that they believe are declining" and around which they draw at least a theoretical "red line." For example, the largest savings and loan association in Baltimore made fewer than 30 home loans in the city in the year 1972. [4c]

Other economic losses in the housing area include the lower degree of public services supplied where Black people live, and the less convenient accessibility of good job locations. (Chapter 6)

Similar discrimination against Blacks as consumers is general and substantial, in everything from the purchase of an automobile to the purchase of groceries. Overall, it is difficult to believe that this factor reduces effective Black incomes by less than 5%, and it seems more likely that the cost is of the order of 10% or more.

This brings the real effective per capita income of Blacks down to the range of 45% to 48% of that of "white-Anglo" people, as of 1969. As indicated in the next chapter, it may have declined further since then.

The above discussion relates to *economic* discrimination against Blacks as consumers, discrimination which could be measured, but which by and large has not been measured in any systematic way. It does not even go into the vast area of social, psychological, health, and other qualitative losses sustained on account of the all-around discrimination against them, losses which in their total impact may exceed strictly economic losses for many Black people, but which cannot be expressed in dollars and cents terms.

Regional and State and Local Differences

In 1970 more than half of all Black people still lived in the southern and border states, lumped together in the broad regional grouping of the South in Census statistics. Economic discrimination remains much more severe there than in the rest of the country, although this regional difference is declining (see Chapter 4). Per capita incomes of Blacks in the South were two-thirds of those in the rest of the country in 1969 (Table 4). Per capita incomes of Blacks ranged between 61 and 67% of those of "white-Anglos" in the three northern regions, but were only 47% of those of "white-Anglos" in the South.

TABLE 4

PER CAPITA INCOMES OF WHITE ANGLOS AND BLACKS BY REGIONS, 1969

REGION	WHITE-ANGLOS	BLACKS	BLACKS % OF WHITE-ANGLOS
Northeast	$3,630	$2,277	63
North Central	3,296	2,206	67
South	3,072	1,439	47
West	3,698	2,274	61
United States Total	3,383	1,818	54

SOURCE: U.S.-C-130, 135, 94

Statistics for individual states, metropolitan regions, and cities reveal wider variations, and shed more light on the reasons for these variations. Table 5 compares per capita incomes in the three Middle Atlantic States.

TABLE 5

PER CAPITA INCOME OF WHITE ANGLOS AND BLACKS IN
MIDDLE ATLANTIC STATES, 1969.

	WHITE-ANGLO	BLACK	BLACK % OF WHITE-ANGLO
New York	$3,956	$2,365	60
New Jersey	3,914	2,243	57
Pennsylvania	3,190	2,152	67

SOURCE: C-48,57 for specified states.

The ratio of Black to "white-Anglo" per capita income was considerably higher in Pennsylvania—67%—than in either of the two neighboring states, but simply because the per capita income of whites was much lower in Pennsylvania than in New York or New Jersey. The per capita income of Blacks in Pennsylvania was a little lower than in the other two states, but by no more than living costs which in Philadelphia and Pittsburgh are lower than in the New York-New Jersey metropolitan area.

However, the statewide ratios, in these and most other states, exaggerate the relative situation of Blacks, because the latter are concentrated in a few central cities where living costs are higher than in the rest of the state. The economic situation of Blacks in the country's three largest metropolitan areas is remarkably uniform. Per capita incomes of Blacks were $2,411 in New York, $2,398 in Los Angeles, and $2,330 in Chicago metropolitan areas. In the three areas they were 54%, 54%, and 55%, respectively of the per capita incomes of "white Anglo" people, or just about equal to the national average ratio.[5]*

The absolute and relative economic situation of Blacks is somewhat better in Michigan than in other major industrial states. Statewide, their per capita income in 1969 was $2,405, or 68% of that of "white-Anglo" people; and in the Detroit metropolitan area it was $2,507, or 61% of that of "white-Anglo" people. This is due to the large-scale employment of Blacks in a relatively high wage basic industry, the automobile industry. It is also relevant that the United Automobile Workers, while not without serious racist faults, has a moderately better record in this respect than some other major unions.

The highest per capita income of Blacks was in Alaska, $2,907, or 67% of the per capita income of "white-Anglo" people. Owing to the extremely high cost of living in Alaska, however, this sum represented no more than the lower money incomes of Blacks in a number of the

* A slight degree of estimation is involved in calculating the per capita incomes of white people for metropolitan areas and cities. They are not given specifically in the Census volumes, but have to be determined by subtracting figures for Blacks and other minorities from figures for the total population. However, while per capita incomes for minorities other than Blacks can be computed from data provided on a statewide basis, this is not possible for individual cities and metropolitan areas. For our calculations, it was assumed that the ratio of the per capita income of minorities other than Blacks in a metropolitan area to the per capita income of minorities other than Blacks in the state was equal to the corresponding ratio for all people in the metropolitan area and the state, respectively. The probable error involved in this estimation is a small fraction of a percent, in the final figure of "white-Anglo" per capita income.

other states. At that, Black incomes in Alaska are bolstered by the fact that the majority of Black gainful workers were in the armed forces or worked for the military and related government agencies.

A striking example of the rooting of extreme discrimination in the country's political structure is illustrated by the situation in Washington D.C., where the main occupation is working for the U.S. government. In the District of Columbia proper, where the Black people comprise a majority of the population, their per capita income came to $2,734, higher than in any state except Alaska, but only 39% of $6,993, the per capita income of "white-Anglo" people in the District. True, the bulk of the white population has moved to the suburbs, and the District per capita is raised by the presence of high income whites in luxury housing in the city center. But in the metropolitan area as a whole the relative situation of the Black people is bad enough. Their per capita income in the area was $2,702, or 56% of the $4,850 per capita of "white-Anglo" people.

The highest ratios of Black to white per capita incomes were in largely agricultural states with very small Black populations and comparatively low per capita incomes of whites. In South Dakota the Blacks had a per capita income of $1,914, considerably lower than in most industrial states. But it was 77% of the per capita average of "white-Anglo" people, only $2,484. But in this state the numerically largest and most oppressed people are the Native Americans. Their per capita income was only $976, or 39% of that of the "white-Anglo" people.[6]

Extremely low per capita incomes prevailed for blacks in a number of deep southern states, along with ratios of Black to white per capita income well below 50%.

TABLE 6

PER CAPITA INCOME OF WHITES AND BLACKS, SELECTED SOUTHERN STATES, 1969

	WHITE	BLACK	BLACK % OF WHITE
Arkansas	$1,950	$ 847	43
Alabama	2,751	1,157	42
Mississippi	2,545	898	35
North Carolina	2,516	1,151	46

SOURCE: C-48, 57, for specified states

NOTE: because of the small "Spanish heritage" population in these states, no adjustment is made to exclude them from the calculation for whites.

The per capita income of Blacks was absolutely lower in Arkansas than in any other state, with a mere $847, and relatively the lowest in Mississippi, where it was only 35% of the per capita for whites. But note that the per capita income of the whites in these states was far lower than in the rest of the country, and in Arkansas well below the per capita income of northern Blacks. We will return to consideration of this evidence of the cost to whites of extreme manifestations of racism against Blacks in a later chapter.

There are a few northern places of extreme Black poverty where per capita incomes of Blacks are no higher than in the deep South. One such place is Cairo, Illinois, where Blacks averaged only $1,088 per capita, or 46% of the per capita income of whites. Cairo is notorious not only for its decaying economy and consequent mass unemployment, but for the aggressively racist local regime, which has provoked repeated bitter mass struggles and engaged in persistent vicious repression of the Black population.

Comparisons with Other National Groups

How does the economic status of Black people compare with that of other racially oppressed national groups and with that of the white "ethnic" groups? Census statistics contribute to an answer, through per capita income figures in the 1970 Census of Population and family income figures in special Census surveys.

The Census statistics have serious shortcomings, arising from the official racism and refusal to recognize the existence of national minorities or nationalities, within the United States. The predominantly "white-Anglo" ruling class, determined to suppress struggles for equality, fears the presentation of clear factual information on the national question. The Census Bureau, therefore, uses a confused conglomeration of "color," "race," and "ethnic" distinctions.

Thus, the Japanese and Chinese peoples, who are certainly of different national origin but of the same race—if that term has any meaning—are classified as belonging to distinct races. The Census statisticians have made a dubious contribution to anthropological science with the "discovery" of a Japanese "race," a Chinese "race," and a number of others equally ridiculous.

The "persons of Spanish heritage" are treated as both fish and fowl. Counted, almost entirely as part of the white race, they are dealt with as a separate race in all social and economic characteristic tabulations. But in other tabulations, and in various special surveys, they are regarded as an "ethnic" group. Furthermore, the Census Bureau uses three different criteria for identifying them, and in the 1970 Census used different methods in different parts of the country, which resulted in the non-tabulation of statistics for about a million "persons of Spanish heritage," other than Puerto Ricans, in the Northeastern part of the country.

Despite the conceptual and statistical limitations, the Census data on per capita incomes contribute towards understanding the comparative economic status of different racially and nationally oppressed groups.

TABLE 7

PER CAPITA INCOME, SPECIFIED NATIONAL/RACIAL GROUPS, 1969

NATIONAL/RACIAL GROUP	POPULATION 1970 (Thousands)	PER CAPITA INCOME, 1969	PERCENT OF WHITE ANGLO
White Anglo	168,823	$3,383	100
Black	22,550	1,818	54
Chicano (part)	4,667	1,850	55
Puerto Rican	1,391	1,805	53
American Indian	764	1,573	46
Japanese	588	3,602	106
Chinese	432	3,122	92
Filipino	337	2,790	82
Others of Spanish Heritage	3,237	2,487	72
All Others	439	2,337	69

SOURCES: U.S. -85, 94; PC(2)-1D, TC1, 12; NY, NJ, PC(2)-1E, T. 1, 9; PC(2)-1F, T. 1, 9; PC(2)-1G, T. 1, 9, 16, 24, 31, 39.

NOTES: Data for Chicanos cover only those with Spanish surnames residing in five southwestern states. Data for American Indians, as most other data in this table, are based on a 20% sample. The full Census count gave a substantially larger total American Indian population. "Others of Spanish Heritage" include Chicanos not covered above, Cubans, peoples of other Latin American, Caribbean, and Spanish "heritage." "All others" include Hawaiians, Koreans, Eskimos, Aleuts, and people of unspecified "races."

The two other largest oppressed national groups, Chicanos and Puerto Ricans, had per capita incomes close to those of the Blacks, and are subject to economic discrimination roughly comparable in severity. However, these national averages conceal one important difference. Most Puerto Ricans are concentrated in the New York metropolitan area, where living costs are considerably higher than the national average. There the per capita income of Puerto Ricans, $1765, was 27% lower than that of Blacks, and only 39% of the per capita income of "white-Anglo" people, as compared with a 54% Black/white Anglo ratio.[7]

The American Indians are the most economically oppressed, with a per capita income of $1,573, or only 46% of that of "white-Anglo" people. The most severe oppression is suffered by Indians living on reservations. On about half of these, the per capita income was under $1,000. On the largest reservation, that of the Navajos, the per capita income was only $776, and on the important Navajo/Hopi joint-use reservation in Arizona, the per capita income was an incredibly low $472. On the second largest reservation in terms of population, the Pine Ridge reservation in South Dakota, the site of bitter liberation struggles in 1972-73, the per capita income was $1,042. The situation is less severe for Indians living off the reservations. In most cases their per capita incomes were equal to or higher than those of Blacks living in the same areas.[8]

The per capita incomes of the Asian and Oceanic peoples are considerably higher than those of other oppressed groups. The per capita income of Japanese people was 6% *higher* than that of white Anglo people, while that of the Chinese people was only 8% lower, and of the Filipino people 18% lower, than that of "white-Anglo" people. While exact figures are not available, comparable data indicate that the per capita income of Koreans was between that of Japanese and Chinese, and of Hawaiians between that of Chinese and Filipinos.[9]

However, the Asian and Oceanic peoples remain subject to significant economic discrimination. To some extent, the per capita income figures exaggerate their real status, since these people are concentrated in high living-cost areas. Thus, one-third of all the Japanese resided in the Honolulu metropolitan area, where living costs are higher than in any other metropolitan area except Anchorage, Alaska. Moreover, the situation is uneven geographically. Chinese people are relatively well off in Hawaii, and not too badly off in California but in New York the large Chinese population is afflicted with poverty and discrimination. Their per capita income in the New York metropolitan area was only $2,655, which was but 10% above the Black per capita income, and 41% below the per capita income of "white-Anglo" people.[10]

Asian people were brought into this country in the last century virtually as indentured workers, subject to the most barbarous discrimination and exploitation, or, in the case of the Hawaiians, treated as colonial subjects on their native soil. The Asian peoples were subject to extremely vicious chauvinistic attacks and victimized by special discriminatory legislation. Yet, it is obvious from the income statistics and other data that economic discrimination against them has been reduced, as anti-Asian chauvinism has been muted.

This does show that even under capitalism, major gains can be won in the struggle for economic equality of oppressed national and racial groups. But it does not mean that similar gains can be won by Blacks or other oppressed peoples simply by "following the example" of the Asians, as some apologists place the question.

A number of special factors, which do not apply to the Blacks, entered into the partial gains of the Asian peoples.

Two-thirds of the Asian and Oceanic peoples live in California and Hawaii. The militant International Longshoremen's and Warehousemen's Union, with Communists prominent in its leadership and with relatively advanced racial policies, became the leading force of the bulk of the Hawaiian working class, winning important gains for the longshore and agricultural workers and, as a result, for all working people. The same union has also been a positive influence in California, especially in the San Francisco Bay area, where many of the Asian people are concentrated.

For particular historical reasons, a substantial proportion of the Japanese and Chinese people were able to obtain a high degree of education or to become small proprietors. As of 1970, 33% of the Japanese males and 40% of the Chinese males were in the professional and managerial groups of occupations.[11] Connections with powerful countries of origin were helpful to some in obtaining jobs with trading firms, or setting up their own establishments.

In recent decades U.S. imperialism has used great resources, and conducted two wars, to establish itself as the dominant power in Asia, under the new conditions when outright colonialism is no longer possible. Evidences of extreme oppression of Asians within the United States, and consequent bitter liberation struggles, would hamper the maneuvers of the U.S. Government and the penetration of U.S. multinational corporations in Southeast Asia and the Far East. Similar considerations apply to the role of Hawaii, with its majority of Asian and Oceanic peoples, as a huge U.S. military base.

The Asian and Oceanic peoples comprise only 4% of the oppressed national-racial minorities in the United States. Concessions to them cost relatively little in comparison with what major gains by the Black people, for example, would cost their exploiters. Moreover, dominant forces in California may speculate on being able to use Japanese and

Chinese against Blacks and Chicanos on the divide and rule principle.

It should be noted, contrary to this possibility, that there are increasing signs both in New York and in California of the development of joint struggles of Asian, Black, and Puerto Rican or Chicano peoples, for equality and against all national and racial oppression.

Various groups among the white population retain a degree of solidarity according to the national origins of their forefathers who first immigrated to this country. Recently the Census Bureau has compiled income statistics for eight of these "ethnic groups," comprising about half the population of the United States, and over 60% of the white population (Table 8).

TABLE 8

MEDIAN FAMILY INCOMES OF ETHNIC GROUPS AND BLACKS, 1971

ETHNIC GROUP	NUMBER OF FAMILIES (thousands)	MEDIAN FAMILY INCOME
Russian	660	$13,929
Polish	1,429	12,182
Italian	2,511	11,646
English, Scottish, Welsh	8,467	11,345
Irish	4,289	11,060
German	7,201	10,977
French	1,437	10,272
Spanish	2,057	7,595
Black	5,157	6,440

SOURCE: P-20, No. 249, T. 9; P-60, No. 85, T. 16.

Except for the small Russian group, the differentiation between the white ethnic groups (other than the "Spanish"—mainly Chicanos and Puerto Ricans), is not marked. The range of medians among the four most numerous white ethnic groups is less than $700. By contrast, the differential between the largest white ethnic group, the British, and the Blacks is nearly $5,000.

The Census does not report a Jewish ethnic group. It may be that a large proportion of those listed as Russians are, in fact, of Russian Jewish ancestry, and that the large proportion of professionals and petty bourgeois, as well as capitalists, among the Jewish people accounts for the high median family income in this group. Also relevant are the high income White Guard Russian families who became part of the U.S. aristocracy.

The important point here is the economic levelling between the descendants of later groups of white immigrants and the descendants of the earliest European immigrants, who came mainly from Britain. Two lines of reasoning can be extracted from this, one misleading, and the other valid.

The false argument concerns the American "melting pot," and its application to the Black people, namely, if the Irish, Germans, Jews, etc., "made it," so can the Blacks. These other groups were all victims of prejudice and discrimination, it is argued, but overcame this situation, and so can the Blacks. If they fail, it's just their own fault. Sometimes it is even claimed that the Blacks "came later," so all they need is a little patience, and their turn to catch up will come also. *Of course, the opposite is the case.* The Blacks, alone among the various large national groups, came here simultaneously with the first Europeans, and amounted to nearly one-fifth of the total population at the time independence was won. The point is that they were brought to this country as slaves, and that the white capitalist class, like the slave-owners before them, has maintained as much as possible the master-slave relationship towards the Black population. To this end, they take advantage of the marked difference in skin color, which makes most Blacks easy to identify. It was not so long ago that blackness as a mark of congenital intellectual and spiritual inferiority was broadly disseminated as a main component of the dominant culture of the United States.

Struggles of the Black people, and changes in the world situation have compelled a reduction of crude racist propaganda and "blackface culture," but it continues in different, often veiled, forms, with a persistence and pervasiveness far outmatching the prejudices directed against any white ethnic group.

Moreover, there is this important difference between the present situation of the Blacks and that of the white immigrant groups at an earlier stage in history. Then, as barriers connected with ethnic discrimination and language difficulties were removed, there was room for successive waves of immigrants to "make it" in a broadly expanding economy. In this generation, the increasingly monopolized and less dynamic United States economy has lost the possibility of making way for large new groups in the population simply by removing barriers against them. Now the disastrous effects of past racist discrimination can be overcome only through far-reaching practical measures *explicitly* directed towards that end.

Yet, there is an important real significance to the fact that the median family income of English, Scottish and Welsh families was not much different from that of other white ethnic groups. In fact, it was only about 3% above the Labor Department's estimate of the intermediate budget needed in 1971 to finance a quite modest standard of living. This means that nearly half of all strictly Anglo families fell below that budget, and that a substantial majority of Anglo families consisted of working people, who themselves were receiving much less income than they produced by their labor, who were themselves victims of exploitation, and not exploiters.

It is true that to this day the largest and most powerful billionaire families, and the owners of a dominant share in the large-scale means of production, are of British origin, with an admixture of German origin. But these comprise a tiny minority of the British-origin families. Historically, and currently, some of the bitterest class struggles in the United States have been by workers, largely of Anglo origin, against exploiters

Chart 3

INCOME BY YEARS OF SCHOOL COMPLETED
males 25 and over, 1971

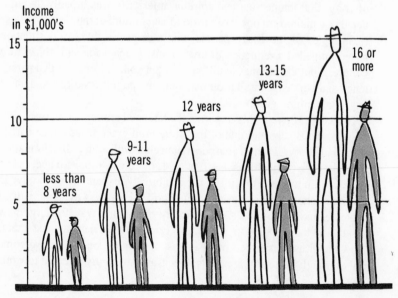

of the same ethnic origin. It is the handful of owners, and not the majority of working people of British or other white ethnic origin, who are the profiteers from racism, and the ultimate founts of racist ideology.

Thus the struggle for equality cannot be rationally waged against "white-Anglos" in general. To be successful it must be waged against the largely Anglo exploiters of both whites and Blacks, through an alliance of the exploited whites and the superexploited Blacks.

Education and Income

A common apologetic argument is that all the Black people need to overcome their disadvantage is more education. Firstly, this overlooks or minimizes the serious handicap imposed on Blacks by their lack of access to equal educational opportunities—beginning with the inferior, and often crudely racist—teaching practices in the largely segregated schools to which most Black youth are limited, and ending with the financial stresses which make it more difficult for Blacks than whites to obtain a higher education.

Secondly, a high school diploma or a college degree, are less advantageous for a Black than for a white. Economic discrimination, relative to education, is severe at all levels of education, and seemingly increases with the amount of education. Roughly speaking, a Black man has to obtain three to four more years education than a white man to rate the same income. Or, to put it another way, a Black man with more than an elementary school education will have an income about 30% less than that of a white man with the same amount of education. (Table 9).

TABLE 9

MEAN INCOMES, BY YEARS OF SCHOOL COMPLETED
OF PERSONS 25 YEARS AND OLDER, 1971

YEARS OF SCHOOL COMPLETED	MALES		% BLACK OF	FEMALES		% BLACK
	WHITE	BLACK	OF WHITE	WHITE	BLACK	OF WHITE
less than 8	$ 4,984	$ 3,912	78	$2,060	$1,761	85
8	6,378	4,877	76	2,465	2,310	94
9-11	8,277	5,909	71	3,127	2,857	91
12	9,772	6,748	69	3,949	3,890	99
13-15	11,248	7,483	67	4,466	5,055	113
16 or more	15,355	10,684	70	6,666	7,464	112

SOURCE: P-60, No. 85, T. 49.

Among females the result is markedly different. Black women high school graduates almost equaled white women high school graduates in income, and Black women who had gone to college substantially exceeded white women with the same number of years of education in income. This is the kind of statistical comparison which is used by apologists to preach the "solution" of the problem of economic discrimination. Yes, there is a trick to it. Black women who have received a high school education or more are almost always required to work so that they can contribute substantially to family incomes. But relatively more white women with a higher education have well-paid husbands, and can afford to stay home and bring up their children. In such cases, they usually have small incomes from savings or investments, hold part-time jobs, or get some work they can do at home a few hours a week. This pulls down the average incomes of white women in such a way that the white-Black comparison among females is misleading. In 1970, 78% of Black women college graduates were employed, as compared with only 56% of white women college graduates.[12]

Of those with incomes in 1971, 17.5% of the whites, but only 7.4% of the Blacks, had incomes of under $1,500, representing income from occasional work or small investments. These recipients of small occasional income artificially pull down the average for the entire group, yielding the false picture of a differential favorable to Black college graduates. Actually, the differential in economic status remains substantially favorable to white women college graduates. Thus 5.2% of the white women, but only 2.4% of the Black women college graduates had incomes of over $15,000.[13]

There is another kind of evidence, which is in some ways more striking, of the tremendous economic differential against Blacks, regardless of education. There are seventeen states where the median educational level of Blacks is equal to, a little more or a little less than that of whites. But in each such case, the median income of Blacks is far lower than that of whites. Again, the comparison is limited to males, because of the mentioned distorting factors influencing comparisons among females. (Table 10)

Not only were the median incomes of Black men far below those of white men in every one of these states, but the record was no better than in states where Black educational levels were significantly lower than white educational levels. In fact, in 8 of the 17 states, the ratio of Black

TABLE 10

SCHOOL YEARS COMPLETED AND INCOMES,
MALES 18 AND OVER, SELECTED STATES, 1970

	MEDIAN SCHOOL YEARS COMPLETED		MEDIAN INCOME	
	WHITES	BLACKS	WHITES	BLACKS
Maine	12.2	12.3	$5646	$3484
New Hampshire	12.3	12.5	6639	3925
Vermont	12.2	12.7	6166	3711
Massachusetts	12.4	12.0	7414	5312
Minnesota	12.3	12.2	7057	5223
North Dakota	12.1	12.6	5366	3530
South Dakota	12.1	12.5	5205	2864
Montana	12.3	12.5	6288	2614
Idaho	12.3	12.2	6168	3300
Wyoming	12.4	12.3	6716	3597
Colorado	12.5	12.3	6739	4679
New Mexico	12.4	12.1	6006	4015
Washington	12.5	12.2	7683	5242
California	12.5	12.1	7818	5573
Alaska	12.6	12.4	8649	4585
Hawaii	12.7	12.4	6436	3327

SOURCE: U.S.-D-344.

to white median incomes for males was below the national average of 61%.

Note that in every one of these states more than half of the Black males (or exactly half in the case of Massachusetts) had gone beyond the high school level in education. And yet in every one of these states Black incomes were far below the norm for white men, even where their educational level averaged lower than this. How can a reasonable person explain away a situation like that existing in Montana, where, with a higher average educational status, Black men had less than half the median incomes of white? Ironically, in each of the four states with the highest median incomes of Black men — over $6,000 — the median educational level of Black men fell below that of white men by more than one year.

Incomes of Black Women

Average incomes among year-around full time workers in 1972 came to $12,166 for white males, $7,809 for Black males, $6,625 for white females, and $5,692 for Black females.[14] Taking the figure for white males as 100, then the index for Black males was 64, for white females 54, and for Black females 47. Situated at the bottom of the ladder, Black women averaged less than half of what white men received, which latter figure might be considered a standard wage in the United States.

paid, as are Black men, and that Black women are paid least of all. But it is not accurate to claim, as some do, that the oppression and exploitation of women *in general* is worse than that of Blacks. The special social and personal oppression of women in a capitalist society is of a different quality than the racist oppression of Blacks, so that attempts at quantitative comparisons of the two evils are apt to be misleading. However, it is possible to talk of economic exploitation and elements of oppression clearly related to it, in common terms.

First, one would hesitate to conclude that the lower average incomes of full-time white working women, as compared with Black working men, represents a higher rate of exploitation. Consideration must be given to the fact that many Black men are employed on the most dangerous, unhealthy, strenuous jobs, on night shifts, and for long hours; that more Black men, relatively, than white women moonlight on extra jobs, etc.

Still, it is certain that many white women workers are very badly off, are severely exploited, whether more or less so than Black men being beside the point. *But this cannot be said of white women in general.* In 1973, 33% of all white women were in the full-time labor force. Two out of three white women worked part-time or didn't work outside the home at all because they did not have to. On the other hand, 40% of all Black women were in the full-time labor force. Only three out of five worked either part time or not at all.[15] And white women received several times more income, per capita, than Black women from ownership of property, and from employed husbands.

A much larger proportion of Black than white women work under the double difficulty of having to care for children at the same time. In 1970, 46% of all Black women in the labor force had children not yet grown up, as compared with 37% of white women in the labor force. Moreover, 36% of the Black women in the labor force with children were also heads of households, as compared with 16% of similarly situated white women.[16]

In situations where both husband and wife are working, the Black woman's burden is apt to be heavier, because her husband is earning much less than the white husband, in addition to her receiving less than the white wife. Similarly, the homemaker's job of a non-working Black wife is apt to be more difficult than that of a white housewife, because of the lower income of the Black husband.

The U.S. Women's Bureau has published these revealing figures on the percentages of families below the official poverty level in 1970. Among those headed by white men, 7%, headed by Black men, 24%, headed by white women, 25%, and headed by Black women, 50%.[17]

Barbara Deckard and Howard Sherman comment:

"Even the median white male wage is under what the Bureau of Labor Statistics considers 'moderate, but adequate,' which is why so many wives must work. Still lower is the white woman's wage, showing even greater economic discrimination. And lowest of all is the wage of the Black woman (whose median is at the poverty level), reflecting the double burden of racist and sexist discrimination."[18]

An eloquent and generally valid summary, except for the qualification cited above, that the lower wage of white women as compared with Black men does not necessarily, or even probably, show "even greater discrimination."

Poverty

Official measurements set boundaries, depending on family size, below which people are regarded as living in poverty. According to the 1970 Census, 9.9% of the "white-Anglo" population, and 35.0% of the Black population, had incomes below the poverty level in 1969. The boundaries, however, are far below realistic levels. A somewhat more realistic measure is provided by the Census count of those living below 125% of the "official" poverty level: 14.0% of the "white-Anglo" population, and 42.9% of the Black population, were below this line.[19]

The Black poor were poorer than the white poor. The "mean income deficit" of an officially poor white family was $1,427, and of an officially poor Black family, $1,832. A larger percentage of the Blacks were working poor, and a larger percentage lived in abominable conditions. Thus 11.7% of the poor white families, but 25.2% of the poor Black families, lived in dwelling units that lacked plumbing facilities.[20] A larger proportion of the Black families live in metropolitan areas, and especially in central cities, where prices are higher and public services lower than elsewhere. The Census does not allow for such differentials in setting its poverty boundaries.

Chart 4
FAMILY INCOME
COMPARED TO BLS BUDGETS, 1971

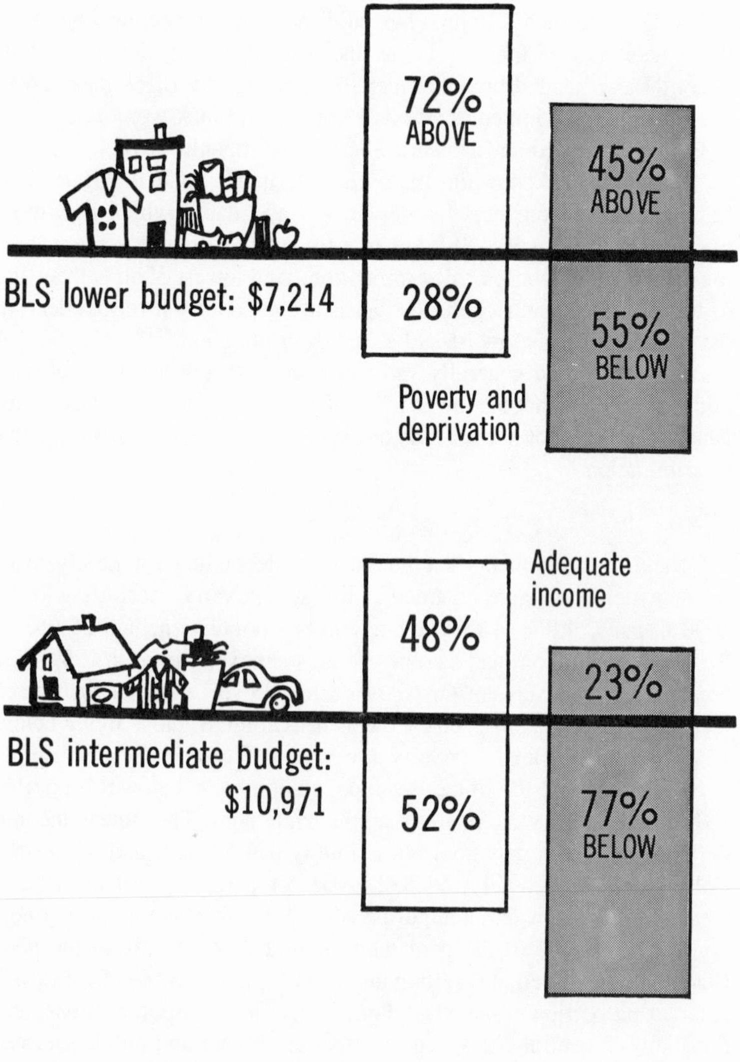

BLS lower budget: $7,214

72% ABOVE

28%

Poverty and deprivation

45% ABOVE

55% BELOW

Adequate income

BLS intermediate budget: $10,971

48%

52%

23%

77% BELOW

Considering all of these qualifications, it seems reasonable to conclude that as much as one half of the Black population are living in a greater or lesser degree of poverty, and that a substantial majority are unable to afford what is generally regarded as a normal, moderate, U.S. living standard. This can be verified by comparison of incomes with the standard budgets of the U.S. Bureau of Labor Statistics.

In 1971 the "lower budget" of the BLS for a family of four came to $7,214.[21] One can say that for a family to fall below the BLS lower budget level of income signifies poverty, or at least "deprivation" as that broader term is sometimes used. In that year 28.3% of the white families, and 55.6% of the Black families, fell below the lower budget income level. So more than one-fourth of the white families (including many of "Spanish origin"), and *considerably more than half of all Black families were below the line of poverty or deprivation.* The white-Black differential, using this boundary, was somewhat wider than indicated by the simple percentages, and not only because of the factors mentioned above. The BLS budget used was for a family of four. The average size of white families was 3.47 persons, but of Black families 4.05 persons.[22]

In order to live in reasonable comfort, if a bit sparsely, a family must attain the "intermediate budget" of the BLS. In 1971, 48.1% of the white families, but only 23.5% of the Black families, reached that level, which was then $10,971.[23]

It is often said that poverty in the United States is not comparable with poverty in countries of Asia and Africa. True, people in the United States are not often found dead of starvation on the streets, as in some Asian cities, or lying on parched ground, as in some African near-deserts.

But it is also true that millions and millions of people in the United States suffer from malnutrition resulting from poverty. It is true that repeatedly senatorial and other investigators have uncovered mass near-starvation of poor Black people in southern states, often leading to permanent brain and muscular damage to children—and that the U.S. Congress has done nothing effective about it. And it is true that countless hungry Black children in northern cities have been poisoned by eating lead-bearing wall flakings while their mothers were away at work. And it is true that the lives of Blacks are years shorter than those of whites, and that infant mortality is much higher among Blacks than among whites, because of poverty. And it is true that the standards of governmental relief for poverty have been deteriorating, even as the need increases with soaring inflation, especially of poor people's, food. It is true that in the year 1974 many poor people turned to eating dogfood and catfood in an attempt to survive.

An expert report to a Senate Committee in 1974 found that "Over the past three to four years, our nation's needy have become hungrier and poorer," that the cost of food has gone up much faster than the allotments for welfare or food stamps, that only 35.7% of the 37 million people eligible for food stamps actually get them.

The report moved towards the root of the matter when it noted that "more than a food stamp . . . or child-feeding programs is at issue. The food programs cannot end their poverty; and fundamentally people are hungry because they are poor."

It called for "a just, dignified, guaranteed income maintenance program that ensures that no person lives without adequate income."[24]

But, still more than that is needed. As examples in the report indicated, a very large proportion of those suffering from hunger and poverty are Blacks, Indians, and other oppressed peoples. No matter what programs are adopted, unless they are accompanied by specific programs to end racist economic discrimination, the evils and suffering of poverty will not be stopped.

Regardless of the absolute comparison of U.S. poverty with that in the "Third World," it is necessary to say that the depths of suffering of the poor and deprived in this, the world's richest country, are most extreme, in relation to the labor output of U.S. workers, the most productive in the world; in relation to the country's rich natural resources, vast territory, and mild climate. And it is necessary to say that the burden of this poverty and deprivation on the substantial majority of the 28 million Black people is the bitter fruit of racist oppression imposed by U.S. capitalism. This poverty must be eliminated as the top priority domestic reform in living conditions.

4. Trends in Incomes

We have seen that per capita incomes of Blacks, realistically estimated, are about half those of "white-Anglo" people. What have been the changes in relative incomes since World War II?

Of course, the real incomes of most Black people have increased, as have those of most white people. But these gains have to be considered in relation to changing living requirements, changing standards and life styles, farm-city migration, and the changing class composition of the population.

The most crucial question is the change in the relative economic position of Blacks and whites. If the real income of the Black family is doubled, but remains half that of the white family, the Black family is just as much discriminated against as before, the social and political consequences are just as severe, the racism and injustice of a social structure which perpetuates this remains deserving of condemnation. Indeed, it is sometimes argued, and not without reason, that this case represents a worsening of discrimination, in that the margin by which the white family can buy more goods and services than the Black family has doubled in real terms. Floyd McKissick writes:

"Even more distressing, however, is the fact that dollar-wise the Black family's economic position is growing worse. The median family income of Black people as a percent of white family income has increased since 1947, but the dollar gap adjusted for price changes has widened.''[1]

In this chapter, we will concentrate on trends in the ratio of Black to white incomes. But the point made by McKissick should be kept in mind, and it is still true that over the past 30 years the gap between white and Black purchasing power has widened considerably in absolute terms, that the Blacks require a much bigger gain in the quantities of goods they are able to buy in order to attain economic equality.

While per capita income provides the best single measure of overall economic status, such figures, for whites and Blacks separately, have been published so far only in the 1970 Census for the year 1969.*

We are able to study the trend of the Black/white income relationship for the entire period since 1945 by reference to the Census Bureau figures on median family incomes. These are provided by the decennial Census for 1959 and 1969, and by the annual current population reports of consumer income for other years. Prior to 1964, the Census Bureau lumped together the income figures for all minority people. Beginning in 1964 they have also given the figures for Blacks separately. This makes a sizeable difference, and one that has been increasing as the incomes of the Asian people have gone well ahead of those of Blacks. For the years prior to 1964, we have made adjustments to the figures for minority families, to arrive at estimates of median incomes for Black families alone.

The calculations have provided a continuous picture of the ratio of family incomes of Blacks to whites extending over a 29 year period. This is shown graphically in chart A, and statistically in Table 11. The results must be surprising to people who have been convinced by official and academic apologetic propaganda that discrimination is rapidly vanishing from the American scene.

In 1973 the median family income of Blacks was 57.7% of that of

---

* From data contained in the 1960 Census, it is possible to make an estimate of Black and white per capita income in 1959. That estimate gives a ratio of 47%. The increase of the 54% ratio derived from 1969 Census figures is consistent with the increase of 8.7 percentage points in the ratio of Black to white median family incomes over the same decade.

Also, since 1967, the annual Census Bureau surveys of consumer income contain data which permit calculation of per capita incomes of whites and Blacks. For the last three years available these show trends inconsistent with the published figures of median family income. This may be due to an excessive dispersion of Black incomes, as reported by the Census, after 1970, and to an excessively speedy reduction in the Census estimates of Black family sizes. Presumably the Census statisticians will publish annual calculations of per capita income, by race, when they consider the data sufficiently reliable.

whites, just 2.4 percentage points higher than the ratio 28 years earlier, when the median income of Black families was 55.3% of that of whites. If the gains continue at that snail-like pace, Black/white equality in the United States will be reached in the year 2467. Hardly anybody can expect, in this day and age, that the moving forces of history will show such patience! Also, remember that the ratios of Black/white median family income should be adjusted downward around 10 percentage points to allow for the combined effects of larger Black family size and the exclusion of most property income from the Census surveys.

TABLE 11

PERCENTAGE BLACK MEDIAN FAMILY INCOMES
OF WHITE MEDIAN FAMILY INCOMES, 1945-1973

YEAR	% BLACK OF WHITE INCOME	YEAR	% BLACK OF WHITE INCOME	YEAR	% BLACK OF WHITE INCOME
1945	55.3	1955	53.9	1965	53.6
1946	51.4	1956	51.3	1966	57.8
1947	49.9	1957	52.1	1967	59.2
1948	52.2	1958	49.8	1968	60.0
1949	49.8	1959	52.2	1969	60.9
1950	53.0	1960	53.8	1970	61.3
1951	51.4	1961	51.8	1971	60.3
1952	55.4	1962	51.8	1972	59.4
1953	54.6	1963	51.3	1973	57.7
1954	54.1	1964	54.3		

SOURCES AND TECHNICAL NOTES: Median family incomes of white families and minority families: 1945-1949 (1946 urban families only), US Dept. of Labor, Bull. 1119, Dec. 1952, *Negroes in the United States*, Table 23, p. 49. 1950-1968, 1970-1972, P-23, No. 46, Table 7, p. 17

Median family incomes of white and Black families, 1969, U.S. C-94 1973, P-60, No. 93, Table 1, p. 4.

Median family income of Black families, 1964-1968, 1970-1972; P-23, No. 46, Table 7, p. 17.

Median family income of Black families, 1945, 1947-1963: computed by formula taking into account changes in ratio of Black to total minority population, and using ratio of Black to total minority median incomes and population, as reported in the 1970 Census, as a base.

Percent Black of white median incomes, computed for all years except 1946. For 1946 derived by interpolation, using as an interpolating parameter the ratios of minority to white median incomes of urban families for 1945, 1946, and 1947, as given in Bulletin 1119, Table 23, p. 49.

The most striking fact brought out by the chart is not the 2-point gain over the entire period, but the flat trend line for the 20-year period 1945-1965. The first year's ratio, 55.3%, was exceeded only once in that twenty years, and then by only one-tenth of a point. And the low of

49.8% reached in 1949 was equalled once later, in 1958. Otherwise the ratio of Black to white median family incomes fluctuated up and down within the 50-55 percent range.

Then, in the last half of the 1960s, the ratio moved out of the range on the upside, reaching a high of 61.3% in 1970, but declining in the next two years to 57.7% in 1973.

What about the longer historical perspective? Rough estimates, based on 1939 and 1949 Census figures that are not quite comparable, suggest that the ratio of Black to white median family incomes increased by at least 10 percentage points during the World War II years, up to the 55.3% recorded for 1945. True, part of that gain may have been a mere recovery of losses in the relative status of Blacks during the grim depression years of the 1930s. Yet the economic gains during World War II were certainly the most substantial realized by Black people at any period, except, of course, in the immediate aftermath of liberation from slavery.

Chart 5

PERCENTAGE BLACK OF WHITE
MEDIAN FAMILY INCOME, 1945-1973

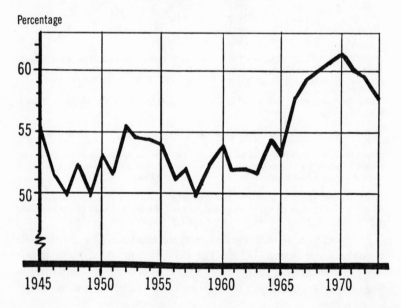

But this status achieved during World War II, involving still gross discrimination in all forms, represented the platform from which the postwar struggles for equality were launched. These struggles had to contend not only with that inertia standing in the way of anything progressive, but also against the continually operating tendencies to undermine and reverse past gains imposed by the workings of an economic system built up throughout its history on racist superexploitation of Blacks, and by the conscious efforts of the most reactionary forces within that society.

The results, for the first two postwar decades, were essentially a standoff, in which the gains of World War II were consolidated, although shakily and incompletely. Then, in the period initiated by the passage of far-reaching civil rights legislation and the launching of the Vietnam War in 1964-65, there was a push forward into new high ground. So far, the decade of the 1970s has again been one of sharpened and roughly balanced economic struggle, between the forces seeking to extend the gains of the late 1960s and the backlashers seeking to stem this tide and move backwards to more extreme profiteering from superexploitation of Blacks and other oppressed peoples. Indeed, if one were to judge only from the income statistics in Table 11, he would have to say the racists have had the better of it in this period.

Will the people of this country tolerate another two decades of stagnation or worse in the relative economic status of Black people, another two decades of the existing extreme discrimination against these 28 million human beings? The growing pace of changes on a world scale will not tolerate this without leading to explosive consequences, disastrous in nature. And it will be white working people, above all, by their attitudes and extent of participation on the side of and together with Black people in this struggle, that will determine whether the gains of the 1960s are resumed and a momentum of progress built up that cannot be reversed.

War and Black Incomes

The chart helps us to identify causes of fluctuations in the ratio of Black to white incomes.

As already indicated, the biggest gain — ten percentage points or more — occurred during World War II, which, in turn, involved the all-time peak of militarization of the U.S. and its economy. After losing ground in the early post-war years, the ratio regained 5 percentage points during the Korean War years, and, later, following another drop, 7 points between the start of the Vietnam War and its peak year of U.S. involvement in 1969.

Only in wartime does U.S. capitalism ever approach full employment. Only in wartime, have labor shortages been sufficiently severe to induce employers to open up previously closed occupations to Blacks, and to provide employment to many Black youth and women never previously able to get regular jobs. Even recruitment into the armed forces significantly increases the per capita income of the Black people as a whole.

Of course, this is a far cry from saying that war is good for Black people. All of the wars mentioned have subjected Black servicemen to the particular brutality of military racism. In the Vietnam War this took the special form of putting disproportionate numbers of Blacks in front line infantry positions, causing a higher percentage of Blacks killed. The wartime monetary gains of Blacks may be largely cancelled out by wartime shortages of commodities and housing, by the greater inflation afflicting the poor. Nor are these monetary gains outstanding in the circumstances. The key conclusion from the figures is that at the peak of World War II, despite the desperate shortage of labor power, the employers were more interested in maintaining racial barriers than in fully meeting their labor requirements in the most efficient way. A really unrestricted use of Black labor power would have resulted in Black family incomes reaching far more than 55% of those of "white Anglo" families.

Booms and Recessions and Black Incomes

In its economic effects, a war resembles to some extent an exaggerated version of a boom in a peacetime cycle. This brings us to a second factor causing fluctuations in the ratio of Black to white income.

The ratio goes down in depression, and goes up in recovery and boom.

The logic of this is simple enough. Since Black workers are last to be hired and first to be fired, the cyclical fluctuations in their employment are more severe than those of white workers. The chart and table help us to trace the cyclical movement of the ratio in non-war periods. The ratio of Black to white family income dropped from 52.2% in the peak boom year of 1948 to 49.8% in the recession or economic crisis year 1949. It rose to 53.0% in the boom year 1953.

Again, the drop from 52.1% in 1957 to 49.8% in 1958 represented the impact of the economic crisis of 1958. With the recovery in the next two years, the ratio got up to 53.8%, only to fall again to 51.8% in the mild recession year, 1961. Finally, there was a gain to 54.3% in 1964, which was the peak year of economic recovery from the 1961 recession prior to the Vietnam War.

There is a lag in the response of Black incomes to economic recoveries. The ratio of Black to white incomes continued to decline in the recovery years 1955 and 1956, and only increased in 1957, the last year of the upturn. This repeated the pattern of 1947 and 1948. Similarly, the ratio stagnated in 1962 and 1963 and only increased in 1964. One might almost say that in past experience, the gains of Black workers in relative economic status have appeared only at the peak of booms, almost as harbingers of the coming crises that would wipe out these gains.

The situation was still worse in the latest cycle. The ratio of Black to white family incomes continued to decline in both of the recovery years 1972 and 1973. There was not even a temporary relative gain before the inflationary slump of 1974 hit the Black population with especial severity. As indicated below, political factors were an important negative influence during this cycle.

Migration and Black Incomes

Migration has played a very important part in Black income trends. *Escape from southern rural oppression more than accounts for the gain in relative incomes of Blacks since World War II.*

The 5.7 million Blacks living in rural areas in 1950 comprised 38% of all Black people, while twenty years later only 4.2 million Blacks, 19% of the much larger Black population, lived in the countryside. Among the white population, on the other hand, the rural population held steady at 49 million, declining from 36% of the total in 1950 to 28% in 1970.[2]

Then as now, the Black rural population was overwhelmingly concentrated in the South. In 1950, even more than at present, the southern rural Blacks lived in the deepest poverty, and were subject to superexploitation and lack of human rights as sharecroppers, farm laborers, woodcutters, and service workers for the racist white ruling class.

By escaping to the cities, partly in the South and even more in the North, Blacks advanced from being victims of racial oppression under a legal, political, and economic structure with important features carried over from slavery, to being victims of special racist oppression within the framework of capitalist industry and bourgeois-democratic laws. Undoubtedly, by making this move, millions of Black people achieved a certain improvement in life. But as the weight of the Black population in the cities increased, the capitalists intensified the extra exploitation of Black urban dwellers.

Within the cities, the income differential against Blacks is wider than it was in 1945.

In 1945, the median income of urban minority families was 66.5% of that of urban white families. A reasonable estimate is that the corresponding ratio for Black urban families was 65.0% of the median for urban white families. But in 1969, according to the latest Census, the median income of all urban minority families was 64.3% of that of urban white families; the median income of urban Black families was 61.9% of that of urban white families.[3]

Moreover, the remaining Black rural population is still largely excluded from sharing in the transformation of farming and country life generally which has resulted from application of the scientific-technical revolution to agriculture. The incomes of rural Black families remain considerably less than half those of rural white families — in 1969 the ratio was 46% for Black and white families living on farms, and 47% for rural non-farm families. Per capita income of Blacks living on farms was only 38% of that of white people living on farms, while the per capita income ratio for rural non-farm people was 41%. The Black country people were even considerably worse off than the Chicano people of the Southwest living on the countryside.[4]

For a large proportion of the white rural population, the gap between country and city living standards has been closed, but not yet for the Blacks remaining in the countryside, not by a long shot. Moreover, with the tremendous increase in land values everywhere, notably in the countryside, the virtual exclusion of Blacks from landownership becomes a factor of increasing economic discrimination, for the most part not reflected in current income statistics.

Migration from South to North by Blacks has meant migration from wider to narrower income differentials. While the Black southern population has continued to grow slowly, as a result of relatively high birth rates, important migration continued, and Black population in the North and West has increased rapidly. In 1950, two-thirds of the Black population lived in the South, but by 1970, only a little more than half of the Black population lived there — 53%. In those twenty years, the number of Black people living in the North and West doubled. By 1975, it is likely that fully half of the Black people live outside the South, despite recent reports of reverse migration.

Census Bureau estimates of the ratio of Black to white median family incomes, by regions, are available for 1959 and for the years 1967-1972. They yield important results (Table 12).

TABLE 12

REGIONAL RATIOS OF BLACK TO WHITE FAMILY INCOME
SELECTED YEARS, 1959-1972

REGION	PERCENTAGE BLACK OF WHITE MEDIAN FAMILY INCOME			
	1959	1967	1970	1972
Northeast	69	65	71	64
North Central	74	77	73	70
West	67	74	77	71
South	46	54	57	55
U.S. Total	51*	59	61	59

SOURCE: P-23, No. 42, T. 19; P-23 No. 46, T.8.

For the United States as a whole, over the thirteen year interval from 1959 to 1972, the gain in the Black/white family income ratio was 8 percentage points. But only in the South, where the gain was 9 points, was that national gain equalled. In the West, where only 8% of the Black population lived in 1970, the gain was 4 points. But in the Northeast and in the North Central states there were *losses* of 5 percentage points and 4 percentage points respectively.

In all regions, except the Northeast, there was a gain between 1959 and 1967, and by 1968 there was a gain in the Northeast as well. But in all regions, including the South, there was a loss between 1970 and 1972, and in the Northeast and in the West these losses were quite sharp — 7 and 6 percentage points respectively.

By moving from South to North, Blacks have achieved absolute economic gains. But within the northern regions, there has been a decided decline in the relative economic position of Blacks since 1959,

---

* This figure differs by one percentage point from that used in Table 11. The figure used in Table 11 is a later revision, but the uncorrected figure is used here for consistency with the regional figures.

and, while comparable statistics are not available, it is certain that there was an even wider decline since the end of World War II.

Since 1959 alone, the gap between the South and the rest of the country in the degree of discrimination against Blacks has been cut in half. In the first years of the current decade, there was a deterioration in the relative position of Black people in every region of the country.

These changes cannot be accounted for solely by economic factors.

The Role of Politics

The political struggles of the Black people and their white allies, and the counteroffensive of racist reactionaries, have been decisive in the gains and losses of the Black people. The balance in these specific struggles generally was correlated with the balance in the overall struggle between progress and reaction in the political life of the country.

Thus, the sharp economic gains of Blacks during World War II were not due only to the labor shortage. They were very much connected with the rise during the 1930s of united struggles and organizations of Black and white workers, for relief of unemployment, for the formation of

Chart 6
BLACK LOSS OF RELATIVE INCOME BY REGIONS, 1970-1972

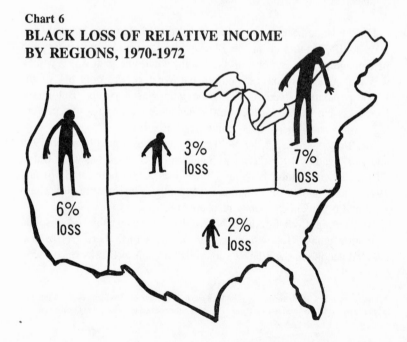

trade unions, for social insurance. These struggles were greatly influenced by Communists, and by the slogan of "Black and white, unite and fight!"

The mass backing for such a course had its influence on the general stance of the Roosevelt administration, which set up a Fair Employment Practices Committee and took relatively advanced positions for the time on race questions. Although their practical actions were limited, Roosevelt and his administration created a climate in which gains could be won more readily.

The participation of the United States in a war against racist Hitler fascism, although marred by U.S. governmental and military racist tactics against its Japanese enemies and against Japanese-American civilians, created a favorable atmosphere for gains against racism at home.

On the other hand, political factors of an opposite character were very much in operation in the 20 years following World War II. After all, the significant long-time demographic and economic factors which contributed substantially to the gains in relative Black incomes during the late 1960s were also operative during the period 1945-1965 — migration from South to North, from farm to city. All other things being equal, these should have led to a steady upward trend in the national average ratio of Black to white incomes. Instead this ratio stagnated.

This can only mean that within each of the regions, or most of the regions of the country, in industry as well as in agriculture, pressures were operating to push down the relative position of Black people. And these pressures can be readily identified.

These were the decades of the cold war, of virulent anti-communism. Anti-communism and racism went together as twins. The infamous Peekskill riots of 1949, the outstanding fascist assault on masses of people during the entire period, symbolized this. It was directed with equal venom against the Communists and against the Blacks, especially Paul Robeson, the leading figure of the occasion. It was not for nothing that F.B.I. agents, hunting Communists, asked the neighbors of suspects if those being investigated had Black visitors. Indeed, this was doubly significant, revealing the racism of the ruling Establishment in its full brazenness.

The anti-Communist putsches in the trade unions deposed almost all progressive leaders, including the main Black leaders who had contributed so much to the organization of the unorganized in the 1930s and

1940s. The defeat of the Communists and other left forces in the unions made it possible for employers to defeat the Communist demand for superseniority for Black workers, designed to break the pattern of "first to be fired" in the postwar reconversion period, and in the subsequent 1949 crisis. Along with the mass expulsion of Communists from factories, there was a reduction in Black industrial employment, a period of several years during which the real income of the Black people declined not only in relation to that of whites, but also absolutely.

The purge of progressives from the Government included the liquidation of the wartime Fair Employment Practices Committee, and the liquidation of those agricultural programs which, for the first time, had given some assistance to Black farmers in maintaining their positions on the land against the assaults of racist large landowners bent on converting to mechanized agriculture with hired labor.

Low cost public housing, as a means of solving the urgent postwar housing shortages, was downgraded in quantity and quality, converted into largely segregated extensions of ghettoes, while subsidies were given for the construction of millions of units of "middle-income" housing, almost wholly limited to whites. Continued inferiority in housing and education facilities reduced the competitive situation of Blacks in the labor market.

The racist war against the Korean people, and racist propaganda against and encirclement of People's China, domestic McCarthyism and the imprisonment of the Communist leaders, made it easier for employers to raise their profits and divide their workers by the full use of racial discrimination. The large-scale importation of fascist and pro-fascist refugees from socialist countries provided an ultra-right base for attacks on Black workers and a buttress for racist right-wing leaders of trade unions.

But underneath, changes were going on in the world and in the United States. Domestic public pressure and the resistance of the Korean people forced an end to the Korean War. The Vietnamese people won independence over French colonialists, who were supplied and financed by the U.S. Government. It became increasingly clear that the U.S. could not "roll back" the boundaries of socialism in Europe or Asia. European capitalist countries began to establish normal trade and cultural relations with them. Popular revulsion against McCarthyism drove its chief protagonist into disgrace. All in all, the politics of anti-Communism began to lose its influence, and so did the racism that went with it.

In 1954 the Supreme Court handed down its famous decision banning segregated schools in principle. It was also the year when the Montgomery, Alabama, mass struggle against segregated seating on buses began.

A decade of civil rights struggles followed. Tens of its participants were murdered by racist police and gangsters. Thousands were beaten up and jailed. But bit by bit the walls of Jim Crow were blasted down. And by the 1960s large trade unions, with hundreds of thousands of members, joined the struggle. A tremendous demonstration was held in Washington, D.C. This stage of struggle culminated in significant legislative victories which outlawed the special regime of legal racism in the South, and insisted on the end of segregated education and of discrimination in employment on account of race or color.

Continued struggles in the South, extending over a period of several more years forced the carrying out of many provisions of the Civil Rights Act of 1965. Legalized and semi-legal segregation of Blacks was ended. Blacks could no longer be barred from public places. They won the right to vote. Overtly, separate job descriptions and lower wage scales for Blacks were ended. True, these formal victories were far from complete and much remained to be done to consolidate them. This was especially true of the economic field, where the immediate fruits of the civil rights legislation were not great.

In the following years civil rights struggles were increasingly reinforced by economic struggles, drives to organize and win contracts and better conditions on the part of some of the most exploited Black workers. There were more cases in the South of cooperative action of Black and white workers in trade unions. Increasing use was made of the courts and the administrative apparatus charged with enforcing the employment provisions of Civil Rights laws.

These actions brought about a significant reduction in the degree of discrimination against Blacks in the economic life of the South, although as can be seen from Table 12, it remains more severe there than in the rest of the country.

Meanwhile, struggles of Blacks in the North were concentrated on the issue of police brutality and around school segregation and community control of schools. Except for spontaneous urban risings, there was little development of a genuine mass movement, as distinguished from struggles of individuals and local groups.

Economic struggles of particular groups of workers, which included large proportions of Blacks, won important victories, as in the case of the New York City hospital workers. Such struggles involved only a small proportion of all Black workers, however. There were prolonged campaigns to overcome the racist exclusion of Blacks from the skilled construction crafts, sometimes backed by community picket lines, but mainly relying on appeals to governmental administrative agencies and courts, and negotiations with the racist trade union bureaucracy.

Meanwhile, the counteroffensive of racist reaction was not without effect. It concentrated on the areas of housing and education. Through the combined action of bankers and real estate magnates, using racist incitation of whites, and offering incentives in improved living conditions, masses of the white population have been moved out of the central cities into suburbs, while the Blacks for the most part remain more and more segregated in sections of central cities and in equally segregated suburban areas.

Simultaneously, more and more factories and business offices have been moved to suburban areas where they are accessible to white residents but not to Black people in the central cities. Thus the social discrimination of organized housing segregation has its direct economic impact. Simultaneously, through housing segregation, gerrymandering of school districts, and other devices of racist school boards, and by the flourishing of racially exclusive private schools, educational segregation has increased in the North, and desegregation partly counterbalanced in the South. Since the Blacks receive inferior education in the segregated schools, this also has its negative impact on their economic welfare.

These factors limited the overall economic gains of Blacks, especially in the northern regions of the country, in the latter half of the 1960s.

In 1969 the Nixon administration, the most overtly racist in modern times, came into office. The president and his top aides directly assisted the racists in their attempts to increase segregation in housing and education, and to defeat enforcement of equal employment policies. Official propaganda supported the formulas of opposition to school busing and opposition to special programs to enforce employment of Blacks in occupations from which they had been effectively barred.

Budget allocations were shifted to leave more discretion to racist school boards and local municipal authorities. Vast sums were spent for training and equipping police forces for "riot control," which meant in effect repression of the Black communities, and the FBI together with local police forces engaged in raids against centers of Black militant organizations, with a number of dead victims among the Blacks. The trial of Communist woman professor Angela Davis on murder charges represented the infamous climax of this drive.

Simultaneously an intense propaganda campaign was launched to divert the Black population to the "Black capitalism" buildup, which succeeded in taking out of action a number of prominent Black militant leaders, and converted them into serving as glorified salesmen for the purveyors of "Black capitalism" bonds.

Encouraged by this government attitude, gangs of racist thugs, often operating under "white ethnic" labels, attacked Black people attempting to attend integrated schools, to establish themselves in formerly all-white areas, and otherwise to exercise their rights.

Undoubtely, this racist turn in the federal government contributed to the decrease in the relative economic status of Black people in all main regions of the country in the early 1970s. The recession of 1970, which continued into 1971, would be sufficient to account for the decline in the ratio of Black to white family incomes in 1971, and even, because of the lag in hiring of Blacks, in the recovery year 1972. But economic factors cannot account for the sharp decline in the ratio in 1973, a boom year. The prime blame must be placed on the cumulative impact of 5 years of government-encouraged intensified racism.

As before, broad national movements and international trends have interacted with the struggles over the conditions of the Black people in the United States. During the latter half of the 1960s, the Black liberation struggles converged with the surging peace movement and student movements to provide an improved climate and substantial practical support for the struggles of the Black people, contributing to the gains that were won.

These positive forces dwindled in the early 1970s, with the winding down of direct U.S. involvement in the Vietnam War and the reactionary counteroffensive of the Nixon administration.

The dictatorial, corrupt Nixon was replaced by Gerald Ford, chosen by Nixon and by the steel and automobile corporations. Ford intensified Nixon's racist offensive, coming out, in effect, for segregated schools, and thereby encouraging racist mobs who attacked Black children trying to attend supposedly integrated schools in Boston. He nominated for the vice presidency the centimillionaire Nelson Rockefeller, who had shown his true position on the race question with the slaughter of some 40 prisoners, mainly Black, at Attica, New York.

To the reactionary attack of the government was added the blows of a new economic crisis, fast on the heels of the 1970-71 recession, and the most severe and complicated since World War II. This crisis of the American workingman's standard of living included a sharp decline in real wages, a slump in production and a rise in unemployment, "double-digit" inflation; a crisis in the international economic and financial relationships of the U.S. and its multinational corporations, a loss of U.S. domination of the world's raw materials.

The burden of all this fell on U.S. workers, but with extra force on the Black people, over and beyond the special losses of Black workers from the operation of the "first to be fired" rule. Every survey showed that inflation was hitting the poor, and especially the lower income ghetto residents, harder than other sections of the population, as monopoly profiteering took the greatest advantage of those with the least physical and financial maneuverability.

The people of the country became increasingly disillusioned with big business and the government, angry at the corruption of corporate America, the profiteering of the ultra-rich from the inflation and depression which was slashing the people's living standards.

Which way would the people turn? Towards action against monopoly and its political representatives, towards demilitarization, towards radical reform, towards a rebuilding of trade union strength, towards racial equality? Or towards following the demagogic spokesmen of monopoly, the anti-Soviet/Pentagon axis, the union busters, the racists?

A new stage in the political and economic struggle was emerging. The political representatives of the most reactionary groups tried to turn the distress of large sections of the white population against the wrong enemies, against the Arabs and other peoples taking control of their own raw materials, against the Soviet Union and other socialist countries, and against the Black people and other minorities at home. The bloody hands of the CIA, behind the fascist terror in Chile, or their domestic equivalent, certainly played their part in inciting the facist riots against Black schoolchildren in Boston. There was an epidemic of police murders of Blacks, Indians, Chicanos, and Puerto Ricans.

But conditions were favorable for defeating this dangerous attempt. The Vietnam Peace Treaty signed in 1973 and the series of agreements for peaceful coexistence and cooperation between the U.S. and the USSR created a climate more conducive to rational dealing with issues. The struggle against racism gained momentum with the victorious liberation struggles of the African peoples of the former Portuguese colonies.

Black workers have become more important in the trade unions. They are prominent in the budding rank and file movements, and gaining many leadership posts. The multiplying election of Blacks to political office puts more power behind the drive of Black people for economic improvement. A nationwide campaign for enforcement of the legal requirements for job equality has developed. Important court decisions raise the possibility of large scale concessions in this area, particularly if there is sufficient support and activity on the part of white trade unionists and white people active in the political arena.

5. Discrimination in Employment and Wages

How can one account for the wide and continuing gap in incomes between Blacks and whites?

Academic researchers commonly "factor out" the difference — so much due to inferior education, so much to lower skill, so much to broken families, etc.; and the balance to racial discrimination. This tends to leave a small balance attributed to discrimination. *But what is worse, the very categories chosen by these researchers are expressions of their own racial prejudices.*

If Blacks have inferior education, that is due to racism. If they have fewer saleable skills, that is due to racism, both in access to training, and in employers' judgments of comparative skills. If they have more broken families, that is due to racist discrimination and segregation.

Yes, either one accepts the fascist-like racism of those who regard Blacks as anthropologically inferior — or one is forced to the conclusion that the economic differential against Blacks is *wholly, 100%*, due to racism. Given a clear understanding that racism is the underlying factor in all forms of economic differential, we can examine the components of the total differential. The main ones are:

- Differences in the kinds of jobs available to whites and to Blacks, including differences in the possibility of promotion to better jobs.
- Differences in pay for the same kind of work.
- Differences in access to any kind of work; that is, in unemployment.
- Differences in ownership of property, and in receipt of property income.

69

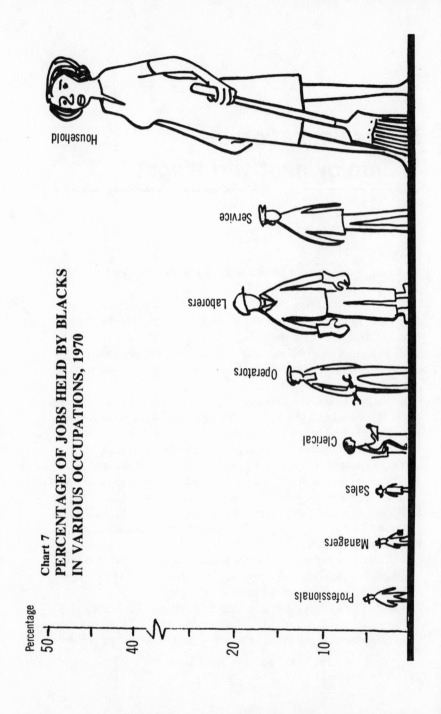

Percentage

Chart 7
PERCENTAGE OF JOBS HELD BY BLACKS IN VARIOUS OCCUPATIONS, 1970

50 —

40 —

20 —

10 —

Professionals   Managers   Sales   Clerical   Operators   Laborers   Service   Household

In this chapter, we consider the first two components, which are, in fact, the two most important components. Differences in unemployment are considered in Chapter 6, and in property income in Chapter 8.

Discrimination in Kinds of Jobs

Table 13 shows the percentage of jobs in each major occupation group held by Black people in 1970. This is sometimes referred to as the penetration ratio of Blacks into an occupation.

TABLE 13

PERCENTAGE OF BLACKS, BY MAJOR OCCUPATION GROUP, 1970

	PERCENTAGE OF BLACKS AMONG TOTAL EMPLOYED
Professional, technical	5
Managers and administrators	3
Farmers and farm managers	3
Sales workers	3
Clerical workers	7
Craftsmen, foremen	6
Operatives, except transport	13
Transport equipment operatives	14
Laborers, except farm	20
Farm laborers and foremen	19
Service workers	17
Private household workers	53
ALL OCCUPATIONS	10

SOURCE: P-23, No. 42, T. 52.

This is a visually striking table. The top six numbers, representing the penetration ratio of Blacks in the "better" occupation groups, are all small one-digit numbers. The lower six, covering the "less desirable" occupations, are all relatively large two-digit numbers. Blacks had 5.4% of the jobs in the first six groups combined, and 17.0% in the next six groups, or three times the penetration ratio in the former six.*

* In Table 13, farmers and farm managers are placed among the favored occupation groups, in accord with earlier Census practice, although now the Census Bureau places them near the bottom, just above farm laborers. This is typical of Census muddling of class and social relationships. Farmers occupy a social position similar to that of non-farm proprietors. While their Census-reported incomes are low, this is a statistical result of calculation of bookkeeping net income for tax purposes so far as *averages* are concerned. Of course, many *really* poor farmers remain, just as there are poor small urban business people.

The overall figures on occupation groups do not reveal the full depths of discrimination. They include within the groups and within specific occupations people really on the fringes of those groups or occupations — and that is more apt to be true of Blacks than of whites. Also they include government employees, among whom the pattern of discrimination is less sharp than in private industry. The exclusion of Blacks from better jobs is more complete in private industry, and especially in those industries which pay the highest wages and provide the best working conditions. A Commerce Department report shows that while Blacks had 3% of the high-paying jobs in all industries in 1970, they had only 1% of the high-paying jobs in high-wage industries, and their overall percentage of employment was moderately less in the high wage industries than in all industries.[1]

Large companies can afford the money to advertise their supposed merits as equal opportunity employers, but the record fails to show them as doing any better than the average of industrial employers. In 1972, employers of 500 or more workers accounted for total employment of 29.8 million, of whom 10.2% were Black. These large companies are required to file reports on Black and Spanish employment at various levels. Compilations of these reports by the Equal Employment Opportunity Commission (EEOC) showed "the Black percentage to be 2.6 for officials, managers and professionals, 6.8 for lower-level white-collar jobs, 6.1 for skilled workers, . . . 14.6 for semiskilled workers, 20.8 for unskilled workers and 25.1 for service workers. . .

"In other words, Blacks have gained easier access to the job market, and they are no longer given entry-level jobs only, but at the same time a disproportionately large number of Blacks remains locked into the bottom half of the employment pyramid."[1a]

But these statistics tell only part of the story. The figures for particular occupations within a group reveal that the picture is much more extreme. Invariably, the share of Blacks is much less in the good jobs than in the poor jobs within a broad group.

Thus, among professionals, Blacks had a penetration rate of only 1% among engineers, lawyers and judges, and 2% among physicians and dentists, but 8% among nurses and health technicians, 15% among social workers.

Just think how much the lack of Black lawyers and doctors contributes to the fact that the proportion of Blacks in prisons is several times the proportion of whites in prisons, and to the lower life expectancy of Blacks. And it isn't mainly because of a crude refusal of white lawyers and doctors to service Blacks, but because of the influence of racism on the quality of service they render, on the financial conditions they impose, on the degree of their concern, involvement, encouragement of the client or patient.

Again, Blacks constituted 3% of the teachers and professors at college and university level, but 10% of elementary school and kindergarten teachers.

In sum, Blacks had only a tiny share of the professional jobs providing relatively high incomes, and, often, considerable ownership of property and participation in management of business enterprises.

Similarly, within the general group of clerical and kindred workers, Blacks were only 1% of the real estate appraisers, but 15% of the messengers and office boys. Among service workers, they were 2% of airline stewardesses, but 61% of the bootblacks.[2]

Discrimination against Blacks in kinds of jobs is more extreme than that against other minorities. Orley Ashenfelter computed indexes of overall discrimination in kinds of jobs against various minority groups as of 1966 and 1967 using data of the EEOC. This showed that among males discrimination against Blacks was about twice as severe as against American Indians, and about one-third more severe as against Spanish-surnamed Americans. Among females the discrimination against Blacks was one and one-half times as severe as against these other two groups. Ashenfelter's indexes failed to show discrimination against Asian-Americans.[2a] Data for 1973 show discrimination against Blacks standing out in comparison with discrimination against other minorities to an even more striking extent.[2b]

Favorable Trends in Black Employment Pattern

Since 1960, especially, there has been a definite improvement in the share of Blacks in "better" jobs. The penetration rate of minorities in white collar occupations increased from 3.8% in 1960 to 6.2% in 1970; and in the middle and better blue collar occupations* from 8.2% in 1960 to 10.4% in 1970. Simultaneously the share of minorities in the poorer jobs, those of laborers and service workers, declined from 26.2% to 21.1% in absolute terms, the number of minorities in white collar jobs increased 117%, and in middle and better blue collar occupations 41%, while their number in service and labor occupations declined 13%. These trends have continued since 1970. The already small number of minority farmers were further decimated during the decade, from 193,000 to 41,000, and from 7.7% of all farmers to 3.1% of all farmers.**

While there are numerous qualifications, by and large these trends represent a shift from worse to better lines of employment for Black people. Generally, the gains were more marked for Black women than for Black men. For example, between 1960 and 1970 the number of minority clerical workers increased from 219,000 to 719,000, or three and one quarter times. The number of minority male clerical workers increased more slowly, from 199,000 to 336,000, or about two-thirds. The number of white female clerical workers increased a little less than one-half, and of white male clerical workers only one-seventh. The number of Black women employed in the professional and sales categories also more than doubled. Altogether, by 1970, the number of minority women white collar workers exceeded those of minority male white collar workers by 55%, while among whites, the number of male white collar workers was 10% fewer than the number of females.[3]

Undoubtedly the increased access of Blacks and Asians to white collar jobs, and especially the increased employment of Black women in these jobs, represented a real improvement in comparison with the kinds of employment available to Black women, and in general to Black men, earlier. *But it was not all gain.* It was part of a process in which white collar employment increased very rapidly, and in which the technical and economic boundary between white collar and blue collar employment became less distinct.

For the most part, the increasing employment of Black women in clerical jobs took place under conditions motivated more by the corporations' drive for high profits than out of compliance with equal employment opportunity rules. Faced with a soaring requirement for white collar workers, employers took advantage of the historic discrimination against women and against Blacks simultaneously to hold down salaries in these occupations as much as possible.

Thus, in 1959 the median earnings of male clerical workers was

---

* In the "middle and better blue collar occupations" we include the Census groups of craftsmen and foremen, operatives except transport, and transport equipment operatives.
** In comparing 1960 and 1970 occupations, we are compelled to refer to minorities rather than Blacks, as the 1960 economic statistics did not separate out Blacks from Asians, Native Americans, and others classified as minorities

$4,785. Ten years later the median earnings of female clerical workers was $4,232, and of Black female clerical workers $4,152.[4] Earnings of male clerical workers increased substantially during the decade, and those of female clerical workers moderately. But there was a substantial relative substitution of female for male clerical workers, and in some occupations, such as bank tellers, an absolute decline in employment of males combined with a continued rise in employment of women. To the extent that employers were able to make this substitution, *they got away with a substantial reduction in money wages, and a more marked reduction in real wages, considering the rising level of prices.* During this decade, also, there was a rapid rise in labor productivity in clerical occupations, along with automation and computerization. This, combined with the reduction in real wages, meant a radical slash in real labor costs per unit of output for employers able to substitute women for men in clerical jobs at much lower wages than would have to be paid the men.

Certainly Black women played a special role in this process. *In a period of rapidly expanding demand for clerical labor, the availability of Black female workers without alternative job possibilities was important to employers in enabling them to hold down the going wage for all female clerical workers.* It was particularly important in large metropolitan areas with increasing Black populations and most urgent demands for white collar workers. In the New York metropolitan area, the largest white collar labor market in the country, Black, Asian and Puerto Rican people, mainly women, supplied one-half of all the additional employment of clerical workers between 1960 and 1970.[5]

The purpose of hiring them was admitted in a private talk by a top telephone company official that later became public. He said:

"What a telephone company needs to know about its labor market (is) who is available for work paying as little as $4,000 to $5,000 a year."[6]

He pointed out that two out of three persons available at that wage were Black, and that is why the company was hiring them. The official's remarks and their significance are discussed more fully in Chapter 8.

Thus the gains of Black women in white collar, especially clerical, employment, while socially important, are diminished in economic significance to the extent that employers use this to hold salaries for clerical occupations down to levels which, relative to wages and salaries in other occupations, are at historical lows. It is a fact that today the average salary of a full time, year-around clerical worker is lower than the average wage of a full time, year-around factory operative; although this is not true if we restrict attention to women workers. Moreover, the traditional advantage in working conditions in most clerical occupations over most factory blue collar occupations is dwindling with the conversion of office work to factory-like conditions. This applies with especial force to such occupations as telephone operator, in which tens of thousands of Black women are employed, under conditions of great physical stress and supervisory oppression (Chapter 8).

Black workers have also made significant gains in factory production-line employment, and again, the gains were most marked for Black women, Between 1960 and 1970 the number of minority women operatives (other than transport), increased 67%, of minority men operatives 32%, of white women operatives 13%, and of white men operatives only 4%. Black and other minority people accounted nationally for 40% of the increase in employment of operatives during the decade,[7] and, if account were taken of Chicanos and Puerto Ricans, this would certainly bring the share of Black and Brown people to at least 50%. Again, as with clerical jobs, it is clear that only by turning to Black workers, and especially Black women workers, could employers find the necessary number of production workers at pay consistent with their drive for maximum profits.

This is particularly clear in the case of textile workers. Formerly kept out of all but janitorial jobs in the textile mills, Black workers are now prominent as production workers in this largely southern industry. The number of Black textile operatives multiplied fourfold between 1960 and 1970, surpassing 60,000 in the latter year, and accounting for 14% of all textile operatives. More than three out of every four additional jobs of textile production workers were filled by Blacks during this decade.[8]

Black textile workers wages remained very low, and about one-fifth below those of white textile workers. But even these low wages represented a substantial economic gain for tens of thousands of Black southern workers previously kept on the fringes of the labor market, limited to service jobs, part-time agricultural work, etc.

The gains in types of jobs have been most marked following the civil

TABLE 14

PERCENTAGE BLACK EMPLOYMENT OF TOTAL
BY LARGE PRIVATE EMPLOYERS
BY MAJOR OCCUPATION GROUPS 1967, 1970 AND 1973

	1967	1970	1973
All Workers	8.7	10.0	10.6
Officers, Managers	1.0	1.9	2.7
Professionals	1.8	2.5	3.2
Technicians	4.3	6.2	7.3
Sales Workers	3.1	4.3	5.1
Office & Clerical	4.2	7.2	8.3
Craftsmen	4.1	5.6	6.5
Operatives	11.8	14.1	15.3
Laborers	21.6	21.8	20.6
Service Workers	27.2	26.3	23.9

SOURCES: 1967: EEOC, Equal Employment Opportunity *Report No. 2, Job Patterns for Minorities and Women in Private Industry, 1967,* Washington Vol. 1, p.52. 1970: EEOC, *7th Annual Report for Fiscal Year Ended June 30, 1972,* p. 43. 1973 EEOC, *Nationwide Summary of EEO 1 Reports,* Xerox Sheet.

rights legislation of the mid-1960s and the increase in court actions and mass struggles to make that legislation effective. Table 14 shows that between 1967 and 1973 there was an increase in the overall proportion of Blacks hired by large employers, and a much faster rise in the proportion of Blacks in the better jobs. Simultaneously, there was a modest decline in the proportion of Blacks in the two lowest job categories. The ratio of the percentage of Black service workers to the percentage of Black officers and managers was 27 to 1 in 1967, 14 to 1 in 1970, and 9 to 1 in 1973.

However, these apparent gains are subject to important reservations. For one thing, note that the pace of gain slowed between 1970 and 1973. Further, the gains were much more marked for Black women than for Black men. The share of Black men went up from 8.7% to 9.9% of total male employment, while the share of Black women went up from 8.6% to 11.8% of total female employment, or nearly three times as much, percentagewise. The qualitative gains, in kinds of jobs, were much more distinct among women, also. *But in all too many cases this simply represented the employers' way of converting previously high or medium-paying jobs into medium or low-paying jobs,* by taking advantage of the desperate need of Black women for employment, as already indicated above.

Finally, the figures are supplied by employers, and are not checked for accuracy. Many employers simply neglect their legal obligation to send in reports, confident that they will not be punished. As the volume and effectiveness of equal employment lawsuits has increased, there has developed an increasing incentive for employers to make a "good showing" in their EEO-1 reports to the EEOC, and especially to show a substantial statistical "improvement," even if little or no improvement exists in reality. Similarly, there is an increasing incentive not to report at all if a really bad, more grossly discriminatory than normal, situation cannot be hidden.

To what extent do these reservations vitiate the significance of the gains shown in Table 14? The apparent gains in the total percentage of Blacks employed contradict statistics for the whole economy showing stagnation in the share of all jobs held by Blacks between 1967 and 1973.[8a] The apparent gains in job quality contradict the data of Chapter 4, showing stagnation in the Black-white income ratio since 1967, and a decline in that ratio since 1970. While none of the statistics involved are fully reliable, the overall conclusion has to be that the apparent statistical gains in the quality of employment are partly fictitious, and have partly been vitiated by the economic deterioration of jobs held by Blacks, so that the immediate positive effect on the economic status of Black workers has been minimal. To the extent that the gains in the quality of Black employment are real, they do provide an improved platform from which to launch further struggles for the achievement of genuine Black economic equality. But it is obvious that the distance so far traversed is but a tiny fraction of the total course.

Discrimination in Promotion

One of the most serious forms of discrimination against Black workers is the failure to promote them to better jobs, or to better pay on the same job, as they grow older. There are countless stories of experienced Black workers training white newcomers, who are then promptly promoted above them, and may even become their bosses, while the Black workers stay throughout their lives at a low rung. The same effect is accomplished by the sectional seniority systems which have prevailed in the steel and other industries, whereby Black workers are channeled into deadends, while white workers have what opportunities there are for advancement. These racist seniority systems have been dramatized by recent court cases and decisions requiring their abolition. In the white collar field the discrimination in promotion is even more notable. In their search for an image, corporations consider it necessary these days to hire some Black managerial personnel. But the complaint among them is that they are consigned forever to the lower and middle management levels, while the higher jobs, and those involving real degrees of power, are closed off to Blacks. The same applies to Black professional workers. This point is developed further in Chapter 11.

A common statistical method of showing the discrimination against Blacks in promotion is to compare the ratios of Black to white earnings by age groups, with the gap widening as workers grow older. (Table 15).

TABLE 15

EARNINGS OF WORKERS BY AGE, RACE AND SEX, 1969

MEAN EARNINGS

AGE GROUP	WHITE-ANGLO	BLACK	% BLACK OF WHITE-ANGLO
Males			
18-24	$ 4,125	$3,436	83
25-34	8,838	5,914	67
35-54	10,856	6,154	57
55-64	9,517	5,268	55
65 and over	6,669	3,424	51
Females			
18-24	3,009	2,679	89
25-34	4,288	3,740	87
35-54	4,484	3,603	80
55-64	4,743	2,950	62

SOURCE: PC(2)-8B, T. 1, 2, 5, 6, 7, 8, 11.

Among Black male youth who managed to get jobs, earnings averaged 17% less than those of white youth in the same age group. There was a gap of about $700, but the Blacks were within striking distance of the whites. However, when white men reached the young adult age bracket, 25-34, their mean earnings more than doubled, while the earnings of Blacks increased much more slowly in the same time period. Blacks were now 33% and $2,900 behind whites. Reaching the so-called prime of life, in the 35-54 year range, white workers enjoyed another $2,000 increase in average earnings, while the earnings of Blacks barely crept forward another $200. Now Blacks averaged $4,700, or 43%, less than whites. The dollar gap was nearly seven

Chart 8
WORKERS' EARNINGS BY AGE, MALES 1969

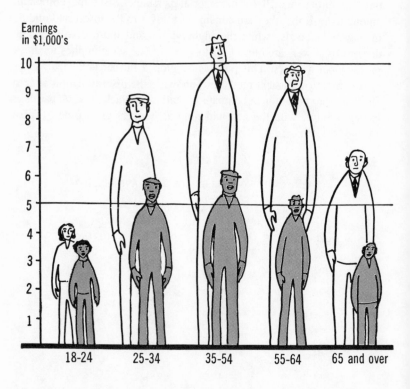

times as wide as when they entered the labor market. In the older age brackets earnings of both whites and Blacks slipped, but more rapidly for Blacks, so that among male workers 65 and over Blacks earned barely half as much as whites.

Among women the situation is similar, although differentials are not so extreme. Blacks earned 11% less in the 18-24 year group, 13% less in the next age group, 20% less than white women in the 35-54 year group, and 38% less in the 55-64 year group. Data are not given for older women.

The President's Council of Economic Advisers has made the "discovery" that discrimination in promotion no longer exists in America. They "prove" this with statistics, and since the matter is of some importance, it is necessary to deal with the alleged proof. The advisers write:

"There is a widespread belief that, compared to white males, Black males are related to poorly paid, dead-end jobs—in which earnings . . . do not rise with experience. This view originated as a result of examining the relation between age and income for white and Black males at a moment in time . . . (there is) a substantial decline for older age groups in the income of Black males relative to white males."

They then give figures similar to those in Table 15, but significantly, omitting those for workers below 25 and above 65.

This is the wrong way to do it, they claim. The correct way "is to follow a group (cohort) as it ages." Thus the ratio of 25-34 year age groups in 1959 should be compared with that of 35-44 year age groups in 1969, since these represent more or less the same individuals, and a change in the ratio might indicate faster promotion for one group than for the other. Examining it in this way, they claim, "the ratio of Black to white annual and weekly incomes either did not decline at all with age from 1949 to 1969, or declined at an appreciably slower rate than in the cross section." Hence, their conclusion that Blacks are not discriminated against in promotion.[9]

The argument is based on a false premise, misinterprets the statistics used, and *still more serious, involves deliberate suppression of the most important data of the type used.*The false premise is that belief in discrimination in promotion "originated" with statistical correlations of age and income. Of course not. This is simply used as confirmation of the accumulated life experience of a people, of innumerable examples of clearcut discrimination against Blacks in promotion.

There is some advantage in following identical groups of persons from decade to decade, as the government economists claim, but there are also certain disadvantages in this procedure, as other factors besides promotion are involved, most notably the large-scale migration of Black workers from the South to areas with higher wage levels.

But the main thing is that the presidential advisers deliberately left out the most important statistics. The most rapid and important promotions come in the late twenties and early thirties of a person's age. This can be seen, for example, in the sharp income jumps shown in Table 15 between those in the 18-24 year age group and those in the 25-34 year age group. If a person is going to "get ahead in the world" that is when he starts moving upward. Above age 35 forward movement slows, and comes to a stop by the mid-forties, except at the very top of the executive suites. Thereafter, employers are often looking for ways of getting rid of workers, or are actually demoting them.

The president's economists left out the cohort or group of workers who were under 25 in 1960, and from 25 to 34 in 1970. For the next group, those who were 25 to 34 in one year and 35 to 44 ten years later, even their statistics showed a decline in the Black to white earnings ratio in each of the four situations for which they made the calculations. They showed no change in the ratio for workers who were already 35 to 44 to begin with, and ten years older a decade later. And ditto for workers in still older groups at the beginning of the comparison. *And this was to be expected,* because promotions are rare for workers in these older groups, and the record becomes increasingly confused by other factors, such as retirement on account of disability or age.

To present reasonable calculations by the cohort method, which would eliminate the effect of migration, we show the results for New York State for the 1960-1970 decade, including the ratios for those workers who were below 25 years of age in 1960, (Table 16).

TABLE 16

PERCENTAGE BLACK OF WHITE MALE INCOME, BY AGE COHORTS,
1959 AND 1969, NEW YORK STATE

AGE OF COHORT		PERCENTAGE BLACK OF WHITE MEDIAN INCOME	
1960	1970	1959	1969
14-19	25-29	131	74
20-24	30-34	86	68
25-34	35-44	68	65
35-44	45-54	66	66
45-54	55-64	64	66
55-64	65-74	65	66

SOURCES: 1960 N.Y. -D-134; 1970 N.Y.-D-193

NOTES: The Census tabulates ages for the Census years, and incomes for the previous years. Ratios refer to all minorities in 1959 and Blacks only in 1969. There is a distortion on account of this, and on account of inclusion of Puerto Ricans with whites. However, correction of these distortions would not essentially change the results.

Consider first the youngest cohort, males who were aged 14-19 in 1960 and 25-29 in 1970. The ratio of Black to white incomes for this cohort declined from 131% in 1959 to 74% in 1969. A special factor entered here, and accounts for the "surprising" appearance of a higher

Black than white income among the youngest groups. Only a minority of these teenagers reported incomes, and the medians used refer to this minority. Of these, a much larger percentage of Blacks than whites were working full time at that early age, and hence obtained larger incomes than teenage whites working part time or obtaining small amounts of non-labor income. Even so, the decline of the Blacks in this group to only 74% of the incomes of the whites in this group, ten years later, signifies a very serious lag in promotion, either on a single job, or by moving to a better job, during the decade.

The record for the next group, those aged 20-24 in 1960 and 30-34 in 1970, is more exact, since most of these young men were working at both times. In 1959 the Blacks in this group obtained 86% of the incomes of the whites, whereas ten years later the Blacks obtained only 68% of the incomes of the whites. The gap, percentagewise, increased from 14% to 32%—more than doubled. In dollar terms, the result was much more dramatic. In 1959 the Blacks in this cohort were $400 behind the whites, in 1969 they were $3,000 behind! But this is the cohort most critically affected by promotions in the 1959-69 interval, *so the result confirms most decisively the correctness of the conclusion that the Blacks were terribly discriminated against in promotion and other forms of economic advancement.*

Among those aged 25-34 in 1960 and 35-44 ten years later, the ratio of Black to white incomes declined from 68% to 65%, while the dollar gap more than doubled, from $1,700 to $3,600. Promotions were not so important for this cohort. Workers aged 35-44 earn little more, on the average, than those aged 25-34. But even so, the loss of ground of the Blacks, especially in dollar terms, was too large to be dismissed as trivial.

For the older age cohorts incomes are already on the decline. For these groups the ratio of Black to white median incomes remained unchanged over the decade, or actually increased a little, because of the tendency for Blacks who were able to hold onto jobs to stay on them longer, since they could not afford to retire. Promotions no longer entered into the picture.

There is a much more direct way of checking out the discrimination against Blacks in promotion than by use of income statistics. That is by reference to changes in occupational groupings. For example, people rarely start out their working careers in managerial or administrative jobs. They get promoted to them. Census statistics indicate that among white males who were 20-24 in 1960 and 30-34 in 1970, 9.0% were promoted to managerial or administrative posts during the decade, as compared with only 2.8% of Black males in the same age group. *Thus a young white man had more than three times the chance of a young Black man of obtaining a high-level promotion.* (Table 17). Examples of this type, at all occupational levels, are legion.

There is nothing mysterious about this. The explanation, in the crudest terms, is in the catch-phrase: "It's not what you know, its whom you know." In a society where capitalists have all the economic power, and there are hardly any Black capitalists, the chances of a Black having family or other social connections with somebody in a position to arrange occupation and financial advantage is very small. With racism deeply ingrained in large sections of the white population, and ethnic quasi-nationalism a significant influence, with those in intermediate positions with power to hire or promote almost all white and connected with friends and relatives in various white ethnic groups, Black workers are handicapped in advancement at lower levels as well.

That is why the discrimination against Blacks in promotion is all too real. It must be ended by *special measures* requiring priority to Black promotion, to make up for the historical discrimination, special measures which cut through the class and racist obstacles imposed by capitalism.

TABLE 17

CALCULATION OF RATE OF PROMOTION
OF YOUNG MALES TO MANAGERIAL JOBS, 1960-1970
(Thousands of Workers)

	WHITE	BLACK
Managers and administrators, 20-24 years old, 1960	134	3
Managers and administrators, 30-34 years old, 1970	544	16
Increase in Managers and administrators, 1960-1970	410	13
Total employed in all occupations, 30-34 years old, 1970	4,536	459
Percent increase in managers and administrators of total employed	9.0	2.8

SOURCES: 1960, U.S.-D-204; 1970 U.S.-D-226

NOTE: minorities other than Blacks in 1960. There are slight distortions on account of this, but insignificant in relation to the dimensions of the contrast brought out by the table.

Lower Pay for the Same Job

The law requires equal pay for equal work. But, in the absence of a working class movement determined to enforce it, employers systematically discriminate against Blacks and other minorities, against women, youths and old people.

The U.S. Commerce Department calculated the 1969 ratios of median earnings of Black to white workers in separate occupation groups and occupations, for males and females separately, and for two different age groups. The calculations are limited to workers who worked the whole year around. This permits isolation of Black/white differentials from those based on age, sex, and part-time employment. However, all of these also operate against Blacks, since larger percentages of Blacks than whites are young and women, a larger percentage suffer from part-time unemployment, and a larger percentage keep on working past retirement age.

Thus the Commerce Department calculations really minimize the discrimination against Blacks in a given occupation. Consider workers in the 35-54 year age range. For each of the 27 occupation groups and occupations covered, median earnings of Black males were lower than those of white males, by percentages ranging from 1% for bus drivers to 62% for farmers and farm managers. The middle ratio of Black to white median wages was 76%. That is, for a typical occupation, the median earnings of Black males were about one-fourth lower than those of white males in the same age group. For all occupations combined, however, the median earnings of Black male workers were only 66% of white workers in the same sex and age group. The 10 percentage points difference represents the effect of Blacks being concentrated in lower paying occupations.

Among women, the differences were much narrower, For all occupations combined, Black women in the 35-54 year age group had median earnings 79% of those of white women in the same age group. But most of this 21% difference resulted from Black women being concentrated on poorer jobs, not from different pay for the same job. In 8 of the 24 occupation groups and occupations covered, the median for Blacks was actually higher than that for whites. In 12 cases the Black median was a little lower than that for whites, and in only 4 cases was it substantially lower.[10]

The minimum wage laws, and in some cases welfare levels, tend to set a floor under women's wages. The biggest gap between white and Black women's earnings was in the case of farm laborers, who were not covered by minimum wage laws at that time. Also, many women seek and obtain part-time work, so that they can have modest earnings, and still have time for household chores. More white women, relatively, than Black are able to afford to work only part-time and to obtain part-time work suitable for their schedules. In 1973, among white women, the number employed part-time by choice equalled 35.5% of the number employed full time, while among minority women, the number employed part-time by choice equalled only 24.5% of the number employed full time.[11]

Thus differentials in Black/white womens' earnings on an annual basis are less than the actual differentials in hourly wage or salary scales.

Table 18 shows pay differentials for the same or similar work in the Detroit metropolitan area, which has a history of militant working class struggles, and where Black workers have an exceptionally strong position within the working class and in the unions. Because of this history, differentials in Detroit are less marked than in most parts of the country (Chapter 3). Yet even here differentials against Blacks are quite serious, far beyond the limits of possible statistical accidents, or causation by secondary factors.

For the tabulation, occupations have been picked with large numbers of workers, or which are reasonably representative of large groups. Discrimination is most marked at the top, among managers and administrators, where Blacks earned 40% less than whites. Nearly as bad was the situation among plumbers and painters. Owing to the exclusionary policies of most craft union leaders, carried out in collaboration with the construction contractors, Black workers in key crafts can obtain employment only on non-union jobs at wages far below the union scale. Even when admitted to unions, they are discriminated againt in job assignments, and so obtain less work in the course of a year.

Discrimination is also relatively severe among manufacturing foremen. Note that the occupations with particularly severe differentials, and with the most notable exclusion of Blacks from employment altogether, are completely under control of the employers. Except for the building trade, the unions have nothing to do with it, and even there, while the unions decide whom to admit into membership, the contrac-

TABLE 18

WAGE AND SALARY DIFFERENTIALS FOR SELECTED OCCUPATIONS
MALE WORKERS, DETROIT METROPOLITAN AREA, 1969

	MEDIAN OF BLACKS AS % MEDIAN OF WHITES
Salaried managers and administrators	60
Plumbers	63
Painters	67
Linesmen and servicemen	72
Manufacturing foremen	77
Truck drivers and deliverymen	84
Motor vehicle operatives	87
Assemblers	92
Mail handlers and clerks	100
Freight, stock, and material handlers	130

SOURCE: Mich-D-175

tors generally select the workers for a particular job. In the supervisory occupations and in the telephone linesmen jobs, prejudices of workers have little to do with the poorer pay and employment opportunities of Black workers. This is evidence against the attempts of apologists for the system to blame discrimination on the attitudes of the white population in general, rather than on the controlling capitalist class.

The 16% differential shown against Black male truck drivers and deliverymen relates to the employers' practice of assigning Blacks to lower paying inner-city delivery jobs, rather than the better paying over-the-road jobs. Here the situation is not nearly so bad in Detroit as nationwide (Chapter 7).

But what about the 13% differential against Black motor vehicle operatives? This refers to the main production workers in auto, supposedly with very uniform wage scales. A more than proportional number of Black workers are forced to work the night shift, on which a differential is paid. They tend to be assigned to the hardest, most dangerous, health-destroying jobs on the assembly lines. They are concentrated on foundries, coke ovens, paint pits, and other most undesirable sections of the auto plants. Demands of Black workers and integrated rank and file groups for higher wages for the bad jobs have not received adequate support from the union bureaucracy, although slight progress was made in the 1973 negotiations, when more favorable retirement terms were granted foundry workers. Because of their job assignments, the Black workers should average more than the white workers. Instead they average 13% less, which means that the auto companies, despite supposedly uniform wage scales, manage to discriminate sharply against the Black workers by systematic application of the many devices open to the employer who controls the production process.

The U.S. auto industry, it should be noted, lags far behind that of the USSR in adjusting compensation to working conditions. At the Volzhsky Works, the newest and largest Soviet passenger car factory, there are add-ons to the base wage scale for various factors, including conditions of work. For each station on the assembly line there is a bonus corresponding to the degree of physical effort or tension required.[12] This is in addition to the special compensation in money and leisure given workers throughout the USSR engaged in strenuous, dangerous or unhealthy jobs, or in intemperate climate. The shop trade union organization has a major voice, along with management, in determining all bonus and incentive systems in the USSR.

Recently, a really sensational innovation has been introduced into the Volzhsky Works. Workers on the assembly line rotate jobs along the entire cycle according to a regular schedule. This is for the primary purpose of minimizing the boredom of assembly line work, and of enabling each worker to learn the entire process of production. But an incidental result is to eliminate the possibility of that kind of favoritism which prevails in job assignments in U.S. factories.

The wage equality of Black and white postal clerks shown in the table is a rare exception, even in government employment. Nationally there was a differential of nearly 10% against Black postal clerks, and in Mississippi Black postal clerks continued to receive 17% less than whites, and had only 8% of the jobs, which pay exceptionally well, in relation to other jobs available for Blacks in that state.[13]

What about the 30% extra average earnings of Black freight, stock and material handlers? It's the kind of thing a Daniel Moynihan or a Voice of America propagandist might pick up to show "how well Negroes are treated in the United States." This is more or less a special situation in Detroit, although the causes are operative to a lesser extent elsewhere. In the New York metropolitan area, for example, Black freight, stock and material handlers averaged 11% less, and Puerto Ricans 24% less, than "white Anglo" workers in the same occupation.[14]

The difference between Detroit and New York can be explained. In the New York area factory wages are relatively low, while those of freight, stock and material handlers are at a decent level owing to the organization of many of them in the effective District 65 of the Distributive Workers Union. Their earnings in New York are actually higher than those of male factory operatives. In Detroit, on the other hand, factory wages, dominated by the United Automobile Workers members, are relatively high, and considerably higher than those of the freight, stock and material handlers.

Consequently, the latter is not a desirable job. Most white regular workers can get better jobs. Many of those whites who do take these warehouse jobs are casual, part-time workers, and 40% are teenagers—often working part-time after school or during summer vacations. Their low annual earnings pull down the median for all white workers. Black youth, on the other hand, do not have the connections to get the part-time and vacation jobs, contributing to the sky-high unemployment rate among them. And this job, which doesn't rate as more than casual labor for older white men, *is at least a job,* which the Black man must hold onto once he gets it.

Detroit area the median earning of Blacks were about 8% lower than those of whites. Thus the appearance of no discrimination, or even "reverse discrimination" in this case, *conceals* the continued existence of wage discrimination, and in access to employment, especially against Black youth. And so it is with the other seeming "exceptions" to the rule of discrimination against Blacks in the U.S. economy.

The combined effect of discrimination in types of jobs, and in pay for the same job, is shown in the comparison of Black and white earnings in particular industries. In 1969, in the Detroit metropolitan area, among male workers, the median for Blacks was 61% of that for whites in the communications industry. That compares with the somewhat closer ratio, 72%, for linesmen and servicemen, a typical industry occupation, shown in Table 18. Blacks earned 66% as much as whites in construction, again lower than the ratio for most construction trades, 70% in non-electrical machinery, 72% as much in motor vehicles, and 98% as much in postal service.[15]

In every case, the industrial ratio was lower than that for characteristic occupations in that industry. Thus the differential against Black automotive operatives was 13%, but against all Black auto workers

28%, or about twice as severe. The influences of unequal pay for similar work, and relative exclusion from better-paying jobs, were about the same in this case.

Black Workers in Low-Wage Plants

An important part of production is carried out in small establishments, often auxiliary to the large plants, and making certain parts or performing specified processes. Other small plants produce items with only a small-scale market, or bulky items which have to be produced for local consumption.

In 1967 in the United States only 0.7% of the manufacturing establishments, with more than a thousand workers each, accounted for one-third of the employment and two-fifths of the payroll. But over 90% of the plants, with fewer than 100 employees each, accounted for nearly one-fourth of employment and about one-fifth of the total payroll. The average wage or salary in the large plants was about one-third more than in the small plants,[16] and Black and Spanish-speaking workers are concentrated in these low-wage plants. Here is an example:

"On November 30, workers at Birmingham Stove and Range, a cast iron foundry in Birmingham, Alabama, went on strike. Virtually the entire plant—except the foreman and supervisors—is Black. And surprisingly, a majority of Stove and Range workers—about 60%—are women, who perform the heavy, industrial work almost always associated with men, including the handling of hot molten iron."

The starting wage is $2.10 per hour. No woman has ever been raised to more than $2.30 per hour, even after working many years. Men's wages may go up to $2.50 per hour, and if they are white, they are usually moved to supervisory roles.[17]

This wage level is about half the national average for foundries. Even in bigger, better paying foundries a large proportion of workers are Black, but not that large a proportion. And many of the Black workers are in shops such as the Alabama stove plant where arbitrary company power, backed by the state's "Right-to-Work" law, imposes extremely low wages and other outrageous conditions, including dangerous, heavy work for women. Conditions such as these, which cannot be conveyed by statistical averages, are a reality for a large proportion of the Black working force.

And not all low-wage plants are small. Entire industries are characterized by very low pay, especially in the handling of agricultural products, in branches of the food, textile and apparel industries, and in some trade and service industries. By and large, the proportion of Black workers is especially large in small plants and in low-wage industries. Conditions in these industries are much influenced by minimum wage legislation. The rapid inflation of the early 1970s, while the minimum wage remained unchanged, resulted in a worsening of the relative position of hundreds of thousands of workers in low-wage occupations, including a large proportion of Blacks, and particularly Black women and Black youth. Finally, after three years of congressional stalling, a revised minimum wage law became effective May 1, 1974. The small increase fell far short of matching rising living costs. (Chapter 14).

Sex Discrimination in Wages

Sex differentials in wages for the same occupation are even wider than race differentials. Among full time clerical workers in 1972, the median earnings of all women were 38% lower than those of all men, as compared with differentials against Blacks, among men, of 17%, and among women of 2%. Among manufacturing operatives in nondurable goods industries, the differential against all women was 44%, as compared with differentials against Black men of 22%, and against Black women of 5%.[18] These examples could be multiplied. The differentials against women in specific narrow occupations are nearly as extreme, and in some cases fully as extreme, as in these broader occupation groups.

There are those, including men as well as women, who, basing themselves on such statistics, regard the fight for women's equality as having priority over the fight for Black equality. There have been numerous recent examples of companies, union leaderships, and government bodies agreeing to small concessions to women workers as a means of evading or minimizing the need to end discrimination against Blacks.

But there can be no ending of discrimination against women so long as discrimination against Blacks continues, and no major reduction of discrimination against women without a corresponding reduction in discrimination against Blacks. As indicated repeatedly in this volume, Black women are the most oppressed section of the population, economically and otherwise, and the most economically active section of the female population. Even with campaigns to end discrimination against women, it is necessary to give special emphasis to ending discrimination against Black women and to avoid campaigns constructed so that they will benefit only white women, sometimes objectively at the expense of Black men and women.

A combined strúggle for Black equality and women's equality is needed, with special priority within that combination for the cause of Black women. But overall, in terms of the stage of political and social development, of the area of really sharp confrontation between the most reactionary, anti-democratic groups and the country's progressive forces, *the priority must go to the struggle for Black equality.*

6. Super Unemployment

Discrimination in access to employment—any kind of employment—is one of the most severe hardships afflicting the Black people. The old rule of last to be hired, first to be fired, continues in effect, by and large. And there remain important occupations from which Blacks are almost totally barred, and hundreds of thousands of employers who bar Blacks from all except menial employment. The burden of unemployment is especially heavy on Black women, and heaviest of all on Black youth.

Official statistics show that over the past quarter of a century the rate of unemployment among Blacks has been generally more than twice that among whites. (Table 19)

TABLE 19

PERCENTAGES OF AVERAGE UNEMPLOYMENT RATES BY RACE 1948-1973

YEARS	WHITE	BLACK AND OTHER MINORITIES	BLACK AND OTHER MINORITIES % OF WHITE
1948-1953	3.77	6.50	172
1954-1963	4.80	10.24	213
1964-1973	4.09	8.26	202

SOURCE: BLS Handbook of Labor Statistics, 1973, T 61, Survey of Current Business, May 1974.

During the 19-year period 1955-1973 there were only three years in which Black and other races' unemployment percentages were less than two times the corresponding percentages for white workers. Throughout that period the ratio of Black to white unemployment has been higher than during the nine years immediately after World War II.

Unemployment in the 7 to 11% range, which persistently applies to Black workers, is associated in economic literature with crisis conditions. On this account alone, then, aside from other economic factors, *the Black population lives in a condition of permanent depression.* U.S. economic growth has slowed down during the 1970s, and now Establishment economists and government financial officials predict and *recommend* a further slowing of the growth rate, as necessary to cope with inflationary, energy, and balance of payments crises. This means hardship and increased unemployment for the entire working population. For the Black people it projects a decline from depression to disaster, unless special measures are taken to end the discrimination against Blacks in employment, along with measures to protect the working population as a whole from the harmful effects of capitalism's failures.

Sometimes a single incident sheds more light on reality than a ream of statistics. A New York newspaper headline in February 1974 read: "163,039 Seeking City Job Where No Openings Exist." The story reported a three-month citywide recruitment drive among minorities which Councilman Matthew J. Troy Jr. called a "cruel hoax." The reason—no vacancies. However, it was expected that 6,000 jobs would open up during the 4-year period of validity of the Civil Service list.[1]

There was nothing glamorous about the job offered—that of sanitationman. And yet the number of people who applied were equal to about five times the total number of officially counted unemployed Black and Puerto Rican males in New York City!* Presumably almost all of the applicants were male members of minorities. While some might have been seeking an improvement over an existing job, it is reasonable to assume that a large proportion, probably more than half, were unemployed. Nor is it believable that *all* unemployed Black and Puerto Rican males in the city applied. After all, it is not every man who can cope with the strenuous job of a sanitationman.

And yet, apparently, something like two or three times the number of officially counted Black and Puerto Rican male unemployed applied for

---

*The Census of Population reported 27,702 unemployed Black and Puerto Rican males in New York City in 1970, out of a total 76,955 unemployed males. (U.S.-C-85, 92, 98). Unemployment in the city was only moderately higher by the winter of 1973-74.

the jobs, with the prospect that fewer than one out of 100 of the applicants would actually get a job in each of the four years for which the list would be valid.

Such incidents are frequent in the United States. And they happen to white workers as well as Black, women as well as men. But relatively speaking, Blacks are victimized in this way to the highest degree, because of the huge mass of Black unemployed workers.

Thus the actual rate of unemployment among Blacks is much higher than the 7 to 11% range shown in government statistics, and the differential impact of unemployment above that on whites is much more than the 4 to 5 percentage points indicated in Table 19. Here are some of the reasons.

First, consider the color or race definitions used by the Census Bureau and Labor Department in compiling the regular reports on unemployment. The basic color division is between white and "Negro and other races." The "other races" include Japanese, Chinese, Filipinos, Koreans, Hawaiians, Native Americans, Eskimos, Aleuts, and some unspecified. Most of these people are Asians. Unemployment among them is much lower than among Blacks, and the Asian population has been growing much more rapidly than the Black population. Hence, the unemployment rate for Blacks alone is considerably higher than the rate for "Negro and other races" and that difference is increasing. On the other hand, the white population includes an increasing proportion of Chicanos and Puerto Ricans, who suffer from extra unemployment as do the Blacks. According to 1970 Census data, the unemployment rate differential between Blacks and "white-Anglos" was 10% wider than that between "Negro and other races" and whites (including Spanish speaking).

Beginning in 1974, quarterly data are published for persons of Spanish origin separately, so that these can be subtracted from the figures for all whites to arrive at an unemployment rate for "white-Anglos" alone.

Another source of understatement is in the non-inclusion of partial unemployment. A worker, generally unemployed, who gets a few hours of casual labor during the week is counted among the employed. In 1973 2.7% of the whites, and 4.6% of the minorities were on part-time jobs "for economic reasons"—that is, because they could not get full time employment. [1a]

Then there are the workers "with a job but not at work," who are counted as employed by the Labor Department. This is reasonable for those who get paid vacations and sick leave. But the approximately 2 million workers in 1973 not being paid should be counted with the unemployed. That amounts to another 2¼% of the civilian labor force. The Labor Department does not report this for whites and Blacks separately, but it must be assumed that it hits Blacks harder than whites, because relatively more Black workers are not covered by paid vacation and illness provisions. Finally, there is the unemployment among 14 and 15 year olds, which is counted, but not included in the published overall totals. The unemployment rate among these young teenagers who are in the labor force is, of course, higher than the average.

But the biggest addition to the official figures must consist of those who are really unemployed but are counted out of the labor force by the Census takers and Labor Department statisticians.

Exclusion of Unemployed Blacks from the Labor Force

Official figures show markedly smaller percentages of Black males than white males in the labor force. In 1973, 80.1% of white males 16 and over, but only 74.8% of minority males 16 and over were counted in the labor force, including the armed forces. In figures for the total population, this is partly compensated by a higher reported participation rate for Black females than white females—49.1% for minority females, 44.2% for white females in 1973.[2]

But the seemingly low participation rate of Black males screens massive hidden unemployment. And the actual differential in the female participation rates is higher than shown, because of large-scale hidden unemployment among Black women. The published statistics tend to buttress the racist slanders about the "laziness" of Blacks; "anyone who really wants a job can find one," etc. A Labor Department report which analyzes some aspects of hidden unemployment comments:

The figures also show that a larger proportion of Blacks than of whites are job-oriented: Those employed plus those seeking work (unemployed) plus those wanting a job but not actually seeking one constituted 66 percent of the Black population and 62 percent of the white population . . . the figures help dispose of the myth that Blacks are less interested in jobs than whites.[3]

Leonard Goodwin, in a Brookings Institution study, finds no difference between whites and Blacks in "work orientation"—that is, in considering work desirable. Owing to their experiences, however, a larger proportion of Blacks, especially poor Blacks, do not think they can be successful in obtaining jobs. Many Black mothers find that they fare worse when working than when on welfare, but this does not cause them to stop preferring a decent job to a welfare subsistence. Blacks as well as whites, poor as well as rich, have a low opinion of "quasi-illegal" activities and prefer honest work by an overwhelming majority. Thus a lumpen existence is not the preference of Black people.[4]

Analysis of Census data permits a partial quantification of hidden unemployment, owing to exclusion of males from the labor force. The 1970 Census shows an unemployment rate of 6.3% for Black males and 3.5% for white Anglo males aged 16 and over.* It also provides a partial breakdown of reasons why people are not in the labor force. Some are students, some are institutionalized. Some are over 65 years old and presumably retired. Others are classified as disabled. For the remaining men, there is no apparent reason for being out of the labor force.**

A few—hardly any would be Black— may be coupon clippers, idle rich. But they would be apt to give an occupation to the Census taker, even if a fictitious one such as "estate management." A few might be criminals or other lumpen elements, but these would be apt to escape the Census taker altogether. By and large this residual group consists of unemployed men. And many jobless students are actually unemployed. There is strong evidence that this affects Blacks more than whites. Many in institutions, notably prisons, are there because they could not get jobs, and a disproportionate number of Blacks are institutionalized because of the racist character of the system of justice. Many over 65 would like to work, or need the income from work, but cannot get it—again this affects Blacks more than whites. Many disabled men would certainly work if they lived in a society that made the necessary provisions, but capitalist society makes such provisions more rarely for

* These figures are considerably lower than corresponding 1970 annual averages based on the monthly Census Bureau sample household surveys. This may be partly due to the decennial Census count being taken mainly in the Spring, while unemployment rates continued to mount rapidly throughout the year. Differences in method may also be involved.

** The same reasoning does not apply to women. Many of those not in the labor force are housewives who do not need to work nor want to work. Indirect evidence indicates that about 50% of the Black housewives and 20% of the white housewives not currently in the labor force want to work. Here we make estimates of hidden unemployment among women in a different, more direct way.

Blacks than for whites. So in all categories there are a certain number of hidden unemployed people, especially among Blacks.

Thus, in counting only those not in the labor force for no apparent reason as actually unemployed, we are making a minimum estimate of hidden unemployment. Adjusting the Census percentages to add these both to the numbers unemployed and to the labor force, and making a minor adjustment to add 14 and 15 year olds who are in the labor force, the 1970 Census unemployment percentages become 13.5% for Blacks and 6.7% for white Anglos.[5]

The percentage gap between Black and "white-Anglo" male unemployment is thereby widened from 2.8 points to 6.8 points. The number of Black unemployed is increased 132%, and of "white-Anglo" unemployed 99%.

In recent years the Labor Department, on the basis of questions asked respondents in the monthly labor force and employment surveys of the Census Bureau, has published statistics on the numbers of those not counted in the labor force who want jobs, and the numbers of those counted in the labor force who intend to look for jobs within the coming 12 months. If the former group want jobs, why aren't they included among the unemployed? They are excluded because they are not actively looking for jobs, or not looking hard enough to satisfy the government criterion for being counted as unemployed rather than not in the labor force.

It's true that not everybody who says he or she wants a job is very serious about it, or might do anything about it even under favorable conditions. And it's true that not everybody who plans to look for a job in the next twelve months will really do so. But the evidence of sociological studies is that a substantial majority of the people in these categories *seriously want to work*, and that this is especially true in the areas of concentrated poverty, and hence especially true of Blacks.

Here is a frequent example: a woman is forced to leave work for advanced pregnancy and to nurse her infant. In a socialist country she would be given ample leave with full pay both before and after birth, and the job would be kept for her until she could return. In the United States such arrangements are made for only a minority of women workers, and an especially small minority of Black women workers. But should not such a woman be regarded as unemployed during her period of forced absence from the job?

The Labor Department refers to those not counted in the labor force, but who are actually unemployed, and would work if jobs were available and—where necessary—if suitable arrangements could be made, as constituting the contingent labor force. Here we will refer to the total of the officially recognized unemployed and the contingent labor force as an approximation to the true scale of unemployment. Since there is no simple or uniform means of measuring the contingent labor force, we take a range. The minimum is taken as equal to those not counted in the labor force but wanting jobs now. The maximum is taken as equal to those not counted in the labor force but planning to look for jobs within the coming twelve months. Labor Department studies of labor market conditions in a half dozen cities suggest that this method provides a reasonable approximation to reality.

We have adjusted the published unemployment figures for 1973 by:

● Counting as unemployed half of those working part time for economic reasons, a standard procedure.

● Including the labor force and unemployment figures for 14 and 15 year olds.

● In the minimum version, including in the labor force and in the unemployed, those officially not looking for work but wanting work now.

● In the maximum version, including in the labor force and in the unemployed, those officially not looking for work but intending to within the coming twelve months.

The percentage unemployment for white males goes up from 3.7% as published to 7.0% by the minimum adjustment and 9.7% by the maximum adjustment.

The corresponding percentages for minority males are 7.6% as published, 14.5% and 17.7%, respectively, by the minimum and maximum adjustments.

For white females, the three percentages are 5.3%, 13.6%, and 18.7%.

For Black females, the three percentages are 10.5%, 25.3%, and 29.7%. (Table 20).

There is no adjustment to correct for the inclusion of other minorities with Blacks, nor for the inclusion of Chicanos and Puerto Ricans with whites.

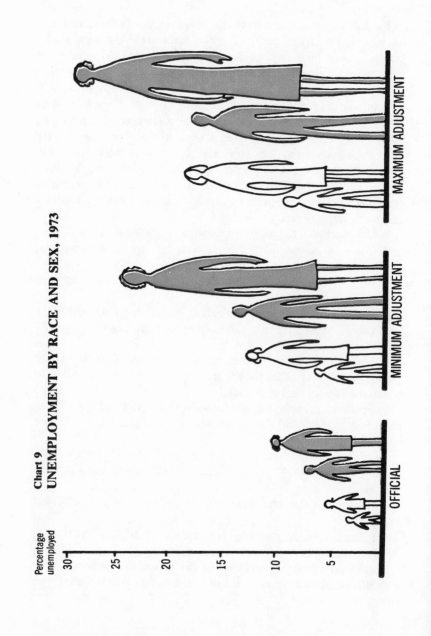

Chart 9
UNEMPLOYMENT BY RACE AND SEX, 1973

Percentage
unemployed

30

25

20

15

10

5

OFFICIAL

MINIMUM ADJUSTMENT

MAXIMUM ADJUSTMENT

TABLE 20

OFFICIAL AND ADJUSTED UNEMPLOYMENT RATES
BY RACE AND SEX, 1973
(Thousands of Persons and Unemployment Rates)

	WHITE		BLACK AND OTHER RACES	
	Male	Female	Male	Female
Official Labor Force and Unemployment				
1. Civilian Labor Force, 16 and over	48,648	30,041	5,555	4,470
2. Unemployed, Number	1,818	1,593	423	471
3. Unemployed, Percent	3.7	5.3	7.6	10.5
4. Labor Force, 14 & 15 years	882	657	82	45
5. Unemployed, 14 & 15 years	94	51	28	16
Part-Time Adjustment				
6. One-half of number employed part-time for economic reasons	516	514	114	116
Officially not in labor force:				
7. Wanting Jobs Now	1,103	2,346	294	719
8. Intend to seek work in next 12 months.	2,647	4,387	526	1,053
Adjusted Unemployment and Labor Force				
A. Minimum Basis				
9. Unemployment (2 + 5 + 6 + 7)*	3,531	4,504	859	1,322
10. Labor Force (1 + 4 + 7)*	50,633	33,044	5,931	5,234
11. Percent Unemployed	7.0	13.6	14.5	25.3
B. Maximum Basis				
12. Unemployment (2 + 5 + 6 + 8)*	5,075	6,545	1,091	1,656
13. Labor Force (1 + 4 + 8)*	52,177	35,085	6,163	5,568
14. Percent Unemployed	9.7	18.7	17.7	29.7

SOURCE: BLS Special Labor Force Report 163, 1974, Tables A2, A6, A28, A33, A38
* Addition of lines from official tables above.

The general conclusions from this table are:

● Unemployment is more severe among women than among men.

● Unemployment is twice as severe among Blacks as among whites, both for men and for women taken separately.

● Among men, the hidden unemployed, on the minimum basis, approximately equal the officially counted unemployed, and equal about one-and-one-half times the officially counted unemployed on the maximum basis.

• Among women, hidden unemployment ranges between double and triple the officially counted numbers.

Thus, hidden unemployment among women is more severe, relative to official unemployment, than among men. The rates of total unemployment, including hidden unemployment or the "contingent labor force" approximate 15% for white women and Black men, and go up to a terrible 25-30% range for Black women.

These figures are significant from the point of view of human welfare and the right to a full participation in life. The official establishment is most concerned about those unemployed who, in their view, pose the gravest threat to social stability. They consider that male heads of families — "breadwinners" — responsible for the support of wives and children, are most likely to organize and struggle against hunger, evictions, and other hardships resulting from unemployment. People in that category are most likely to be counted in the official ranks of the unemployed. Also the percentage of unemployment among them is lower than among all males. Officialdom, also, focuses on the unemployment rate among white males in this category, which is still lower, on the assumption that the Black unemployed, being concentrated in ghetto areas, will not be able to join forces with the white unemployed. The latter, so long as they are a scattered minority among a more than 96-97% employed men heads of families, are not apt to crystallize into an effective movement of the unemployed.

However, the broader concept of unemployment can become politically relevant and even decisive when there spreads among the population a sufficient consciousness of the *right of every person* to a job, the *need* of every person for work and a decent income, and *the necessity of struggle to realize that right and satisfy that need*. With such a recognition, it is clear from Table 20 the numbers of whites as well as Blacks, of men as well as women, who are deprived of that right, are sufficiently huge, sufficiently dense in the population as a whole, as to provide a formidable base for struggle, and to win the participation of workers currently employed, many of whom have been unemployed themselves or know that they are likely to become unemployed in the future. This realization comes more readily during a serious economic crises such as the present one of 1974-1975, when unemployment rates become formidable even among white male heads of families.

The New York Poverty Areas

Formal statistics, referring to numbers placed in predetermined boxes, edited by Census clerks operating under instructions which ensure a bland picture, only start to penetrate into the depths of the problem of jobs in the Black ghettoes of the United States.

A more fully-dimensioned picture is provided by a Labor Department study of working age nonparticipants in the official labor force in New York City poverty areas. It is the best of a series conducted by the department in a half dozen cities in 1968-69, a period of peak cyclical employment. The New York data covered representative households in Harlem, East Harlem, South Bronx, and Bedford Stuyvesant. Of the population 16 and over, 63% were Black, 22% Puerto Rican, and 15% of other nationality, including "white-Anglo". The survey results were "blown up" to provide estimated total figures for the population of the areas covered.

Of 388,800 people 16 years and older, only 218,700 were counted in the labor force, representing a considerably smaller proportion of the total than in the national count. 170,100 were counted as not in the labor force. Of those considered as in the labor force, only 14,800, or less than 7%, were counted as unemployed.[6]

But the majority of those officially excluded from the labor force were found to actually want work. Of the 170,100, 46,000, or more than three times the number officially unemployed, said they wanted a job "now." Another 63,000 said they didn't want a job immediately, but would want one if specified problems could be solved. Many of these had quite recent work records. Adding these groups to the officially unemployed gives a total of 124,700 of what the Labor Department statisticians call the "unemployed and contingent labor force entrants." The total labor force, including all of the "contingent entrants" or hidden unemployed, comes to 328,600. And of these 203,900 or 62% were employed, while 124,700, or 38% were unemployed. The remaining 60,200 persons aged 16 and over were definitely out of the labor force with no desire for jobs.[7]

Statistical breakdowns between men and women are incomplete. The percentages of official unemployment among men and among women were about equal. But the numbers of women not counted in the labor force and wanting a job now were 2½ times as numerous as similarly situated men. While exact statistics are not given, the report makes it evident that at least twice as many women as men were also among the group that said they would want a job if specified problems could be solved.

Thus it seems that total unemployment, including hidden unemployment, was about twice as severe among women as among men, and could range up towards 50% of the female population. Reasonably enough, the author of the report, Horst Brand, writes:

"The total for 'contingent labor force entrants' is overstated by the number of persons whose problems preventing their labor force entry cannot be solved."[8]

Who can say how large that number is? Given the existing social structure, that problem will be solved for a number determined by the intensity and quality of organization of the mass struggle for a constructive solution. Under socialism, it would undoubtedly be solved for the overwhelming majority. But even if we count only those who say they want and could take a job right now, we get a labor force of 264,800, and an unemployment total of 60,800, or 23% including a 16% rate for men and a 30% rate for women. This may be regarded as the lower bound of actual unemployment in New York City's poverty areas, and the figure of 124,700, or 38%, as an upper bound. It is notable that 82% of those who said they wanted a job now had previous work experience. Most of the remainder were youths who hadn't yet succeeded in getting their first jobs and were going to school.

Whatever the "true" figure, it represents an outrageous mass deprivation of the right to work to the Black and Puerto Rican people reflected only in the palest semblance of reality in official statistics.

Health and family responsibilities were the main problems keeping the "contingent workers" out of the officially recognized labor force:

"One fourth of all persons not in the labor force in the City's major poverty areas cited health problems as the primary reason for not working or looking for work." This included 11% of all Black men in the prime working ages, 25-54, as against 2% of all men in this age bracket nationally.[9]

Two-fifths of the people out for health reasons said they wanted a job. Many required special arrangements, like frequent rest periods, light work, or part-time work. Most said they would be available immediately or within a month if such arrangements were made:

"Nearly all reported chronic conditions. . . . Three fifths reported organic ailments, such as heart or digestive disease, the remainder reported functional disabilities, such as hearing defects, missing limbs, and so forth."[10]

Consider the situation of an employer's or corporation executive's relative with any of these ailments. Almost certainly, he or she would be placed in a type of employment taking into account his or her disability. A white working class person would have a certain chance of being "taken care of" by a "good boss" who might, in fact, obtain normal or better profit out of the handicapped person's labor by paying a subnormal wage. The chance of a Black worker getting such special dispensation, or being provided with special arrangements for getting to work if handicapped in travelling, is, however, close to zero.

About 45% of the "contingent labor force" almost all women, said the main obstacle to their working was family responsibilities: "Close to one-half of all Negro women nonparticipants with child care responsibilities, as against one-fourth of their Puerto Rican counterparts, said they wanted a job. . . . Problems of finding proper care for their children probably were among the more important reasons why women who wanted a job did not actually look for one."[11] Lack of an available child care center was the most frequent specific problem raised. Another was inability to find or afford baby sitters.

In many cases, the wages paid working women in New York were insufficient to make it worth-while for mothers to switch from welfare to work. At the time of the survey, the weekly welfare allowance for a woman with two preschool children was $51. If she got a job, her work-related expenses would be at least $23 per week, so she would need $74 to maintain her effective family income. But one-third of all women heads of households employed in New York and living in poverty areas were paid less than $75 per week, and the average for all such women was $84, or just $10 net over welfare for putting in a full week's work, and having the home and children to take care of in the bargain![12]

Increasing Severity of Black Unemployment

According to Table 19, the average rate of Black unemployment during the past decade has been moderately lower than during the previous decade, and the ratio of Black to white unemployment also was slightly reduced. Yet the table shows Black unemployment, both absolutely and relative to white unemployment, at considerably higher ratios

than during the immediate postwar years. But the actual trends have
been considerably worse than indicated by this table. The arbitrary
exclusion of Blacks from the officially counted labor force has been
rising, and with this the non-counting of Black unemployment has been
increasing. Key figures for understanding this are show in Table 21.

TABLE 21

MALE LABOR FORCE PARTICIPATION
AND UNEMPLOYMENT RATES 1940-1970

| | PERCENTAGE IN LABOR FORCE | | | PERCENTAGE UNEMPLOYED | | |
| | | | DIFFERENCE | | | RATIO BLACK |
YEAR	WHITE	BLACK	WHITE-BLACK	WHITE	BLACK	TO WHITE
1940	78.9	80.0*	-1.1	14.6	17.8*	122
1950	79.0	76.9	2.1	4.6	7.7	167
1960	78.0	72.0	6.0	4.6	8.9	193
1970	73.8	64.9	8.9	3.7	6.5	176

SOURCE: US-C-77. Refers to males 14 and over. Total labor force includes armed forces, but
unemployment percentages computed on civilian labor force.

* Covers all minorities.

In 1940 the percentage of Black males in the labor force was slightly
higher than that of white males — 80% as against 78.9%. This could be
expected, as relatively fewer Black youth could afford to continue their
education, and relatively fewer older Blacks could afford to retire.
Thus, in 1940, 46.1% of minority males aged 16 and 17 were reported
as in the labor force, as against 27.4% of whites aged 16 and 17; and
49.0% of minorities aged 65 and over were reported as in the labor
force, as against 41.2% of whites in that age group.[13]

These same considerations were operative in postwar years. But in
1950 the reported labor force participation rate of Blacks was 2.1 percentage points lower than that of whites, in 1960 it was 6 percentage
points lower, and in 1970 nearly 9 percentage points lower!

Over the 30 year interval there was a decline of 5.1 percentage points
in the white male participation rate, and 15.1 percentage points in the
reported Black male participation rate. These masses of Blacks have, in
fact, been relegated to the semi-permanent reserve army of the unemployed. Forced to the very fringes of the labor market, they are permitted to work only under conditions of extreme shortages, or are drafted
into the armed forces in time of war. Otherwise, they are simply not
counted as workers, or as students, or as any other socially meaningful

category of persons. In fact, they are treated as non-persons by the Establishment.

A word of explanation is in order concerning the exceptionally sharp drop in labor force participation rates for both whites and Blacks between 1960 and 1970. This is due largely to demographic factors, the rapid increase in the teenage population—about 50% in the case of whites, even more in the case of Blacks. Since the teenage participation rate is always less than that of older men, and with the added influence of the tendency to stay in school longer, this accounted for much of the decline in the white and Black participation rates over the decade. But it did not account for the widening gap between Black and white participation rates. This occurred in almost all age groups.

A minimum estimate of the actual Black labor force, including all who would be available for work if given a real chance, as well as those qualifying under the formal definitions of Census takers, would assume participation rates at least equal to those of whites. The *at least equal* should be stressed for two reasons. The compulsions to work remain stronger for Blacks than for whites. And the figures for whites include those for Puerto Ricans and Chicanos, many of whom are counted out of the labor force in the same ways as Blacks.

We have made alternative calculations, assuming that in *reality*, the percentage of Black males available for employment in each of the postwar decennial years was equal to that for white males. For the reasons cited, this must be regarded as a *minimum* assumption. But it results in showing a radical worsening of the unemployment situation of Blacks, absolutely and relatively. (Table 22).

TABLE 22

ADJUSTED MALE LABOR FORCE PARTICIPATION AND UNEMPLOYMENT RATES
1940-1970

| | PERCENTAGE IN LABOR FORCE | | PERCENTAGE UNEMPLOYED | | |
YEAR	WHITE	BLACK	WHITE	BLACK	BLACK % OF WHITE
1940	78.9	80.0	14.6	17.8	122
1950	79.0	79.0	4.6	10.1	220
1960	78.0	78.0	4.6	15.9	346
1970	73.8	73.8	3.7	17.8	481

SOURCE: Black percent in labor force for 1950, 1960, 1970, assumed equal to white percent in labor force. Black unemployment rates for 1950, 1960, and 1970, computed by adding to Black unemployment and labor force the increases represented by the adjustment of the Black labor force participation rates for those years. Data for whites and Blacks in 1940, as in Table 21.

This table shows Black male unemployment moderately more severe than white male unemployment in 1940, more than twice as severe in 1950, three and one-half times as severe in 1960, and nearly five times as severe in 1970! Moreover, the Black unemployment rate for 1970 is seen to equal that of the deep depression year of 1940. Was Black unemployment *actually* as bad in 1970 as in 1940? Probably not. The unemployment figures for 1940 were certainly incomplete, and we have attempted to take account of this incompleteness, at least in part, in the adjusted figures for 1970 and other postwar years.

But it is close to being as bad, sufficiently so as to justify the frequent saying that *for the Black people, the postwar period has become one of permanent depression.* The figures, in Table 22 strongly indicate, that *the permanent unemployment crisis of Black people is tending to become deeper, and the extent of real discrimination in unemployment against Blacks has become catastrophic.*

For Black men, the calculated rate of unemployment in 1970 shown in Table 22 is almost the same as the "maximum basis" rate for 1973 shown in Table 20. However, among white men Table 20 gives a radically higher "maximum basis" figure—9.7%, as compared with the 3.7% figure for 1970 shown in Table 22. Obviously, there was no such real deterioration in the situation of white workers in those three years.

How can we explain the inconsistency between the results of these two tables?

Table 20 reflects the subjective views of white and Black people not counted in the labor force, to the extent that they express themselves to enumerators. While it makes clear that the actual unemployment of both Blacks and whites are considerably higher than officially counted, it does not increase very much the ratio of Black to white unemployment, in comparison with the official figures.

Table 22 reflects the objective fact that the potential proportion of Black adults available for work must be at least as large as the corresponding proportion of whites. It gives a more accurate picture than Table 20 of the extreme and widening gap between the percentages of Black and white unemployment. But it fails to make any allowance for uncounted white unemployed workers, and to that extent, still falls short of a full count of both white and Black potential workers.

For women workers, it is not possible to make a historical comparison with the same significance, because of scientific and technical progress, and corresponding social changes, which have led to a rapid increase in the percentages of women working and seeking work, both white and Black. According to the official figures, the rates of white and Black unemployment among women were nearly equal in 1940—13.1% for whites and 14.4% for minorities. But in the postwar years, while the rates for both declined sharply, the improvement was more marked for whites, and the rates for Black women were 1½ to 2 times higher than for whites. In the 1970 Census, a rate of 4.9% for white women and 7.8% for Black women was reported.[14]

Among women, as among men, the adjusted unemployment percentages in Table 20 reflect the existing extent of recognition of and pressure for employment among white and Black women. But in a situation of real equality, there would be a tendency for increases in employment leading to approximately equal percentages of white and Black women employed, with remaining differences corresponding to any persisting national/cultural differences affecting choices between working for wages or salaries and maintaining a home full-time.

Mobile Jobs and Immobilized Black Workers

The weight of evidence is that discrimination against Blacks in unemployment is increasing. How is this possible, when so many companies are advertising themselves as "equal opportunity employers," and when jobs previously closed to Blacks have opened up, at least partially?

One answer is that housing discrimination increasingly curtails the kinds of jobs, and the number of jobs, available to Blacks, relative to the Black population.

The trend of industry and trade is to move from central cities to suburbs and semi-rural areas, in the search for lower costs, more space, easier transportation, and more affluent customers. *But as the percentage of jobs in the central cities declines, the percentage of Blacks concentrated in central cities increases.*

Between 1960 and 1970, the share of central cities in total employment of the fifteen largest metropolitan areas declined from 63.0% to 52.4%. The absolute number of jobs in these central cities declined 7%.[15] The pace of decline has quickened. A similar tabulation for 14 of these cities for the four year interval between 1969 and 1973 showed almost as large an overall percentage decline, and a decline of 6% or more for 8 of the 14 cities.

The central city job declines in manufacturing, where the better jobs available to most Blacks are concentrated, has been even faster. Between 1967 and 1972 manufacturing employment declined 13.8% in New York, 18.8% in Philadelphia, 21.7% in St. Louis, etc.[16]

The decentralization of industry is a logical trend, in terms of improving urban environmental conditions, making use of modern transportation facilities, and making it convenient for the population to spread out over larger areas. But the decay of central cities that goes with it is neither necessary nor desirable in any absolute sense. It is a product of the anarchy of capitalist society, where changes corresponding to technical progress take place only in accord with the drive for maximum corporate profits, and at the expense of the majority of the working population, instead of to their benefit. It is a product of the greed of the capitalist class, who are willing to have tax money spent only on the restricted residential areas where they live. It is a product of the racism of U.S. capitalism, which is particularly callous about the needs of the Black population.

White people move out of the city even faster than the jobs, some retaining their city jobs as commuters. Within the white population there is a definite stratification. The majority of white factory workers remain in central cities or smaller towns. Millions of white workers and their families have been stranded in towns and cities of declining industry. But what happens to sections of the white working population, happens most universally and drastically to the basic mass of the Black population. Black people are prevented from moving out of the city in substantial numbers, their overall city population increases rapidly, and more and more Black people are forced to compete for a diminishing number of jobs.

The Tragedy of Black Youth

The catastrophic situation of Black youth has been well publicized. It is true that more and more Black youth are able to get into college, or at least into two-year community colleges. But the great majority still cannot, and these are often subjected to inferior secondary education by the notorious "tracking" system and by segregated school systems. This majority—and many who go to college—enter the job market early, and against very severe handicaps. Amongst youths aged 16-21 in 1973, the official unemployment rates were 10.6% for white males, 11.0% for white females, 21.3% for minority males, and 29.1% for minority females! But the real contrast is much worse than indicated by these figures. The government statisticians, who count 69.8% of the white male youths and 53.9% of the white female youths as in the labor force, count only 58.7% of the minority male youths and 40.4% of the minority female youths.[17] It is obvious that any realistic measurement would show *larger* percentages of Black youth of both sexes in the labor force than white youth, if only to offset the larger percentages of white youth in school or college. Adjusting merely to equalize the labor force participation rates for Black youth raises the indicated unemployment percentages to about 34% for males and 47% for females, and more than doubles the reported number of Black youth unemployed, to a total of nearly 800,000.

The way the Census Bureau has distorted reality is indicated most sharply by their statistics for 16 and 17 year olds. As noted earlier in this chapter, in 1940, 46.1% of the minority males in this age group were classified as in the labor force, as against 27.4% of the white males. But by 1970, the Census Bureau reversed these percentages, placing 37.8% of the white males and 22.5% of the minority males in the labor force.[18] There was a similar switch in the percentages for teenage females.

While the difference is not so marked as in 1940, it is certain that today also the percentage of Black youth needing jobs is considerably larger than that of white youths.

The unemployment situation of Black youth is dramatically summarized in a 1971 report of the Twentieth Century Fund, from which extensive quotation is in order:

At the height of this country's economic boom in 1969, more than one out of four nonwhite male and female teenagers in the central cities of our twenty largest metropolitan areas was unemployed. This was about seventeen times the unemployment rate of 1.5 percent for white males in the entire country.

Since 1969, the softening economy has led to a serious deterioration in the overall employment situation. But its effect on Black youths has been a disaster. As against a white adult unemployment rate of 5 percent in March, 1971, the overall rate of Black teenage unemployment was 30.3 percent — or six times greater. In the poverty areas it was 41.2 percent. For Black adults between the ages of twenty and twenty-four, the unemployment rate was 16.5 percent.

Even so, the official figures do not portray the extent of the problem. An additional number of the ghetto jobless are never found by the enumerators. At the very least, 100,000 young Black people — a most conservative estimate — have given up hope and have stopped looking for jobs.

. . . Compounding the hardships of slack in the job market and the handicap of race is the sex disadvantage with which Black women must contend. They are held back by multiple layers of discrimination. The highest unemployment rates of any group are those for Black female teenagers in low income areas of central cities. Their unemployment rate in recent years has seldom been below 33 percent and is often as high as 50 percent. . . .

While many Black youths in urban ghettoes are on tracks that do not lead into society's mainstream of legitimate gainful activity, their rural brothers in the farmlands and small towns of the South have even fewer employment prospects.

The report notes that the long economic expansion of 1961-69, and the Vietnam War expansion of the armed forces, "decelerated but did not negate the growth of Black youth unemployment. . . . But the moderating influence of these factors no longer exists. Now, opposite trends are at work" — namely, a slowing economy, with a "halting" recovery from recession at the time of the report, and a partial demobilization.

Further, the report notes, the majority of those Black youth who do get jobs are little better off. "Their jobs provide fewer hours of work than those of whites, less pay, little permanence and fewer prospects for advancement . . . they have not escaped the frustration of a dead-end work life."

Typical of the liberal "do-good" approach, the focus of this report is that the plight of the millions of Black youth constitutes "social dynamite" which puts the future of the society in "grave jeopardy," that action is needed to protect "our society" from "violence." Its recommendations are pale and toothless — a little bit more of each of the half measures and appeals to the generosity of employers which have not yet stayed the deepening economic and social crisis of Black youth.[19]

No, the problem is not to save the corrupt and rotten social order which is responsible for these conditions. It is to save the millions of youth, the tens of millions of working people of all races and national origins, whose economic conditions are worsened and undermined when such a large section of the population is excluded from remunerative employment, and first of all to provide a chance of life for the Black youth who are being cheated of this most elementary right by contemporary American capitalism.

The programs necessary to accomplish that must go far beyond the bounds of past pseudo-reforms. They must be radical in content, decisive in extent, and forceful in execution.

They must be based on an understanding of the reasons for Black unemployment and of economic discrimination in general. They must be directed against those who are responsible for the evil. In the following chapter we identify them and establish their guilt.

7. Blaming the Victims

Economic life is the resultant of the social relations of people in the process of production. Under capitalism the principal dividing line is provided by ownership of capital, of means of production.

Those who own substantial amounts of capital, either directly in the form of a privately owned aggregate of structures, machines, and means of transportation; or indirectly, through ownership of large numbers of shares of stock in important productive aggregates constitute the capitalist class. And those who work for wages and salaries constitute the working class.

Between the upper and upper middle sectors of the capitalist class, on the one hand, and the overwhelming majority of the working class, there is a tremendous, rarely bridgeable gap in wealth, income, and standard of living. Even more, the top sections of the capitalist class are able to procure control over the instruments of government on a federal, state, and local level, as well as over the process of production. The gap between capitalists and workers, then, is not only one of income and wealth, but also a qualitative gap between power and powerlessness, between control over the production process and alienation from its results.

115

There are many people in various intermediate positions — small owners of capital who also work, very highly paid salaried people who enjoy the living standard of capitalists, etc. But, with all their variety and range, this intermediate group comprises a distinct minority.

The big majority of the population is of the working class. The economic dispersion within the working class, while substantial, is trivial compared to the gap between the working class as a whole and the upper strata of the capitalist class, those few tens of thousands who own the bulk of the shares of America's corporations. And the vastness of that gap is most apparent when one considers the complex of indicators — wealth as well as income, leisure and freedom of choice, power and control.

But in the United States there is one *major* modification of this standard pattern of capitalist economic life. And that is the drastic and persistent economic, social, juridical and political discrimination against Blacks and certain other peoples — notably Chicanos, Puerto Ricans, Native Americans, and some Asian peoples.

This discrimination has a decisive racial component. It is directed against people of darker skin. True, most Chicanos and Puerto Ricans are counted as "white" in the Census, but in real life they are treated as "darker" people, as "brown" people.

That discrimination goes far beyond the quantitative economic indexes discussed in this book. Blacks receive inferior education, they are limited to inferior housing and excluded from vast residential areas, they are subjected to disproportionate numbers of arrests and more severe terms of imprisonment, they are kept from a proportional share of political offices.

And yet, *the key element* in the entire pattern of discrimination is economic. To end this economic discrimination will be a decisive step towards ending discrimination in all phases of life.

This discrimination is not a result of natural laws, nor of the simple operation of economic laws. It is part of the social relations of people, and is caused by the actions of people. People are responsible for it. *Which people?*

Blaming the Victim

Establishment sociologists and economists, writers of government reports, and politicians, give a whole series of explanations which can be summarized in the phrase *Blaming the Victim,* which happens to be the title of a powerful and passionate book by William Ryan.

The crudest version of that is the unscientific, lying theory of the genetic inferiority of Blacks. The essential genetic equality of all races has been well established by science. Racist genetics is an ideological hangover of the slave system, adapted to present-day conditions by ideologists of a decadent capitalism. It reached its most vicious form in the ideology and practice of German fascism, which annihilated tens of millions of Jews, Russians, Poles, Gypsies, and other peoples of supposedly inferior races. Today it is the cornerstone of the official ideology and legal structure of the fascist regime of the South African Republic.

And it has no more validity when directed against Black Americans or Black Africans than when it was directed against white Jews and Russians.

As the struggle for Black equality has gained momentum, the attempts to revive and popularize theories of genetic inferiority of Blacks have been stepped up. Moreover proponents of these theories are given access to college lecture halls, the media, the respectable publishing houses—all in the name of freedom of speech. But racist theories directed against Blacks in the United States are just as criminal as were racist theories directed against Jews in fascist Germany. *These are criminal theories, disseminated with criminal intent, and their toleration can have disastrous results.*

More widespread today are the more subtle racist theories. Some seem quite harmless, and have a degree of plausibility. For example, the idea that Blacks are handicapped economically because they have less education. True, Blacks on the average, receive less education than whites, and qualitatively inferior education. But as shown in Chapter 3, discrimination against Blacks is severe as compared with whites having equal education. Moreover, the inferior education of Blacks is imposed on them, it is maintained despite persistent struggles, especially in recent decades, for more and better education.

Until quite recently, in large sections of the country separate and grossly unequal education was enforced by law. And to this day de facto segregation and inferior education is imposed by school authorities, by housing segregation, by establishment of whites-only private schools, and other devices.

No, the inferior education of Blacks is part of racist discrimination, and *not* an independent causal factor.

But the Blacks are charged with not being capable of learning.
Ryan writes:

> What is wrong with the victim? In pursuing this logic, no one remembers to
> ask questions about the collapsing buildings and torn textbooks, the frightened,
> insensitive teachers, the six additional desks in the room, the blustering, fright-
> ened principals, the relentless segregation, the callous administration, the ir-
> relevant curriculum, the bigoted or cowardly members of the school board, the
> insulting history book, the stingy taxpayers, the fairy-tale readers, or the self-
> serving faculty of the local teachers' college. We are encouraged to confine our
> attention to the child and to dwell on all his alleged defects. Cultural deprivation
> becomes an omnibus explanation for the educational diaster area known as the
> inner-city school.[1]

Indeed, in addition to being subjected to qualitatively inferior education, the Blacks are deliberately educated for lower-income, dead end
jobs, through the notorious tracking system.

It is said that part of the reason why many of the Jewish people in the
United States have "made it" is because of their tradition of being
"people of the book"—their striving, and self-sacrifice for education.
But Ryan shows that sociological studies reveal the same traits among
Black people, the same extra striving, extra sacrifice for education.
Clearly, the real trouble is that they are deliberately barred both from
high quality education and from enjoying its fruits. The discrimination
is more determined, more persistent, more absolute, than that which
Jewish people faced in anti-Semitic discrimination in the educational
system in the past, and still face to a limited degree.

For the past decade, since Daniel Moynihan became the favorite
sociologist of Presidents, the main target of "victim-blaming" has been
the Black family. Families headed by women, absent fathers, illegiti-
mate children, welfare mothers who do not work—all these phenomena
are taken to be predominant, relatively exclusive, and blameable attributes of the Black people. None of these charges are valid, and even if
they were, they would in no way excuse the existing economic discrimination against all Blacks, regardless of family status.

Robert B. Hill drives a sharp spear into this approach in his small
book, *The Strengths of Black Families*. He concludes that the main
strengths of Black families are strong kinship bonds, strong work orientation, adaptability of family roles, strong achievement orientation, and
strong religious orientation. Concretely, he finds:

Contrary to the widespread belief in a 'matriarchy' among Blacks, our findings reveal that most Black families. . . are characterized by an equalitarian pattern in which neither spouse dominates, but shares decision making and the performance of expected tasks. . .

Most Black babies born out-of-wedlock are kept by parent and relatives, while most white babies born out of wedlock are given away. . . .

. . . Contrary to the belief that dependency is characteristic of most families headed by women, . . . three-fifths of the women heading Black families work—most of them full-time.

. . . The high achievement orientation of low-income Black families is reflected in the large numbers of college students from these families that attend college. For example, three-fourths of the Blacks enrolled in college in 1970 came from homes in which the family heads had no college education.[2]

The majority of Black families, like white families, have a "normal" structure consisting of a husband, a wife, and children. True, a larger proportion of Black families than white deviate from that norm. But far from being the *cause* of the economic and social discrimination against Blacks, this is the *effect* of that discrimination. Poverty, poor housing, unemployment, all impose great psychological and emotional strains on family life, and undermine family stability. But even that isn't the main thing. The patterns of discrimination directly aim at breaking up the Black family. When the Black husband can only obtain employment in a distant city or construction project where there are no living facilities available for his family, this obviously tends to destroy that family's structure. When Black men are subjected to discriminatory police and court treatment, and more often sent to prison than whites, that obviously tends to destroy families.

And when the U.S. Government and local authorities have contrived a welfare system that penalizes the presence of a husband, it most directly operates to break up poor Black families, and to exaggerate the reported number of families headed by women, including in that category many where the husband must remain hidden from view to avoid the starvation of his family.

In the complementary situation, neither the Census takers nor revenue agents pry into rich white men's second mistress-headed households, nor into the "mate-switching," etc., fashionable in upper class suburbia. Nor are the participants in these practices economically penalized.

The 1974 Economic Report of the President, besides its statistical attempts to hide discrimination (Ch. 5) engages in "blaming the victim.'' The authors try to "factor out" income differentials by standard statistical devices, but do not get very far. They explain:

> Several factors can be mentioned to explain why Black males still receive lower earnings than white males after adjustment for schooling, age, region and marital status. Prior investments made in the child at home are important in determining the extent to which a student benefits from schooling. Black youths are more likely to come from poorer homes where the parents have less schooling, to have poorer diets, and to be less healthy. They are likely to start school with fewer advantages and skills than the typical white youth. Moreover, at least in the past, there was discrimination against Black youths in public school expenditures. Later on, as adults, Blacks have poorer health, and may have poorer information about better jobs. Some of the current wage differences may thus be a consequence of past discrimination.

Since, according to the authors, many of these factors are difficult to measure, "one cannot reliably measure the extent of . . . discrimination that now exists," or its effects on earnings.[3]

This agnostic conclusion, as well as the tenor of the entire discussion, aims to convey the impression that discrimination today is either negligible or non-existent. Note the overt expressions of racial prejudice, such as the claim that Black parents do not *"invest"* enough in their children, and that Black children *start* school with less "skill" than white six-year olds. The main thing however, is that insofar as some of these "factors" are accurate descriptions of reality, they merely describe *aspects of discrimination,* rather then independent circumstances.

A year later, the President's economists tried to justify the terrible crisis increase in Black unemployment. Their attempts to "factor out" unemployment differentials according to various alleged causes left a significant residual due to racist discrimination. Like the damned spot on Lady Macbeth's hand, they couldn't get rid of the differential. In fact, they admitted that the spot is spreading, the differential widening. So they turned to a new line of argument, blaming it on equal employment legislation! Here is the tortuous reasoning:

"Even if discrimination in the labor market were widespread, it could result in lower wages instead of higher unemployment for Blacks relative to whites with the same skill and other relevant characteristics. If there were no equal opportunity legislation or other restrictions on wages, and if employers discriminated against Blacks, Blacks might work for less pay than similarly qualified whites; this would provide an incentive for employers to hire them. . .discrimination could take the form of reduced compensation, inferior jobs, or segregation, rather than higher unemployment."

Employers may prefer to discriminate in employment, the authors explain," because it is sometimes more difficult to prove discrimination in hiring than in overt pay differences. . ." [3a]

This has no logical or factual basis. Equal opportunities legislation is supposed to apply to employment and wages equally. to explain violation of the former requirement by compliance with the latter is to tacitly condone the violation. Moreover, as shown in Chapter 5, the legislation has not brought about equal wages for equal work, while discrimination in hiring has been more often and more easily proved than discrimination in wages.

The intent of all this is to convince employers and white workers that Blacks should be forced to work for substandard wages, regardless of the level of their work, "in their own interest." Heavy unemployment among Blacks is their own fault for pressing for equal opportunity legislation. To remove any doubt of their intent, the presidential economists add this crudely racist sentence:

"Moreover, the prospect of equal pay may encourage Blacks to quit jobs with low pay and search longer for more promising positions." [3b]

This is the modernized version of the southern plantation owner complaining about his "uppity" field hands!

Banfield

Academic propaganda in the 1960s seeking to justify economic discrimination against Blacks avoided, for the most part, overt racism, and relied on the method of "factoring out" supposedly independent causes, leaving racism as a relatively minor residual. Professor Gary Becker was a leading exponent of this method.

The 1970s, with the political rise of racist Governor George Wallace, and the accession to the presidency of Richard Nixon with his "southern strategy," created a market place for a more sinister scholar who would use a flimsy veneer of socio-economic analysis to barely disguise blatant racism and incitations to anti-Black repressions. Professor Edward C. Banfield, who served in 1970 as head of President Nixon's task force on model cities, is the leader of this "school."

He admits that racial prejudices are a factor in the inferior economic situation of Blacks, but he gives them only a marginal role:

"Cultural differences—and conceivably even biological ones as well—also account in some degree for the special position of the Negro, as they do for that of every ethnic group."[4]

Here Banfield pays his respects to the Jensens, the Shockleys, and the other "scientific" carriers of the slaveowners' rationalization that the Blacks are really some inferior sort of animal by nature. But to tread lightly, he doesn't quite commit himself, leaves a path for retreat by the qualifying "conceivably." However, when one examines the "cultural differences" Banfield talks about, it becomes clear that he intends to convey the impression that they are so deeply and lastingly ingrained in the Black people that for all practical purposes they might as well be biological characteristics. And yet again he tries to cover himself with the phrase "as they do for that of every ethnic group." This, however, proves to be a mere pretense of even-handedness. Either the differences from the norm of the other groups are positive instead of negative, or they rapidly get over their negative characteristics, in contrast to his version of the Black culture.

Here is one of Banfield's stereotypes of the alleged cultural inferiority of Blacks. Referring to areas vacated by whites, and occupied by Blacks:

"Looking at the neighborhoods they had left a decade or two before, suburbanites were often dismayed at what they saw—lawns and shrubbery trampled out, houses unpainted, porches sagging, vacant lots filled with broken bottles and junk . . ." The people moving in "cared little or nothing for lawns and had no objections to broken bottles."[5]

Some years ago I spent some time in a working class area of Detroit, with street after street of separate two-story houses, inhabited by the "block-busting" system: solid Black blocks sandwiched in between solid white blocks. Conscious of the Banfield-type slander, I walked from block to block to study the relative cleanliness, neatness, etc. In every respect the Black blocks were as good or better. And in more cases, Black householders were improving their homes. I also drove through Cleveland, not long after vast areas had been bulldozed by "urban renewal" programs which turned out to be "Negro removal" programs—areas looking as if bombed out by war. To a Banfield, the damage was done not by avaricious landlords and their governmental collaborators, but by their Black victims.

Under the guise of citing a sociologist's description of what "the community" thinks of "the scum of the city" Banfield characterizes typical Blacks as criminals with no self-respect, given to "delinquency, sexual promiscuity," "perversion," "incestual relations," as "loud," "vulgar," "lazy" belligerent alcoholics. But again there is a cover-up. The quoted description is of an all-white community. So, asks Banfield, if this is true of lower class whites, why is it racist to use it as a description of lower class Blacks?[6]

This "class" characterization of the Black masses is the cornerstone of Banfield's "scholarly" contribution. His social classes have little in common with the Marxist social classes, which are determined by the relation of people to the means of production, by their role in the country's economic life. No, his classes are defined by cultural-ethical-psychological qualities. He defines four classes, from the best to the worst. If it just happens that the description of the best class clearly refers to the big tycoon's image of himself; and of the next-to-the-worst class to the capitalists' image of the worker he exploits; and the worst class to the racists' view of the majority of Blacks, so be it. It's the tycoons, with their class and racial prejudices, who endow his professorial chair and promote his books.

The upper class individual is most "future-oriented," not only for his family, but for the community, the nation, for all mankind. This paragon is "self-respecting, self-confident, self-sufficient . . . tolerant." He places "great value on independence, curiosity, creativity . . . consideration of others." And it's clear from details given that he is also rich.

The "middle class" has less of these good qualities, and is more interested in "getting ahead" personally, in being a conformist.

The "working class" man lives for the present. He emphasizes "cleanliness, neatness, obedience." He cares naught for world affairs, for culture. He is family-centered, has few friends, only companions. He likes crowds, noise, smells, has no use for privacy. In brief, a useful, if vulgar, robot.

The "lower class" individual "lives from moment to moment." He lacks self-discipline, works "only to stay alive and drifts from one unskilled job to another." He's a sex maniac, "suspicious and hostile, aggressive yet dependent," without any loyalty to group or mate.[7]

According to estimates favored by Banfield, 58% of all Blacks are "lower class," 37% "working class," 4% "middle class," and only

1% "upper class." But among whites 17% are lower class, 50% working class, 21% middle class, and 12% upper class.[8]

This fits in with his blaming the Blacks themselves for their miserable lives in the ghettoes, and the working class majority of whites—with their crude narrow-mindedness—as responsible for what little racism he is willing to concede as part of the picture.

Banfield, in explaining away economic and housing discrimination, also uses the factors generally used by earlier apologists for racism, but with special emphasis on migration:

"The misfortune, amounting to a tragedy, is not that Negroes got to the city but that they got there so late and then in such great numbers in so short a time."[9]

In fact, for more than fifteen years, the Black people have been more urbanized that the white. A quarter of a century ago, in 1950, 61.7% of Blacks and other minorities, as compared with 64.3% of the whites lived in cities[10]. By 1970, 72.4% of the white population, and 80.7% of Blacks and other minorities lived in urban areas. That means that a majority of Blacks living today were born in cities, and a majority of Black workers grew up and were educated in cities. Moreover, the proportion of Blacks with a rural background is hardly, if at all, larger than the proportion of whites with a rural background.

If migration from the countryside accounted for the Black people's hardships, this would have been at least a generation ago, and the effects long since worn off for the majority, *unless racist discrimination maintained and intensified whatever disadvantages were associated with the farm-to-city move*. Moreover, there is absolutely no evidence to indicate that those Blacks in families that have been citified for generations are better off than the recent arrivals. It may well be the other way around!

Banfield writes:

"Today, the Negro's main disadvantage is the same as the Puerto Rican's and Mexican's: namely, that he is the most recent unskilled, and hence relatively low-income migrant to reach the city from a backward rural area . . ."[11]

In 1969 the per capita income of Chicanos in families whose head was born in the United States of native parentage was $1,418, the per capita income of Chicanos whose family head was born in this country of Mexican parentage was $2,132, and the per capita income of Chicanos whose head was born in Mexico was $2,376.[12] Apparently the Chicanos whose ancestors have lived here the longest, and in most cases much longer than the Anglos, are the most subject to oppression and economic discrimination!

The same applies even more sharply to Puerto Ricans. Those with a family head born in the United States of Puerto Rican parentage had a per capita income of only $670, while those with a family head born in Puerto Rico had a per capita income four times as large, $2,620.[13]

Without trying to explain these superficially surprising results here, or claiming their direct comparability with the situations of Black migrants from the southern countryside, the statistics certainly confound Banfield's assumption that the migration accounts for the low income of Blacks. And, of course, it is specifically migration from the southern countryside that Banfield emphasizes. Discussing the reasons why Blacks live in all-Black neighborhoods, he writes:

"The physical separation may arise from various causes—his having a low income, his being a part of a wave of migration that inundated all of the cheap housing then available . . . his having cultural characteristics that make him an undesirable neighbor. . . . On the other hand, there are groups—rural Southern whites, for example—whose handicaps are much like the Negro's and must be explained entirely by nonracial factors. . . . Much of what looks like 'racial' poverty is really 'rural Southern' poverty."[14]

Note that here again Banfield reveals, if in passing, his blatant racism, in referring to the "undesirability" of Blacks as neighbors. But let's examine his argument.

The southern countryside has been a prime source of recruiting white workers by the automobile manufacturers. In Michigan in 1970 there lived 465,000 whites and 355,000 Blacks who were born in the South.[15] But these southern-born whites may reside where they wish in Michigan, including such towns as Dearborn, Dearborn Heights, Lincoln Park, Livonia, and Royal Oak, from which Blacks are barred. They may live in the cities and whites-only suburbs, subject only to income restrictions, no matter where they were born. They may join the churches and other social groupings which provide contacts leading to better jobs.

Now let's examine the picture nationally. As of 1970, 27% of the Blacks living in the Northeast, 32% of the Blacks living in the North Central states, and 41% of the Blacks living in the West, were born in the South.[16] In no case did the southern-born Blacks constitute a sufficient percentage of the total to account for the gross differentials against Black people in incomes and employment, especially since significant, although smaller proportions of whites had also migrated from the South. Moreover, the ratio of Black to white median family income is highest in the West, where the percentage of Black migrants is highest.

As already noted, there is no evidence that incomes of southern-born Blacks living in the North are lower than those of northern-born Blacks living in the North. Certainly, if there were an effect, it would be most apparent in the early years after migration. But of the total Black population of the country, only 3.2% had migrated to their present state of residence from another, southern state, in the five years before the Census, as compared with 2.8% among whites. Moreover, Blacks showed as much residential stability as whites—with 81.2% living in the same county as five years earlier, as compared with 75.8% among whites.[17]

Finally, Banfield's explanation totally collapses when applied to economic differentials in the South itself, where half the Black population still resides. Not only that, the collapse is most complete in the rural South. Yes, the rural South is backward. Yes, whites and Blacks living there have been subjected to inferior education, inferior cultural opportunities, and living conditions below the urban standards. But equal, as Banfield implies? Hardly! In 1969 the per capita income of rural southern Blacks was only $1,003, which was a mere 43% of the $2,353 per capita income of rural southern whites.[18]

Economic discrimination against southern rural Blacks is of the "purest" (sic) racist variety, carried forward for more than a century from the period of human slavery. There is no identity between the situations of rural whites and Blacks in the South, and that gross discrimination is carried over, only partly moderated, when the rural people, Black and white, migrate to the cities, South and North. Moreover, Banfield is absolutely wrong when he claims that the handicaps of rural southern whites must be explained entirely by nonracial factors. It's exactly the opposite. The handicaps faced by southern rural whites, while milder than those faced by southern rural Blacks, are *entirely* the products of the racist oppression of Blacks. If the southern countryside is the core area of Black oppression, it is *exactly* that circumstance which makes it the area of deepest white poverty. (Chapter 10)

That Banfield's racism is closely associated with his loyalty to the employer's profit interests is evidenced by his chapter on unemployment. He attributes Black unemployment to the alleged inferiority of the Blacks as workers, and to the allegedly excessive minimum wages, which makes it impossible for employers to hire them without losing money. This is giving a particular racist twist to the standard employer argument against *any* minimum wage, or against any increase in the minimum, which they use to profiteer at the expense of all workers, Black and white, and especially youth and women.

Banfield opposes all governmental programs against racism, or directed to providing better conditions for the poor. He sees no end to segregation, and blithely justifies it:

> The increasing isolation of the lower class is a problem, to be sure, but it is hard to see what can be done about it. The upper classes will continue to want to separate themselves physically from the lower, and in a free country they probably cannot be prevented from doing so.[19]

As for the lower classes, his program is:

1. Encourage the Black to realize that he himself, and not society or racism is responsible for his ills.
2. Get them out of school at 14, and put those unable to get jobs in the army or a "youth corps."
3. Give cash subsidies to the "competent" poor, but only goods to the "incompetents" and encourage or force them to reside in an institution or a semi-institution, such as a "supervised public housing project."
4. "Intensive" birth control "guidance."
5. Increased police powers against Black areas and people, more "stop and frisk" and the like, including jailing those "likely" to commit violent crimes.[20]

In short, a sinister, cynical, Apartheid program for the United States.

Blaming White Workers

It remains to deal with the argument that discrimination in employment and income is the result of the prejudices of white people in general, and white workers especially. That most white people have prejudices against Blacks cannot be denied. However, people are not born with prejudices. They are implanted by the laws, physical arrangements, and dominant culture of the social system under which they live. Racism was deeply implanted into generations of whites by the Jim Crow laws of the South. These were not written by white workers or poor farmers, but by the southern landlord class, abetted by their conquerors and saviors, the northern capitalists. Racism was deeply implanted into generations of whites countrywide by blackface vaudeville comedians, cartoons, motion pictures, radio and then television shows degrading and insulting the Black people, by a caricature of history taught in the schools which by omission and distortion created an image of Blacks as subservient objects of history with no accomplishments and no efforts on their own hehalf. Racism was deeply implanted by the physical separation of Blacks, by their appearance in real life only in positions of inferiority, in menial positions, in dirty jobs. Racism was implanted by the many-sided propaganda to make whites fear Blacks as threats to their jobs and to their physical security.

The cultural environment has been and remains controlled overwhelmingly by the capitalist class. The physical separation and placing in inferior positions of Blacks is the work of bankers and real estate men, private and governmental employers. The working people of this country did not initiate these practices, nor did they influence them significantly.

Yet it is true that generations of white people, with the exception of a minority, tolerated racist institutions, culture, and economic patterns. It is true that too many white workers have participated in outrages against the Black people, and that most participate in everyday racist practices. It is true that people are responsible for their actions, and share responsibility for their acquiescence in actions of an exploiting, racist ruling class.

White workers are not the source of discrimination and segregation in the United States. But white workers must play a leading part in ending these evils, and it is in their vital self interest to do so (Chapter 10). And there is reason to believe that this is being perceived by a growing number of working people.

Powerful forces in the world are combating racist ideology and practice. These include the national liberation movements in Asia, Africa, and Latin America. They include the abolition of racist oppression and the practice of racial and national equality in the USSR and Cuba, as integral parts of the gains of all working people under socialism. They include, not least of all, the long struggles of the Black people of the United States for equality.

The public response to these struggles makes it clear that most white people know that their racist prejudices are wrong, and favor the ending of discrimination against Blacks. That was necessary to get through Congress, which is more conservative than the population at large, major Civil Rights legislation. That was necessary to bring about the election of more and more Blacks to office in cities and states where Blacks are a minority, and sometimes a small minority, of the electorate.

For decades it was said that white workers would refuse to work alongside Blacks, hence Black workers had to be placed in separate and inferior jobs. Similarly, it was argued, white customers would be driven away by Black salespersons and receptionists, hence Blacks could not have "front office" or "counter" jobs. These myths were disproven when, in industry after industry, in offices and trading places, for the first time Blacks broke through to work alongside whites, there was no difficulty whatsoever. The penetration of tens of thousands of Blacks to production jobs in southern textile mills, a process beginning even before the end of legal segregation, proceeded so smoothly that it was scarcely noticed. Undoubtedly there was resentment on the part of some white workers in these cases, but it was, for the most part, subdued and short-lived. In industry after industry Blacks now deal with customers as bank tellers, airline stewards, hotel clerks, and in many other ways. And there are no reports of whites shifting their custom in protest.

But it is true that employers for decades resisted hiring Blacks for these jobs, while placing the blame for their own racist actions on their workers. And when they finally had to permit the breakthrough, often after unfavorable publicity from federal or state fair employment or human rights commissions, they tried to use it as a lever to hold down wages.

What about the role of white workers as a group, organized into trade unions? We'll deal with that in Chapter 12.

8. Capitalist Responsibility

Economic discrimination takes place mainly at the place of employment—in access to jobs, in the kinds of jobs available, and in pay for similar work. As shown in Chapters 5 and 6, almost all of the income differential against Blacks can be accounted for in these terms.

Control of employment, outside of government, is almost exclusively in the hands of capitalists. Only a few tens of thousands of workers are hired through a union-employer hiring hall system, such as that of the International Longshoremen's and Warehousemen's Union—and this shows up both in a high percentage of Black, Chicano and Asian workers and in relatively high wages for all West Coast longshoremen and other members of this union. Much larger numbers of workers are referred by union locals, or require union cards in order to work, but decision on employment remains in the hands of the employer. In building trades unions where this system prevails, the union leadership and the employers share responsibility for employment patterns.

But employers exclusively control the hiring of more than 90% of all private employees. For the roughly one-fourth of wage and salary workers in unions, there is a subsequent influence on firing, and to some extent on promotion. The extent of this influence depends on the strength and character of seniority systems written into contracts, and on the militancy and power of the particular union. But in any event the influence is limited, and never goes beyond the range of employment covered by the union's jurisdiction. Thus it never covers the engineering, managerial, and supervisory personnel, and rarely does it cover the clerical personnel.

So it must be said that if every private industry in the country grossly discriminates against Black workers in employment and wages, that is because the employers deliberately do so. True, the degree of discrimination varies from industry to industry and from individual employer to individual employer.

A rough indication of the allocation of blame for discrimination by its victims is indicated by the identity of those charged with discrimination in complaints submitted to the EEOC. Six out of seven charges filed with that agency during fiscal 1972 were levied against employers. As against the 86% of the total against employers, 6% were levied against unions, 5% against employment agencies, and the remaining 3% against some combination of the three.[1]

There is one line of thought that the main culprits are certain small employers, that major corporate employers try to reduce discrimination. To encourage that viewpoint, top officials of giant corporations have set up various "do-good" organizations in the racial field, such as the National Association of Businessmen and the Urban Coalition. Ostensibly devoted to providing training and employment for Blacks, these organizations have in practice been devoted mainly to providing publicity for their sponsors, serving as attempts to defuse mass struggles against poverty and discrimination among the Black population.

One may also mention the exhaustive "Negro in Industry" series put out by the Wharton School of Finance of the University of Pennsylvania. The general line of these studies is that corporations formerly did have racist employment practices, but are now trying to comply with civil rights legislation and are making rather rapid progress towards achieving equal employment practices.

True, the pressure of the mass movement, and the passage of the Civil Rights Act of 1964, caused most corporations to adapt to the new conditions. Generally, some of the most brazen forms of discrimination were ended. There was an increase in overall employment of Black workers, more because of conditions in the labor market during the Vietnam War than because of civil rights legislation. However, the essential pattern of discrimination was little changed, and some changes in the pattern of employment ended up changing the form of discrimination, but not reducing it in degree.

Ma Bell—the Country's Largest Employer

The American Telephone and Telegraph Company, employing over a million people, is the country's largest and most profitable corporation. It is also the most ubiquitous monopoly, powerful in 50 states, with the most ramified political and economic ties. It represents not just one particular set of big capitalists, but a coalition of the most powerful financial groups, the Rockefellers, the Morgans, the First National City Bank, together with Boston and Chicago financial interests. Economist Stanislav Menshikov writes:

"AT&T has truly become the collective possession of a number of the main U.S. financial groups. The company needs annually about $1,000 million in loans, an operation impossible without the coordinated action of the main New York banks and insurance companies." [1a]

Since this was written, the dependence on the bankers has multiplied, with new borrowings surpassing $4,000 million in the single year 1970. Its racial policies may fairly be appraised as the quintessence of the policies of American big business as a whole. *The deliberately racist character of these policies* is graphically described in a 1972 report of the Equal Employment Opportunity Commission (EEOC). It is a devastating indictment of the practices, and exposes their motivation—extra profits. It deals also with discrimination against women and Spanish speaking people, but in this book we concentrate on its revelation of discrimination against Blacks.*

Through most of its history, the company followed a deliberate and open policy of whites only, except for the cleanup jobs traditionally reserved for Blacks.

"From the earliest times Black workers were almost completely excluded from employment in the telecommunications industry. In 1930,

---

* The report deals only with the telephone subsidiaries of AT&T, and not with the manufacturing, research, and armament subsidiaries, which account for about one-fourth of its total employment.

when Blacks constituted 9.7% of the total population in the United States, they represented only 0.7% of the workers in the telecommunications industry and were exclusively concentrated in the service worker and laborer jobs."[2]

The first increase in Black telephone employment was during World War II, with its huge demand for labor, but even then, Black workers got up to only 1.3% of AT&T jobs by 1950. During the following decade Black women telephone operators were hired in northern metropolitan centers, but few other Black workers were hired anywhere, and the percentage of Black employment actually declined in the South. During the 1960s, especially with the outbreak of the Vietnam War in the middle of the decade, there was a shift to large-scale employment of Blacks, which reached 4.6% of system employment in 1966 and 9.8% in 1970.

However, the pattern of Black employment remained grossly and deliberately discriminatory. After the Civil Rights Act of 1964 was passed Bell Telephone finally began to open up some previously closed jobs to Blacks, but only on a token basis.

"Somehow, Black employment was being concentrated in the lowest-paying, least desirable, dead-end jobs in the Bell System. Blacks still had not obtained a significant number of high-paying craft jobs in any area. This fact emphasizes the futility of the employment advances made by Blacks in the Bell System since 1930."[3]

Blacks remain almost totally excluded from managerial positions, except at the lowest level supervisory jobs. Furthermore:

"Not only are Blacks generally underrepresented in the telephone crafts, they are almost totally excluded from the top craft jobs of Switchman, Cable Splicer, PBX Installer-Repairman, etc."[4]

The exclusion of Blacks from skilled craft employment is more complete in the telephone industry than in industry generally. In the New York area, the percentage of Blacks in telephone company craft jobs was less than one-third the percentage of Blacks in craft jobs in all industries. In Jacksonville, Florida, in 1967, there was not a single Black in a telephone company craft job, and this was not a unique situation.

The 10% participation rate of Blacks in 1970 telephone company employment remained abnormally low, considering the circumstances of the industry.

". . . the low overall participation rate of Blacks in most Bell System companies . . . is quite surprising for three reasons. First, due to extraordinarily high turnover among non-management employees, the Bell System hires approximately two hundred thousand persons every year. Second, Bell System employment is concentrated in SMSA's (metropolitan areas—VP) which contain the bulk of the Black population. . . . Third, virtually all of the new employees hired by Bell System companies each year possess minimal job skills. . . . The low utilization of Blacks in the South is easily explained by deliberate and racially discriminatory hiring practices. Elsewhere, the lag . . . is largely explained by Bell System pre-employment criteria which tend to *screen out Blacks and screen in whites.*"[5]

No previous training or education is relevant to the specific craft skills of the telephone industry. *All training is done on the job.* Thus the discriminatory pre-employment criteria are no more accidental than the overt racism in the South. The racism of the Bell Telephone system is nationwide, expressing itself in slightly disguised form where forced to do so. In many respects, the corporation brazenly violated civil rights law provisions, as in continuing to place racist advertisements, at least as late as 1968.

A revealing incident occurred early in the 1970s, when there was a crisis of disrepair and lag in installation of new phones in the New York metropolitan area, owing to a shortage of craft employees. Civil rights organizations demanded that the telephone company employ Black residents. But instead, the company imported crafts workers from other parts of the country for long periods, paying them huge living subsidies while away from home in order to avoid hiring Blacks in these jobs.

Discrimination against Black males is particularly severe. While 47% of Anglo employees are male, only 21% of Black employees are male. Black women are overwhelmingly concentrated in the operator jobs.

. . . "they have the lowest-paying major job in the System. Since 'female' jobs are appropriately identical to low-paying jobs, it is no surprise that when Blacks entered the System in substantial numbers, they would be Black females . . . most Blacks in the Bell system suffer a double handicap of race and sex. The myriad Bell policies which discriminate against females because of their sex also clearly affect Blacks much more than whites. . . . turnover among operators has continued to escalate, reaching astounding levels in major urban areas. It is these areas that are becoming increasingly Black and in which the operator's wage is no longer attractive to whites. The combination of these factors is rapidly converting the Traffic Department (where operators work) from simply a 'nunnery' into a 'ghetto nunnery' "[6]

It isn't only the low salary that drives away so many operators. It's also the abominable working conditions, the speedup, the petty disciplines imposed by the company, and the brutal pressures of supervisors.

"The Operator job is, quite pointedly, a *horrendous* job. No greater testimony to this fact exists than the unbelievably high rate at which employees bolt from the job. The Bell System's response is amazing: rather than restructure the job, improve the wages, and provide important new avenues for promotion and transfer—changes which even common sense would suggest—AT&T has decided to keep the wages depressed and simply hire more and more Black females.

"The inevitable effects of these policy decisions are all too obvious. Most of the Blacks in the Bell System will never have a real chance at a good job. The economic realities of the labor market will force large numbers of Blacks to apply for operator jobs. After all, *any* job is better than no job, any job except operator. The realities of the operator job will thus force Blacks to quit as fast as they are forced to apply. This sad situation appears to be AT&T's major answer to the cries for equal opportunities."

The greed for rising profits dictates this extreme of racist oppression and discrimination against women. It decrees intolerable job conditions. It inevitably contributes to the deteriorating service of the system, as it decrees the constantly rising rates charged for that service, the demands on pliable Public Service Commissions for higher and higher rates of return.

The motivation of telephone company racism has been blurted out by a number of its officials. A 1970 report complained that in some central city areas, applicants for low level jobs were 90% Black. The president of Pacific Telephone admitted that "our wage levels have become less competitive over the years." The full philosophy was spelled out by Vice President Walter Straley, in charge of personnel, in a 1969 talk to the assembled presidents of all Bell companies:

What a telephone company needs to know about its labor market (is) who is available for work paying as little as $4,000 to $5,000 a year."

According to Straley's remarks, two out of three persons available at that wage were Black:

It is therefore just a plain fact that in today's world, telephone company wages are more in line with Black expectations—and the tighter the labor market the more this is true . . .

Population and labor force projections are not at all encouraging . . . Most of our new hires go into entry level jobs . . . at comparatively low rates of pay. That means city people more so than suburbanites. That means lots of Black people.

There are not enough white, middle-class, success-oriented men and women in the labor force . . . to supply our requirements for craft and occupational people. And from now on, the number of such people who are available will grow smaller even as our need becomes greater. It is therefore perfectly plain that we need nonwhite employees. Not because we are good citizens. Or because it is the law as well as a national goal to give them employment. We need them because we have so many jobs to fill and they will take them.[7]

What Straley left unsaid is that the telephone company "needs" workers at the very lowest wage because it "needs" superprofits, because it "needs" $5 billion per year in net profits and interest payments to bankers, more than any other corporation in the world, and as much profits per employee as the wages of a telephone operator.

The blatant racism of this official needs no comment. Nor the obvious linkage of racism, in his consciousness, to the drive for superprofits. Nor his confidence that the government will do nothing to seriously interfere with his racist practices — (We hire them "not . . . because it is the law.")

Yet another motive is barely hinted at in the speech. What does Straley *mean* when he speaks of "white, middle-class, success oriented men and women" . . . for craft and occupational jobs? (Note, by the way, the similarity of his characterization of middle class people with that of the racist Professor Banfield).

The telephone company has traditionally sought for its better jobs, blue and white collar, workers of a definite type, attached to the capitalist system, conservative poltically, belonging to ethnic groups supposedly having anti-Communist tendencies, not too "intellectual" or "over-qualified." Representing the main groups of high finance, it strives to follow personnel policies serving not only its own profit interests, but also buttressing the political position of big capital as a whole. From the upper echelons of telephone and utility workers are drawn a large proportion of the jurors, the members of veterans and other pro-establishment organizations, people expected to be anti-union or supporters of the right wing within the unions.

Of course, Black workers are just as "success oriented" as white workers. But the telephone official means this in a special way—he is searching for workers oriented on getting places by subservience to the capitalist class, to the hierarchy of the telephone company, willing to climb the ladder at the expense of submerged minority employees, contemptuous of working class customers. And he knows that Blacks are less likely to meet these requirements than certain kinds of whites.

The Equal Employment Opportunity Commission Report gave examples of the racist practices of company officials. In 1954 a Black worker named Hereford was refused transfer to the job of stockman by Southwestern Bell Telephone Co. The Communications Workers of America filed a grievance on his behalf, and the case went to arbitration. The arbitrator ruled in favor of the company on technical grounds, but made these sharp observations:

"The one real question to be answered is that of race qualification. . . The fact of his race permeated the whole hearing. The officials high-up in administration of the Company's affairs were not worried about Hereford's education, they were worried about his race."[8]

Internal speeches and reports, such as that of Straley cited above, show that there has been no essential change in this ideology. But, because of the pressures of the Black liberation movement and legal concessions to that movement, company officials have put on a false front of change. In 1962 the Pacific Telephone Co. adopted a "Plan for Progress" and claimed that it:

"does not constitute a new policy on our part. But it does serve to reemphasize our continuing policy to ensure that all telephone people, including members of minority groups, are (equal as) regards recruiting, placement, transfers, promotion, training and use of facilities."

And in 1963 ATT Board Chairman Frederick Kappel talked of a "fundamental social change" on this issue.[9]

But the record shows that there was no essential change. Earlier we cited figures showing that the ratio of Black to white median wages of telecommunications industry workers in the Detroit area was considerably lower than in other major industries in that area (Chapter 5). The same applies on a national scale. In 1969 the median income of Black male workers was 68% of that of all male workers in the entire economy. It was 67% in mining, 63% in construction, with its racist-led craft unions, 71% in manufacturing, 70% in transportation and utilities, 69% in trade.

But the ratio for communications, dominated by the telephone industry, was only 61%. Fewer than 10 of the 75 industries for which figures are given show such a low ratio.[10]

We stress this because the telephone industry is under the unchallenged control of the most powerful financial groups in the country. The extreme differentials in this industry persist because of *their* decision to keep Blacks in a markedly inferior position, and thereby negatively influence the position of Blacks in the entire economy. The deliberate character of that decision becomes evident when we recall that three-fourths o the buildup of Black employment in the industry took place during the 1960s. There were already substantial social and legal pressures for equal employment opportunities. The company was not "locked into" former patterns of Black employment—it had none. The generation of Blacks coming into the labor market was better educated than earlier generations—the old excuse of "lack of qualifications" could not go very far. The industry had growing employment requirements at all levels, and a rapid labor turnover, so that hiring of Blacks at all levels would not involve the displacement of white workers.

Thus we are justified in concluding that the extremely unequal employment pattern of the Bell Telephone System developed because the powerful magnates who control it wanted it that way. And these are men of the same financial groups which dominate the entire national economy.

There is interesting corroboration of this conclusion when we examine the other exceptionally low ratios of Black to total male median earnings. Some of these occur in especially low-income occupations, or those where a geographical factor is important, such as agriculture and sawmills. But other exceptionally low Black/white earnings ratios occur in high and medium-wage industries, namely:

banking and credit agencies	61%
advertising	52%
ordnance	61%[11]

The banks, the very apex of the economic power structure of the country, turn out to have as low a ratio of Black/white male earnings as the telephone industry, and are the largest in terms of employment, with such a low ratio. It is matched by the ratio in the ordnance industry, of the notorious military-industrial complex, and "surpassed" by the parasitic advertising industry, with its ratio of 52%.

AT&T, in its 1973 annual report,[11a] claimed substantial improvement in hiring and upgrading minorities, especially women, between 1970 and 1973. Some improvement should have occurred, in view of the court decision requiring it at the beginning of 1973 (Chapter 13). But two years after this decision, the *Wall Street Journal* reported: "PRESSING AT&T: Federal agencies fault its job bias performance. Two years after AT&T pledged to provide better job opportunities for minorities, and women, federal agencies aren't happy, particularly with 1973 results . . . Some staff members at the EEOC insist AT&A should be found in contempt, but Chairman Powell says he hasn't decided whether the original goals are unrealistic."[11b]

Utilities

The electric and gas utilities, like the telephone company, enjoy complete monopolies, and are decisively controlled by the same syndicates of financial interests which float their bonds and hold the control blocks of shares. Moreover, their rates and other terms of operation are subject to government regulation, and if that regulation were effective, they should have good records in complying with such official policies as fair employment practices.

William H. Brown, III, then Chairman of the Equal Employment Opportunity Commission, wrote in the Foreword to an EEOC report on the utility industries:

"Our study of the utility industry indicated that systems of pervasive exclusion have been responsible for the near total absence of women and minorities in better jobs. Statistics elsewhere in this booklet document this exclusion. But one statistic should be repeated here because it is so sadly typical of this industry: Among the 23 largest industries in America—those with 500,000 employees—gas and electric utilities rank last in the employment of Blacks."[12]

The report revealed that:

"One-third of all the utility establishments filing EEO-1 reports with the Commission in 1970 had no Black employees."[13]

The industry was revealed to have one of the most extremely unbalance employment structures of Blacks, ranging from 0.6% of the officials and managers and 1.0% of the professionals, and 2.5% of the craftsmen to 25.8% of the laborers and 33.2% of the service workers.[14]

The hearing was especially interesting in exposing the lack of reliability of general assurances of equal treatment. Thus, William Hancock, Assistant to the President of Louisville Gas and Electric Company, submitted this statement of company policy:

"Louisville Gas and Electric Company is committed to voluntary affirmative action. . . Until balance is achieved, the program envisions that in selecting from a group of qualified applicants for a particular job opening a Negro will be given preference . . . the Company has had a long history of minority employment and promotion. . . Negroes held supervisory and foreman positions with the Company 40 years ago. . ."

But under questioning by Chairman Brown he was forced to admit that in 32 out of 39 classifications the company employed absolutely no Blacks, whereas, in the job of boiler repairman, "dirty, filthy work," all 11 employees are Black, and that in the dirty job of conveyor operator, 22 of 23 workers are Black!

The authors of the report made this comment on this and another case:

"The contrast between stated policy and observed performance . . . is typical of the pattern found throughout the utility industry . . . almost all companies had lines of job progression and seniority systems which effectively lock minorities and women into less desirable jobs."[15]

These hearings brought out specific examples of the promotion of whites above Black co-workers, as in the case of John Latham, a Black lineman of the Philadelphia Electric Company:

Chairman Brown: You have been a lineman for 21 years. Is that correct?
Mr. Latham: Yes, sir.
Chairman Brown: Did your white counterparts who came into the category of lineman, remain in that category?
Mr. Latham: Well, my individual white counterparts have disappeared around me.
Chairman Brown: Which lines did they go into?
Mr. Latham: I know some who are in the safety department, some are in work dispatchers and estimating and detailing, the more lucrative jobs . . . the pay is higher and they did not necessarily have to take tests for these jobs.
Chairman Brown: Do the Black linemen with the company retire as linemen?
Mr. Latham: We have had quite a few Black linemen retire as linemen.
Chairman Brown: This means climbing poles until they are 65 years of age?
Mr. Latham: Yes, sir.

142

Chairman Brown: Do you have white linemen who retire as linemen?
Mr. Latham: We have one that we know of in the 21 years I have been there.[16]

General Expressions of Attitude

The primary role of big business in sponsoring and perpetuating racism is epitomized in some recent items. In a report of the very conservative National Industrial Conference Board, the author, Ruth Schaeffer, notes that despite decades of laws and Executive Orders, and the pivotal Title VII of the Civil Rights Act of 1964:

"Until 1968 the Federal nondiscrimination regulations had almost no impact on most major business organizations." And four years later, in 1972, in the words of one business executive she cites:

"Let's face it . . . Our company is not in compliance with Title VII and the other non discrimination laws. Neither is any other company I know of."[17]

Professor William Fellner, when nominated for a post on the President's Council of Economic Advisers in 1973, set the anti-labor aim of raising the official unemployment "goal" from 4% to 5%. He explained that because of the uneven impact of unemployment, when the rate gets down below 5%, there are only women and youth left on the labor market. He evidently considered completely "natural" and not undesirable permanent high rates of unemployment for these large groups of workers. But in one press conference, he blurted out the racist content of this discrimination, in addition to the sex and age components:

"Attempts to reduce the unemployment rate to 4 percent would create . . . shortage of the types of workers most employers (want)—which he identified as adult *white* males." (My emphasis—VP)[18]

Even in times of so-called "full employment" there is no shortage of adult male white workers. However, if one adds Black, Chicano, etc., then it becomes clear that there is no shortage, but always a substantial surplus of adult male workers. That's what employers want to maintain at all times. And Fellner, as their economist spokesman, wants to have the government follow policies that will make sure that the surplus is ample, and that it is concentrated among Black and Brown workers, to fit in with the employer strategy of dividing the working class. Fellner even said he would prefer "subsidization of idleness"—e.g., more welfare payments, to reducing the level of unemployment to an official rate of 4%.

Subsequently, Kenneth Rush, former chief executive of Union Carbide Corporation and then special economic adviser to President Nixon, raised the "goal" to 6% unemployment, claiming that 4% official unemployment represented, in reality, zero unemployment, so that 6% was, in reality, only 2% unemployment!

And not long thereafter, the new president, Gerald Ford, in his first budget message, submitted what amounted to a five-year plan for unemployment to remain above 6%, with the level ranging between 7.5% and 8.1% for the three years 1975-77. True, this was presented as a forecast, but the levels were meant to represent the result of policies framed by the administration, on the basis of the president's "philosophy" that such a high level of unemployment was necessary in order to contain inflation. During this five-year period profits were projected to rise far beyond the previous peak.[19]

The "predicted" unemployment rates would mean official unemployment rates of 15% for Blacks, and actual Black unemployment rates of 25-30%, year after year. Of course, this was not the program of a president in an ivory tower, but of a person reflecting the consensus of views of the most powerful big business groups in the country.

9. *Extra Profits from Discrimination*

The Bell Telephone Company hired Black workers in order to hold down wages, and thereby increased profits (Chapter 8). The EEOC report which brought out this motivation presented calculations showing that Black telephone workers in 30 metropolitan areas lost $225 million per year because of this discrimination, and that Spanish-surnamed workers lost $137 million per year in the same way.[1]

These 30 areas had about half the Bell System operating employees, including about half the minority employees. We assume, therefore, that the lost wages nationally come to $450 million per year for Blacks, and $274 million per year for Spanish-surnamed people, making a total of $724 million per year for these two groups combined. These figures omit the extra profits from discrimination by the non-telephone subsidiaries of AT&T.

The $724 million extra profits derived in this way amounted to about one-fifth of the $3½ billion profits before tax of AT&T, excluding Western Electric, in 1970. But that isn't the end of the matter. The ability to obtain Black workers at low wages enables the company to keep down wages for white workers also, and a large majority of telephone employees are still white.

A partial quantitative check is possible. The telephone company concentrated on hiring Black women, especially as operators. Some 79% of all Black employees were women, as against 53% of white Anglo employees.[2] This contributed significantly to the overall salary discrimination against women, white and Black. The EEOC report estimated that discrimination against women in the 30 metropolitan areas cost these workers $422 million per year.[3] Assume that 79%, or $178 million, of the $225 million lost by Blacks in these areas on account of discrimination were sustained by Black women. That leaves $244 million of the loss sustained by white women.

It would seem, then, that the telephone company made more extra profits *indirectly*, by holding down the wages of white women to the level at which Black women could be hired, than the extra profits made *directly* through the low wages paid Black women.

While the same would not apply as strongly in the case of men, owing to the relatively small number of Black men hired, here also there are considerable extra profits made *indirectly* through the impact on white men's wages of low wages paid Black men.

There's a scientific language for this in terms of Marxist political economy. Briefly, the difference between the values created by a worker's labor and his payment for that labor is known as surplus value, and measures the amount of exploitation of labor by capital. We refer to the exceptionally high profits which a corporation makes by paying lower than normal wages to Black workers as superprofits, resulting from the superexploitation of the Black workers.

And when we consider the *direct* and *indirect* superprofits accruing to the Bell System through superexploitation of minority workers, *we have to conclude that this comes to more than a billion dollars a year before taxes.*

The telephone company is merely one example, but hardly a trivial example. The generality of Black inequality as a source of extra profits is admitted, of all places, in the 1974 Economic Report of the President. Discussing tendencies towards increased employment of Black workers in industry, and certain decreases in wage differentials, the authors say:

"Two important factors served as catalysts enabling these changes to take place. First, the American economy is highly competitive, and business firms whose white owners or white workers have less discriminatory attitudes toward Blacks will be likely to employ more Blacks. *These firms prosper if Blacks receive lower wages.* When such firms expand, the demand for Black workers increases and the discriminatory differential declines."[4] (my emphasis—V.P.)

And note, that even if the discriminatory differential *per worker* declines as more Black workers are hired, the total profits from that differential may well increase, owing to the larger number of workers involved. Moreover, to the extent that the hiring of additional Black workers enables employers to avoid raising wages of the white workers, still the majority, there is an even larger volume of superprofits derived *indirectly* from continued discrimination against Blacks.

We may discount the nonsense about owners "with less discriminatory attitudes" hiring Black workers and being rewarded with prosperity as a result! The owners who hire most Blacks are those who see the possibility of the highest profits thereby, and their attitudes may be fully as racist as those hiring no or few Blacks. As for the discriminatory attitudes of white workers, these have never been a major factor in preventing the employment of Black workers when employers were really interested in obeying the equal employment laws.

Amount of Superprofits

Since World War II there have been a number of estimates of the extra profits of employers from racism. This writer estimated the sum as $4 billion in 1947, based on 3½ million Black workers in agriculture and industry, and a median differential of $1,100 per worker.[5] Using a similar technique, the Union Research and Information Service of San Francisco came out with a total of $4½ billion for 1949.[6]

We have made a calculation on a somewhat different basis for 1972, covering wage and salary workers in the private economy. The mean earnings of 6.9 million such Black workers was $2,321 less than the mean of white workers, making a total difference of $16 billion.[7]* Even

---

* The 1947 calculations included self-employed workers, to take into account the remaining large number of Black sharecroppers and tenant farmers subjected to especially severe superexploitation by landlords, although not in the form of wage labor. The 1972 calculations, while omitting self-employed persons, take into account wage and salary workers in the trade and service industries, who were omitted in the 1947 calculations. Both calcula-

allowing for the depreciation of the dollar's value in 25 years, that's more than double the 1947 extra profits in real terms.

These calculations are conservative in a number of ways. They omit the extra profits made from the many Black workers not counted in government surveys. They are based on the difference between the earnings of Blacks and all whites, rather than on the somewhat wider difference between the earnings of Blacks and "white-Anglo" people. They omit the profits made from selling commodities and services to Black people at higher prices than charged to whites. And they omit the extra profits of capitalists and their corporations corresponding to their tax savings from the deprivation of Blacks of normal public services. A case in point is provided by the tax-exempt municipal industrial development bonds used so widely in the industrial expansion of the South in recent decades. In effect, the corporations which obtain factory buildings through this device avoid any payment of local real estate taxes. The southern municipalities are able to afford to forego these taxes because they do not spend the pro-rata amount on services to the Black population.

A roughly estimated total of extra profits made from superexploitation of Chicano, Puerto Rican, Native American, and Asian wage and salary workers in the private economy comes to $7 billion in 1972. Added to the $16 billion derived from Black workers makes a total of $23 billion in superprofits from racism. This amount increases yearly, for even when the relative differential diminishes, the absolute amount of the difference continues to increase, as does the number of workers subjected to it.

Corporate profits before taxes in 1972 amounted to $98 billion, income of unincorporated farm enterprises to $55 billion, and of farmers to $20 billion, for a total profit of employers and other self-employed persons of $173 billion.[8] Direct superprofits from superexploitation of Blacks exceeded 9% of this amount, and from superexploitation of Black and Brown workers combined 13% of the total.

tions omit government workers. The 1947 calculations covered all minority workers, while those for 1972 are restricted to Black workers. The 1947 calculations covered 70% of Black gainful workers, the 1972 calculations 73%. Note that the 1972 calculations include extra profits realized in service industries where, according to Marxist concepts, no fresh values are created. However, employers in these industries are just as interested as are those in commodity-producing industries in getting extra profits from super-exploitation of Black workers, even if these are regarded as secondary distributions of surplus value created by workers engaged in commodity production.

This calculation does not take into account the indirect extra profits made from exploitation of white workers through the negative effect on their wages of discrimination against Black workers. Judging from the case of AT&T, and from other evidence adduced in Chapter 10, it seems likely that the indirect extra profits are at least as large as the direct extra profits. If so, the total extra profits attributable to racism came to $46 billion in 1972, or 27% of business profits generally.

A word of caution is in order. In calculations of this sort, especially at the secondary level of the influence on white wages of discrimination against Blacks, this factor becomes intertwined with many others, and the chain of causality becomes tangled. So the figure cited should be regarded as representing a very rough order of magnitude. But, even assuming a wide margin of error in either direction, the conclusion is inescapable that the extra profits capitalists obtain through racism are enormous, providing an incentive that the capitalist class—whose primary drive is for profits— *will never give up until forced to do so* by stronger and more united social forces.

Black Losses from Discrimination

We have been discussing extra profits capitalists make from discrimination against Blacks. Another side of the matter is the loss of income suffered by Black people owing to discrimination. The two amounts are not equal. Besides loss of income owing to lower wages in private industry, Blacks lose because of discrimination in government employment, because of the heavier weight of unemployment, and because they get only a tiny fraction of the total property income, or surplus value, created by the people's labor. Besides money, Blacks lose additional billions because of the lower purchasing power of the money they receive, and because they do not receive their pro-rata share of socially provided income in the form of public services, education, etc.

During the 1950's, officials translated the income differential against Blacks into a loss of purchasing power. John Roosevelt, a son of the late president, and a member of the President's Committee on Government Contracts in the Eisenhower administration, told the elitist Commonwealth Club of San Francisco:

"that discrimination cost $30,000,000,000 a year in lost purchasing power."[9]

Chart 10
**GAINS AND LOSSES
FROM RACISM, 1972**

Capitalist
GAIN

$46
BILLION

Minority
LOSS

$70
BILLION

The idea was that if Black incomes were increased, they would have more to spend, which would be good for business.

However, during the eight years of the Eisenhower administration there was no improvement in the relative income situation of Blacks *and the absolute gap widened*. Moreover, none of the more than a dozen government agencies charged with enforcing fair employment practices then, or later, has enforced the requirement of non-discrimination on account of race in government dealings by refusing to let or cancelling a single significant government contract.

Naturally, the loss of income due to discrimination has increased since the mid-1960s. Adjusted calculations for 1972 show per capita income of Blacks at $2,391, or $1,991 less than that for whites.[10] Applied to the 23,144,000 Blacks in the officially estimated population, this amounts to a loss of $46 billion in income. The corresponding loss by other racially oppressed peoples comes to about $20 billion, for a grand total of $66 billion. Further allowance for the large numbers of Blacks, Chicanos, and other minorities not counted in official estimates raises the lost income to over $50 billion for Blacks alone, and over $70 billion for oppressed peoples as a whole.

Nor does this exhaust the matter. An increase in Black incomes to the level of white incomes would remove the downward pressure on white wages resulting from discrimination against Blacks. This would result in increases of tens of billions, in the incomes of all working people, white and Black.

Discussions of figures of this sort are usually accompanied by the suggestion that it would be in the interest of business to encourage the equalization of Black incomes, as that increase would be reflected in increased sales of consumers goods, and corresponding increases in business profits.

Of course, this too-simple argument has a flaw. It certainly is true that sellers of consumers goods and services would enjoy higher sales, and to that extent tend to have higher profits. But employers as a whole, including consumers goods and retail employers, would have to pay out the full $50 billion in higher wages to Blacks. Even if the full $50 billion of higher Black income were spent on consumers goods and services, far from all of that would be translated into profits.

Hence the capitalist class as a whole would endure reduced profits from the equalization of incomes between Blacks and whites. At least that would be the result in the first instance. That is why employers generally stubbornly resist genuine equality of employment and wage practices, and why progress in this direction is achieved only through persistent struggle.

It's ironic that the appeal to employers to raise Black wages in order to realize higher profits is consistent with a standard employer argument directed against all workers—namely that there is no purpose in their striving to win higher wages, because they will only have to pay for it in higher prices. The assumption here is that profits will be inviolate regardless of how much wages go up.

The argument, of course, is self-serving. The employers know that rising wages are basically at the expense of profits. And therefore they persistently resist higher wages, and strive to preserve all weapons, especially those which divide the working class by race, sex, or other characteristics, which help to impede the payment of higher wages.

Isn't there a longer run case to be made, that raising of Black incomes to the level of white incomes will do much to eliminate poverty in the country, to create conditions for a major upsurge in the consumer economy, and consequently better conditions for business? This is definitely the case. The very big gains won by U.S. workers during World War II helped create conditions for a stabilized marked increase in the level of business activity and profits after that war. The important increases in real wages won by Japanese workers, and those of some West European countries in the past two decades have provided much of the underpinnings for the sensational growth of the entire economic scale in these countries.

But in such cases the gains of workers were won through struggle, and not through the "far-seeing" wisdom of employers. Moreover, the improvement in economic conditions was the result of a complex of factors, of which higher mass consuming power was just one.

What can be said is that ending the economic gap between Black and white people will create a potentially much more healthy economic situation for the entire country, and create conditions under which all working people will have a much better chance to influence national economic policy in a progressive direction.

"Welfare Loafers"

The racist myth has it that Black people are responsible for the high taxes paid by honest industrious (white) workers, that they prefer being on the welfare rolls to working, etc. Undoubtedly this kind of argument has a certain influence, not only amongst the more ignorant of the petty and not so petty proprietors, but also among some groups of better off white workers.

This is a particularly vicious lie.

More than any other national or racial group in the country, the Black people earn their way through labor. And less than any other national or racial group, do they receive income created by the labor of others, or as their share of socially contributed labor. Property income is income created by the labor of others. Social security benefits, welfare payments, veterans benefits, medicare benefits, are all forms of socially contributed labor distributed via taxation and the budget. Generally, the recipients themselves or their parents were among the contributors to the funds distributed, as workers.

Table 23 shows the distribution of income received by white and Black people, by source, for the year 1972.

The income figures are as presented in the Commerce Department report on consumer income in 1972, adjusted according to correction factors provided in that report. The point is that wage earners, for example, tend to report their wages fully to the government survey takers, while property owners tend to keep silent about a lot of their income especially for a survey where they are not under legal compulsion to present a truthful answer. The government statisticians estimated that 98.3% of wages and salaries were reported, but only 45.0% of dividends, interest, and other forms of property income. For other forms of income, generally intermediate percentages of completeness were reported.

TABLE 23

PERCENTAGE DISTRIBUTION OF PERSONAL INCOME BY RACE, 1972

		% OF TOTAL	
TYPE OF INCOME		WHITE	BLACK
1.	Wages or salary	70.3	77.9
2.	Nonfarm self-employment	6.6	2.8
3.	Farm self-employment	2.0	0.2
4.	Dividends, interest, rent, etc.	9.3	1.2
5.	Social security	4.7	5.1
6.	Public assistance & welfare	0.8	7.6
7.	Unemployment & workmen's compensation, veterans' payments, etc.	3.3	3.2
8.	Private pensions, annuities, alimony, etc.	3.0	2.0
	Total	100.0	100.0

SOURCE: compiled from P-60, No. 90, Table 44, adjusted by Table K

Line 4 includes income from estates or trusts and net royalties; Line 5 included railroad retirement benefits; Line 7 includes government employee pensions.

For Table 23 the reported figures of different types of income were adjusted up to full coverage. That is, the $33.8 billion of property income reported in the current population survey was divided by 0.45 to bring it up to the $75.1 billion "benchmark" estimate by the government statisticians of the actual amount of property income received by individuals. Similarly the $597.1 billion of reported wage or salary income was divided by .983 to bring it up to the $607.7 billion "benchmark" estimate of total wages and salaries.

Identical adjustment factors were applied, for each type of income separately, to white and Black incomes of that type.

Wages and salaries accounted for 77.9% of Black incomes, a considerably higher percentage than the 70.3% of white incomes. Nonfarm self-employment income accounted for 6.6% of white income, and 2.8% of Black income. The widest gaps were in the shares of income associated with ownership of farms and ownership of stocks, bonds, structures, etc. Dividends, interest, etc., accounted for 9.3% of the income of whites, only 1.2% of the income of Blacks. For the main form of public pensions and benefits, the proportions were about the same for whites as for Blacks, but public assistance and welfare accounted for only 0.8% of the incomes of whites, as contrasted with 7.6% for Blacks.

The Census Bureau regards wages, salaries and self-employment income as earnings, as distinguished from all other types of income. Here we use a different classification. We regard wages and salaries as earnings, properly speaking. Self-employment income is partly earnings—partly the equivalent of wages received by the self-employed person for his or her labor—and partly surplus value or profit, derived from the labor of employees by virtue of the self-employed person's ownership of means of production or distribution. Here we include in one broad category all income associated with ownership of income-yielding property, that is, farm and nonfarm self-employment income and "pure" property income derived from ownership of stocks, bonds, real estate, etc. And we include in a third category all forms of socially provided income and other "transfer payments"—that is, income not associated directly with current economic activity or property ownership. These include social security benefits, welfare payments, veterans benefits, private pensions, etc.*

---

* None of these categories are really "pure." Wages and salaries include salaries of corporation executives, which generally include a portion of profits as well as payment for managerial labor. And the group of private transfer payments—private pensions, annuities and alimony—include items associated with property ownership, notably annuities. On the other hand, certain forms of property income are totally omitted—capital gains, profits hidden in expense accounts, etc. Overall, the statistics in Tables 22 and 23 substantially understate the amount of ownership and property income.

Combining the figures of Table 23 into these three groups, we find that whites obtained 70.3% of their total income from wages and salaries, Blacks 77.9%; whites obtained 17.9% from ownership of property, Blacks only 4.2%; whites obtained 11.8% from transfer payments, Blacks 17.9%.

The disadvantage of Blacks in receipt of property income is only part of their loss from lack of property ownership. In this capitalist society, ownership of productive property gives access to better jobs, to the expense accounts, bonuses, liberal pensions and other perquisites of the corporate and government bureaucracy, ability to get good treatment, including material subsidies, from government agencies, banks and insurance companies, etc. These indirect benefits may amount to more, in total, than the nominal amount of property income.

All property income, direct and indirect, overt and covert, consists of that part of the values produced by labor which is not received by labor. It is the measure of the exploitation of labor in a capitalist society. Hence, a substantial portion of the economic disadvantage of Blacks corresponds to their almost exclusively working class composition (Chapter 2), and their trivial position within the capitalist class (Chapter 10). True, ownership of income-producing property is heavily concentrated among a very small minority of white people, and the revenues of property ownership are most unevenly distributed.

But the extensive middle layers of society—overwhelmingly white—receive parts of the property income. And through family and "ethnic" ties, as well as pure and simple racial prejudice, the owners and managers of big enterprises, and the top men in government, prefer whites for the better jobs, those which are easier and which involve some of the "gravy" which spills over to the upper groups of salaried employees and officials, private and public.

Looking at the percentages, one might answer the argument about Blacks depending excessively on welfare by pointing to the fact that the dependence of white propertied persons on unearned income, even in percentage terms, outweighs the dependence of Black poor people on welfare. However, when we examine per capita dollar figures the refutation is much sharper. (Table 24).

Table 24 shows that per capita income of Blacks from labor was only three-fifths the per capita income of whites from labor, even though a larger proportion of the Black population works than of the white population, and despite the fact that Blacks are much more dependent on labor than whites. The per capita income of Blacks connected with ownership of property was only one-eighth that of whites. Then, finally, we turn to the entire group of transfer payments, or, in the main, socially provided income. Theoretically, such income is distributed in part as a partial compensation for past labor or other services (pensions), and in part as a social recognition of the basic needs of people not provided by the capitalist economy. It certainly cannot be argued

TABLE 24

PERSONAL INCOMES BY BROAD CATEGORIES
BY RACE, TOTAL AND PER CAPITA, 1972

| | TOTAL INCOME (Million $) | | PER CAPITA INCOME (Dollars) | | |
	WHITE	BLACK	WHITE	BLACK	% BLACK OF WHITE
Wages and salaries	$557,231	$43,240	$3,094	$1,868	60.4
Ownership & property	142,568	2,280	791	99	12.5
Transfer payments	93,071	9,984	517	431	83.3
TOTAL	792,870	55,504			
Population (thousands)	180,125	23,144			

SOURCE: As Table 23.
The population covered is the civilian non-institutional population and a specified portion of the armed forces.

that Black people are less entitled than whites to compensation for past services—either as old age pensions, workmens' compensation as a result of industrial injury or accident, veterans pensions, etc. And it is certainly clear that Blacks, owing to their lower income from labor and from ownership of property, are more in need of socially provided income to meet certain basic needs.

Thus, altogether, one should expect per capita receipt of transfer payments by Blacks to exceed that of whites. But the opposite is the case. The average white person received $517 in transfer payments, the average Black person $431, or five-sixths as much, as the average white person.

Examining this in detail brings out the fact that Black people receive far less than whites in the form of old age pensions, unemployment insurance, veterans benefits, etc., owing to a whole series of discriminatory exclusions, inequalities, and inequities built into the laws governing these forms of transfer payments, compounded to some extent by discrimination in administration. And, while Blacks receive more per capita than whites in distributions according to need—that is public assistance and welfare payments,—this is insufficient to make up for the deprivation of Blacks of a proportional share of the benefits provided socially for past labor.

The myth of the "welfare loafer" is not only a gross slander against Blacks, and the poor and superexploited of all races, but in fact hides a gross discrimination against Blacks in the distribution of social benefits.

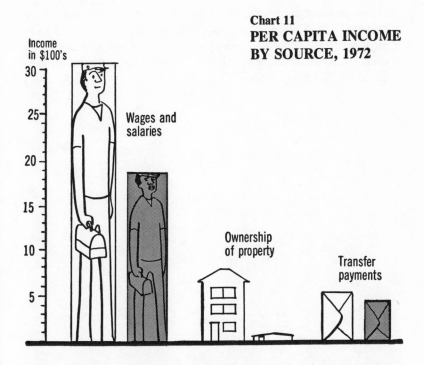

Income in $100's

30

25

20

15

10

5

Chart 11
PER CAPITA INCOME BY SOURCE, 1972

Wages and salaries

Ownership of property

Transfer payments

There is another point that needs to be made in relation to public assistance and welfare payments. A large proportion of families receiving such payments include one or more worker. The welfare payments become necessary because the wages received are too low to support the family. The worker is paid less than the value of his labor power, less than a living wage. He or she is the victim of superexploitation, and the employer is deriving superprofits from that labor. *The welfare payments, are in effect subsidizing the superprofits of the employer.* There are other forms in which welfare payments, rather than benefiting the recipient, are actually contributing to ridiculously high profits. Thus, in New York City, welfare payments include scandously high earmarked rents to landlords for rat-infested, crowded, unmaintained, slum dwelling units.

Property income is highly concentrated. The $791 of property income per capita for all white people consists mainly of property income accruing to a few hundred thousand white people, each of whom receives amounts in the tens and hundreds of thousands, and even of millions. The shortage of wage and salary income of most Black workers is translated into a significant portion of the property income of this small section of the white population, and that of an infinitesimal handful of the Black population.

10. What Whites Lose

T he key argument of racist propaganda is that the Black worker's loss is the white worker's gain, and vice versa. The essential arguments used to try to convince white workers of this are:

• If Black workers are hired, white workers will lose their jobs.

• If Black workers are promoted and their wages are raised, it will be at the expense of higher wages and promotions for white workers.

• If Black workers move into an area where white workers live, it will drive down the value of white workers' homes.

I am not dealing here with the openly racist propaganda about the supposed "inferiority" of Blacks. While most white workers are infected, to some degree, by racism, in this environment that is so saturated with it, today most white workers reject the more vicious forms of fascist-type racist propaganda. However, many are influenced by the more subtle propaganda, which pictures the Black workers as economic rivals.

There is a fundamental fallacy in these arguments. It goes on the assumption that there is a fixed number of jobs, a fixed total of wages, a fixed supply of housing, to be distributed among the working population as a whole, so that the gains of a group of workers are at the expense of other workers. This goes back to the notorious "wage fund" theory popularized at the start of the nineteenth century by Thomas Malthus, John R. MacCulloch, James Mill, and other economists who provided the theoretical basis for the extreme, brutal exploitation of labor on which British industrial dominance of that period was built.

Malthusianism also includes the concept that the earth can only support a fixed population, already reached at the time of his writing. The idiocy of the whole theory is proven by the many times multiplication of both population and total wages in the past 175 years, and the special rapidity of their increase in the past 25 years.

But Malthusianism, in all its main variants, has been vigorously revived recently, with the particular purpose of spurring racist attitudes in both domestic and foreign affairs.

A modern version is the argument that any increase in wages causes a corresponding increase in prices, so that real wages do not advance. A more "reasonable" form is the argument that the share of wages in the total product cannot increase, so that wages cannot increase more than the average productivity of labor.

But this is contrary to the basic principal of labor organization and labor struggle at the most elementary level of trade union consciousness. The workers' position, throughout the history of the labor movement, has been that workers' gains are at the expense of capital, that the total social product can increase and labor's share in it can increase as well. In this respect, workers have really followed the position pioneered by Karl Marx in his practical work with the British trade unionists. And this includes, of course, a majority of U.S. workers who are ignorant of Marx's work.

Under the Malthusian principle, it would appear that any gain of white workers would have to be at the expense of some other group of workers, most notably Black workers, and, on the other hand, that any gain of Black workers would be at the expense of white workers.

However, the main policies of the U.S. labor movement have been anti-Malthusian. For example, organized workers provided the momentum for enactment of minimum wage legislation, and led campaigns for raising and broadening the coverage of the minimum wages. Workers at all levels know that raising minimum wages helps improve their own wages and working conditions.

Workers often strike for the reinstatement of workers discharged by the arbitrary action of a supervisor, or as a penalty for militancy. They know that the security of their jobs will be enhanced, not reduced, by saving the jobs of those let go by the employer.

Trade unions lead the fight for more federal jobs for the unemployed, knowing that these jobs are not at the expense of existing jobs, but help to protect them from unemployment, and strengthen the bargaining position of privately employed workers.

And now there are more than 10 million Black workers who have been systematically discriminated against. Many have never been permitted to hold a steady job. The *majority* have never been promoted to jobs matching their capability, or given the special training required where that is necessary. They have been concentrated in special job categories with lower incomes, and discriminated against in a thousand different ways.

Will ending this discrimination injure the position of white workers as a whole, or of a majority of white workers, or of individual white workers? On the contrary, it can only contribute to improvement of the situation of white workers as a whole and need not injure the situation of a single white worker.

Logically, campaigns for equality for Black workers should be accompanied by campaigns providing gains for all workers. Usually groups struggling for equality do include both kinds of demands such as fair employment for Blacks in the skilled construction crafts, plus a big expansion in the housing program and construction employment overall. But it is only when whites and Blacks unite around both halves of such programs that, under the real conditions existing in the United States, major gains can be won. When trade unions and other organizations try to campaign *only* for the general goals of workers, without simultaneously taking up the special needs of Black workers, they lack the power to win, in view of the real alignment of political forces in the United States today.

Here is what happened in Westchester County, home of the Rockefellers and other super-rich families, along with many people, including 100,000 Blacks subject to the customary discrimination and poverty. They are concentrated in ghetto areas of certain towns, and virtually barred from most of the county. In 1972 the New York State Urban Development Corporation proposed a very modest program of low and moderate cost housing units in the exclusive areas of the county. Some of these units would be available to Black workers.

Racist elements, including local officials, launched a furious campaign against the proposal. They succeeded in defeating it, despite some middle class support for integrated housing. The construction trades unions took a passive position on the issue.

Two years later, as the housing industry went through its worst crisis since World War II, thousands of Westchester building trades workers demonstrated against the mass unemployment afflicting their ranks, and against a big developer using non-union labor from outside the state.

But the demonstrators, supported by other county unions, failed to pinpoint the reasons for 30 to 50% unemployment in the construction trades when so many families lacked adequate housing. The private housing and banking industries make maximum profits by concentrating on raising prices, and catering to the "exclusiveness" and prejudices of upper income population sectors. Only government-controlled integrated housing, which does away with profiteering and caters to the needs of masses of workers of all races for decent housing, can assure steady employment for contruction workers. And these workers can win this steady employment, and win a union shop in the industry, only if they actively fight for mass integrated housing, and open their ranks, across the board, to Black and other minority workers.

The lesson was underlined not long after this incident. The banking-real estate crowd hated the Urban Development Corporation because it attempted, however weakly, to combine social purposes with the private profit motive; because it gave business to Black contractors; provided some housing for Blacks; tried to improve the quality of housing for moderate income people. The bankers refused to lend the funds to finish its projects—many nearly completed—early in 1975, throwing the agency into virtual bankruptcy and thereby threatening the jobs of thousands of workers all over the state and the completion of homes for tens of thousnads of families.

Discrimination is a weapon of employers, an instrument for greater profits at the expense of Black and white labor. That is why employers attempt to convince white workers that any reduction in discrimination is at their expense, as exemplified by a *Wall Street Journal* article under these headlines:

UP-THE-LADDER BLUES
White Males Complain They Are Now Victims of Job Discrimination
They Say Companies Favor Women, Racial Minorities in Filling Manager Posts
Prodding from Uncle Sam

The story begins:

New England Telephone & Telegraph's top executives recently got a long letter from a young white male in middle management who complained that his future looked pretty dim because of the company's push to advance women and members of racial minorities into management slots. Are guys like him going to have "to pay for (this company's) discrimination practices during the past century?'' he asked. The top brass sent him a long-winded reply that boiled down to: Yes.

Generalizing, the article stated that most complaints by whites to the EEOC charging "reverse discrimination" in promotion came from management personnel, not ordinary employees and workers.[1]

So far as the corporate burocracy is concerned, undoubtedly bitter competition for advancement will continue, and we cannot be upset about the ambitious ones who fail to get ahead in the already overblown management staffs.

But the propaganda is directed to all workers, not just managerial employees. And the issue is common at all levels. It is the issue of favoritism. Where workers succeeded in establishing unions they acted to end company favoritism. One instrument for this policy was the establishment of seniority systems. But racism and male supremacy have often permitted favoritism to continue in the form of seniority systems which keep Blacks indefinitely in inferior departments, and women in lower-paying jobs.

Successful trade unionism requires an even more vigorous campaign against group favoritism than against individual favoritism. The steel industry presents a typical example of special relevancy.

A recent court decision required steel companies to end unit seniority systems which discriminate against Blacks and women. The national leadership of the United Steelworkers of America, and some local leaders, opposed these moves, and are attempting to sabotage them and water them down.

They were promoting the superficial view that opening up the better departments to Blacks would take jobs away from white workers. But this is not a situation similar to the scramble for promotion among managers. Labor turnover, more adequate manning of stations, and curtailment of overtime can ensure against any white worker losing his present job. The ending of separate Black and white departments will make it possible to unite all workers into a powerful force that can improve the economic, health and safety conditions of every worker throughout the plant.

Moreover, this type of discrimination directly backfires against white workers. Thus, in March 1974, the U.S. Steel Corporation closed the wheel mill at its Gary works. The 200 workers there were transferred to other sections of the plant. Using the unit seniority system, the company reduced the grade and pay of many of these workers. A white worker,

Lee Lane, filed a complaint with the National Labor Relations Board, charged that his 10 years of experience had been ignored, and that he had been reduced to the rank of laborer, with a radical reduction in pay. Lane said:

> The Fairfield decision is one of the most important things steel workers have got. Plantwide seniority is something we all need. They say its only for the Blacks, but unit seniority hurts white workers too, and I don't see why we can't work together.[2]

General Posing of White Losses from Racism

Michael Reich succinctly explains how employers use racism as a social and psychological weapon to advance their profits at the expense of white workers:

> Wages of white labor are lessened by racism because the fear of a cheaper and underemployed Black labor supply in the area is invoked by employers when labor presents its wage demands. Racial antagonisms on the shop floor deflect attention from labor grievances related to working conditions, permitting employers to cut costs. Racial divisions among labor prevent the development of united worker organizations both within the workplace and in the labor movement as a whole. As a result union strength and union militancy will be less the greater the extent of racism . . . the economic consequences of racism are not only lower incomes for Blacks but also higher incomes for the capitalist class and lower incomes for white workers.[3]

In a study of metropolitan areas, Reich found a quite significant correlation between the degree of income inequality between whites and Blacks and the degree of income inequality among whites. In those areas where the white/Black differential was greatest, the percentage share of white income received by the top 1% of the whites—that is, the top capitalists, was highest, and the general spread between wealth and poverty among whites—the so-called Gini coefficient of white incomes—was greatest. An even higher correlation of the same type among states was computed by S. Bowles.[4]

Reich puts the political factor in the most general way . . . that racism helps to legitimize inequality, alienation and powerlessness, providing a legitimacy for these characteristics that is necessary for the stability of the capitalist system as a whole[5]

But the damage is also concrete and immediate. Racism facilitates anti-labor legislation. It isn't an accident that so-called "right-to-work" laws are nearly universal in the southern states, the traditional stronghold of racism. Racism favors militarism and aggression. Again, the role of the South as the political center of militarism is quite clear. Racism and anti-Communism have been the *main* political weapons used by reaction to divert, weaken, or wholly eliminate the positive social directions charted by New Deal reform policies. These include the right to work, in the genuine, not the union-busting sense; the right to escape from poverty; the right to equality regardless of race, sex or creed; the right to education and medical service; the right to decent housing; the right to freedom from governmental repression; the right to own and operate small farm and non-farm enterprises; the right to freedom from fear of war.

On the other hand, the very struggle for Black equality provides a dynamic force for every one of these progressive directions which, given the cooperation of the majority of white working people, can become absolutely decisive in winning a positive course of policy in all of these domains.

Income Loss of Southern Whites

As of 1970 somewhat more then half of all Blacks still lived in the South, as broadly defined by the Census Bureau to include the border states. Economic discrimination against Blacks remains much more severe than in the rest of the country. Table 25 consolidates the data for the three northern and western regions shown in Table 3, in order to isolate the southern differential.

TABLE 25

PER CAPITA INCOMES OF WHITE ANGLOS AND BLACKS
BY REGIONS, 1969

PER CAPITA INCOMES

	WHITE ANGLOS	BLACKS	BLACK % OF WHITE ANGLOS
North & West	$3,505	$2,257	64
South	3,072	1,439	47

SOURCE: U.S.-C-130,135.

In the South, the per capita income of Blacks was less than half that of "white-Anglo" people, while in the rest of the country it was less than two-thirds that of "white-Anglos". The differential in percentage points was one and one-half times as severe in the South as in the rest of the country.

If the majority of the southern white population were gaining from this very severe discrimination against Blacks, they would be better off than the northern and western white population. But instead, the per capita income of southern whites was $433 less, or about one-eighth less then in the rest of the country. Totalled over the 47,634,000 southern white Anglos, *this adds up to a total loss of $20.6 billion in annual income*. That's quite a bill to pay for the "privilege" of upholding the myth of white supremacy!

Whatever advantage whites may gain from their more complete racial monopoly on better jobs in the South, they lose much more because the existence of a deeply oppressed Black population is used by employers to lower the incomes of *all* workers, on *all* kinds of jobs.

These per capita income figures understate the impact. Because of the higher rate of exploitation of labor associated with lower southern wages, the proportion of property income in the total is higher in the South than in other regions. Among wage and salary earners, especially among hourly wage workers, the losses of southern whites are relatively sharper than indicated by statistics for the entire population.

This is brought out dramatically when we compare the earnings of key occupation groups of Black and white male workers in the North Central states and in the Southern states. (Table 26.) The North Central states include the main concentrations of heavy industry of the country, and have the largest Black population outside the South. But the contrast between the South and the other two northern and western regions is similar.

TABLE 26

MEDIAN EARNINGS, BY SPECIFIED MAJOR OCCUPATION GROUPS, MALE
WORKERS, BY RACE, NORTH CENTRAL STATES AND SOUTHERN STATES
1969

| | MEDIAN EARNINGS | | | | PERCENTAGE RATIOS | | | |
| | North | | South | | Black/White | | Southern Whites/ Northern | |
	White	Black	White	Black	North	South	Whites	Blacks
Professionals, etc.	$10,609	$8,477	$10,008	$7,012	80	70	94	118
Managers,etc.	11,658	8,363	10,003	6,419	72	64	86	120
Craftsmen, etc.	8,968	7,536	7,223	4,731	84	65	81	96
Operatives	7,508	7,084	5,809	4,386	94	76	77	82
Service Workers	5,294	5,204	4,460	3,503	98	79	84	86

SOURCE: Compiled from U.S.-D-296

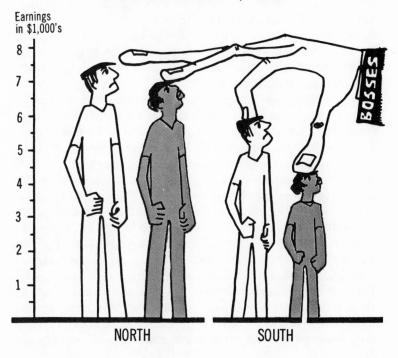

Chart 12
**EARNINGS OF OPERATIVES
NORTH AND SOUTH, 1969**

Earnings
in $1,000's

8 -
7 -
6 -
5 -
4 -
3 -
2 -
1 -

BOSSES

NORTH   SOUTH

Until fairly recently, Black people in the South were not significant potential competitors of white professionals and capitalists. The number of Black male professionals in the South was only 6%, and of managers 3%, of the respective numbers of white males in these groups. And the great majority of Black male professionals were teachers, clergymen, or technicians—generally in segregated schools or working as assistants to white professionals. Hence, discrimination did not pull down the income of white men in these occupation groups to a major extent. White professionals in the south had median incomes only 6% less than white professionals in the North Central states. White southern male managers had incomes 14% less than those of white male managers in the North Central States—and in part that was due to a difference in the distribution of specific occupational categories.

But in the blue collar occupations, the situation was quite different. There traditionally, much of the work was done by Black men in the South, although under conditions of gross discrimination. In recent decades many Black craftsmen have been pushed out of jobs in the South, but even so, they equalled 11% of the number of white craftsmen in the region. And Black operatives equalled 24% of the number of white male operatives, Black male service workers 44% of the number of white male service workers.

In each case, the white workers in the South earned much less than white workers in the same occupation group and of the same sex in the North—19% less in the case of craftsmen, 23% in the case of operatives, other than transport, and 16% less in the case of service workers.

But what is most dramatic—in each of these blue collar groups, the southern white workers earned less than northern Black workers. Despite the continued gross discrimination against Black skilled craftsmen in the North, the "privileged" southern whites earned 4% less than they did. Southern male white operatives averaged $1,275, or 18% less than northern Black male operatives. And southern white service workers earned $744, or 14% less than northern Black male service workers. In each case, southern whites were earning much more than southern Blacks in the same occupation group. The southern Black males were subjected to double superexploitation—but the "privileged" southern white male blue collar workers were also subjected to extra exploitation, in comparison with the standards achieved by the working class nationally.

Much the same can be seen for women workers, although here the differentials are not so sharp. Occupational breakdowns of earnings of women, by races, are distorted by the much larger proportion of white women who prefer part-time work. The distortion is partly overcome by considering the medians of women who worked 50-52 weeks per year—but only partly, because many women, especially white women, work all year around but for short work weeks. For this comparison we do not have medians for white women alone, so the figures for all women, as a rough approximation, are used. Again, the figures for North Central states are taken as more or less representative of the North generally.

Among professional and clerical workers, southern women as a whole had median earnings 4% less than those of Black women in North

Central states. Among operatives, all southern women had median earnings 19% less than those of North Central Black women, and by a same percentage less than those of all North Central women. Among service workers, the figure for all southern women was 22% less than that for North Central Black women. In each of these groups, the median earnings of southern Black women ranged between 4 and 10% lower than those of all southern women. Evidently that advantage over the Blacks did not help the southern white women. In the North Central states on the other hand, the medians of Black and white women were either close together, or, in the case of service workers, substantially higher for Black women. Again, this lack of obvious discrimination against Black women over and above the general discrimination against women as a whole did not hurt the northern white women.[6]

While white southern women workers made more than the triply superexploited Black women southern factory workers, that could be little consolation for the badly underpaid, largely unorganized, white women textile, cigarette, and electronic workers in the South.

A particularly striking case is that of the bus drivers. Until the ending of Jim Crow laws in the South less than a decade ago, the white bus drivers were the enforcers of the vicious apartheid regulations on the Black people, who provided a disproportionate share of the bus passengers, because so many of them could not afford other means of transport.

In recent years this has changed, and Black workers have gotten jobs as bus drivers in the South, and in large numbers in the North. Table 27 shows the median earnings of male bus drivers, by regions, in 1969.

TABLE 27

MEDIAN EARNINGS OF MALE BUS DRIVERS, BY RACE AND BY REGION 1969

REGION	WHITE	BLACK
Northeast	$7,643	$8,293
North Central	6,480	8,397
West	7,290	8,315
South	4,753	3,767

SOURCE: Compiled from U.S.-D-296

White southern bus drivers had median incomes about a thousand dollars more than the pitiful incomes received by Black southern bus drivers. But the white southern bus drivers generally received about $2,500 less than white northern and western bus drivers, and $3,500 less than Black northern and western bus drivers. In all three northern regions, Black bus drivers had higher median incomes than male white bus drivers.

Needless to say, this is not because of "reverse discrimination" against whites. It is partly because the Black bus drivers are concentrated in big city routes, with good union contracts, and often with municipal ownership. More of the white bus drivers are in smaller towns, and especially, many of them are part time school bus drivers. The same applies to southern bus drivers.

But with all due allowances, it is fair to conclude that the great majority of southern bus drivers are subjected to poverty wages, and this is a price they are still paying—white and Black—for two generations of rigidly segregated transportation arrangements for passengers and for workers.

There is still circulating the rationalization that the white southern worker is compensated for his low pay by being able to hire Black houseworkers for next to nothing.

Here's an example, from a work by a generally progressive economist, Michael Tanzer. He enumerates the supposed "beneficiaries" of discrimination against Blacks, including the following:

"Another beneficiary group is the largest single employer of Black females—white families in which the women are able to work outside of the home because Black females run their households and raise their children. These millions of white women encompass a great range, from teachers and professionals in the North to factory workers in the South. A classic example highlighting this relationship involved the white female textile worker in Montgomery, Alabama who discharged her Black female housekeeper for refusing to ride the bus during the Black community's historic 1956 bus boycott. The textile worker then quickly had to rehire her Black domestic because without the latter's willingness to work for fifteen dollars a week she could not continue to earn her forty dollars a week in the textile mill."[7]

There were 590,549 Black female household workers in 1970, hardly enough to provide "millions" of white families with housekeepers, to "run their households and raise their children," especially since only 35% of all private household workers were on full-time schedules in

1970. Many houseworkers today do only day work, for different customers. Of those who work full time many, probably the majority, work for wealthy or well-to-do families where the woman does *not* work. There can be little doubt that the majority of Black household workers are exploited by families of the capitalist class and upper layers of the petty bourgeoisie—from the professional and managerial groups.[8]

Most of the Black women household workers were in the South, and continued to be terribly exploited, with median earnings of $1,327 for year-around-workers. Yet, it is unlikely that many of the white women southern textile operatives, with their median earnings of $4,063, could afford the luxury of employing a full-time household worker. Certainly there also, the majority of these Black women were employed by the well-to-do and rich southern exploiters.[9]

Whether the story about the Montgomery textile worker and household worker is true or apocryphal, it is atypical, and a vestige of the past. The number of Black private household workers has been declining rapidly, and it is no longer a predominantly Black occupation. By 1973 only 12.9% of minority women workers were private household workers, and they constituted 39% of the total number of women private household workers.[10]

It is part of the Establishment propaganda line to spread stories such as that cited, in order to reenforce beliefs that white workers are the main source of racism. Such propaganda is a trap which progressive writers should avoid.

The actual situation is that the continued reservoir of hundreds of thousands of poor superexploited Black women in the southern labor force contributes decisively to the substandard wage and employment position of southern factory workers, white and Black. The losses of southern white workers resulting therefrom exceed many times what a few of them may gain from receiving cheap personal services from Black workers.

We have seen, from numerous examples, how in the areas of maximum discrimination against Black workers, this pulls down the earnings of white workers. By extension, it is reasonable to conclude that wherever discrimination exists, there is the same effect. Owing to the universality of discrimination in the United States, there is no existing situation of equality against which to measure the losses of white workers in northern areas from discrimination against Blacks.

Other Losses of White Workers

Discrimination against Blacks adversely affects white working people in many ways, in addition to the downward drag on earnings.

Consider the issue of working conditions. Factory workers spend one-half their waking hours in conditions which often involve excessive strain, excessive danger, and downright unhealthy conditions. These issues have become especially important in recent years, as evidenced by the fight of the coal miners against silicosis, of the automobile workers against speedup, and the chemical workers against industrial poisoning. As employment of Black workers expanded in the automobile industry, employers concentrated them in the worst jobs, such as the foundry, paint department, body shop, and on the worst stations on the assembly line.

During the accelerated hiring of Blacks in Michigan during the auto boom of the late 1960s and early 1970s, this was accompanied by a state-wide racist campaign against school busing—that is, for segregated schools. Thomas Dennis describes how this related to the auto industry:

"The superexploitation prevalent in the foundries was extended to the production line via stepped up speedup. What happened in Chrysler's is a good example. Jobs which were done by three or four white workers were given to two, maybe three, Black workers. Production standards were raised dramatically when large numbers of Black workers were put on the job. Then the company put Black foremen over Black workers to get even more work out of each worker. This move alone got 10% to 15% more production than before.

"The fight of the Black workers against this speedup was not supported by the union leadership or the white workers. The racist anti-busing campaign made it easier for the company to play the old divide and rule game—white against Black. The amount of work put out by the Black workers became the norm. White workers who complained about the greater work loads were told that if they couldn't do the job there were people who could.

"Thus this extra speedup became the way of life for the white worker also."[10a]

It is in southern states with the widest margins of economic discrimination against Blacks that the smallest percentages of workers are members of unions—and not by choice, but by the successful campaigns of textile and other employers to prevent unionization. The Ku Klux Klan and other racist organizations are employed to beat up union organizers. State and local governments dominated by racists use the police forces and the National Guard to break strikes, and white workers are hit by this as hard as Black workers. Moreover, the social separation and job separation of Black and white workers makes it difficult to build the labor unity which alone can defeat ruthless employers and to replace company-owned officials.

In 1970, when nationally 27.9% of nonagricultural employees were members of unions, the corresponding percentages in southern states were Alabama, 20.3%, Arkansas, 17.9%, Florida, 13.9%, Georgia, 16.2%, Louisiana, 18.4%, Mississippi, 13.2%, North Carolina, 7.8%, Oklahoma, 16.1%, South Carolina, 9.6%, Tennessee, 20.6%, and Texas, 14.4%.[11]

All of these states except Louisiana and Oklahoma had so-called "right-to-work" laws, which prohibit the union shop and make it extremely difficult to firmly establish a trade union in a plant.

On the other hand, some of the high points of labor activity in the South have been on the basis of Black and white unity. This was true of the Brotherhood of Timber Workers in the 1910-1914 period; the successful organization of U.S. Steel and its iron mining subsidiary, Tennessee Coal & Iron Co., in the Birmingham area in the 1930s; and the successful strike of timber cutters in Mississippi in the 1970s.

In recent years U.S. unions have been at a low ebb of effectiveness. They have not succeeded in winning monetary gains for their membership corresponding to rising living costs, let alone increases in productivity. The historical wage advantage of U.S. workers over those in other industrialized capitalist countries has been largely lost.

Edward J. Carlough, president of the Sheet Metal Workers International Association, AFL-CIO, eloquently attacked the big business-government inflationary drive against the living standards of the workers. He wrote:

We so-called great and powerful American trade unionsts have become a tray of cream puffs. We're being gouged by the price fixers and clobbered by the tax collectors, while all the time our unemployment rate continues at over 5 percent nationally, and over 10 percent for construction workers. We're so puffed up and polite with our middle-class status—we great 'silent majority' that the jackals are eating us alive.

It's time to remember where we came from. It's time to remember again what militant trade unionism is all about. It's time to start marching to the sound of a different drummer—that old drummer who screamed and got us where we are. . .[12]

But what really has happened to the militancy of construction workers? Where *is* the stain?

It's exactly in the policy of Mr. Carlough, who runs what is notoriously one of the most racist of all trade unions in the United States. Can he seriously expect that workers will militantly fight the monopolies when their attention is focussed by their leaders on preserving a monopoly of jobs at the expense of that large and growing sector of the blue collar working class who are Black, Puerto Rican, Chicano, Indian, Asian; when men like himself exclude from leadership that sector of the working class which, by virtue of its subjection to superexploitation and their traditions, is today bound to be prominent in the leadership of a more militant, advanced period of struggle of the U.S. working class?

Housing and Education

Discrimination and segregation in housing and education are important parts of the overall pattern of inequality to which Black people are subjected. It isn't within the compass of this book to examine the facts of this. Here we are concerned with its effect on white people. Housing and education are vital features of living, around which the most intense racism has been generated, and over which courageous struggles against racist discrimination are conducted. Tanzer regards discrimination in housing as even more important than discrimination in trade unions. He writes:

. . . the majority of white Americans are home owners and their house is by far their most important economic asset. One of their greatest fears is that the entry of Blacks into their neighborhood, whether in private or public housing, will drive down property values because whites will flee. This makes most homeowners strong allies of the real estate agents and builders in their fight against nondiscriminatory housing.[13]

This places *the wrong emphasis* on the subjective side of racism in housing, and fails to counteract the standard racist distortion about the objective economic consequences of integrated housing. There have been a number of demonstrative campaigns against the entry of Black people into lily-white areas, generally those where white skilled workers and white collar employees predominate. But the enforcers of segregated housing generally operate more quietly. They are the bankers who decree where loans shall be made or not made to Black buyers. They are the real estate agents who show houses or apartments in some areas to whites only, in others to Blacks only. Their weapons include zoning ordinances which make suburban areas economically beyond the means of almost all Blacks, and regulations barring low-cost public housing from certain areas.

And they are the same forces which inspire, if they do not directly organize, those campaigns carried out with extreme viciousness and frightful violence against Black families who have the courage to defy exclusionary attempts. Generally such violent attacks are carried out by a relative handful of racist thugs. The majority of the white population normally remains passive. Their guilt lies in toleration of the racist assault, and not in being "strong allies" of the racists.

There have been cases where white homeowners have cooperated with Black residents in mutual efforts to defeat the attempts of blockbusters and other racists to destroy the integrated character of particular urban areas, or to defend the right of Blacks to move into previously all-white areas. What has been lacking has been a strong organizing base, such as the trade union movement of a given city, or a labor-based political organization, to fight for housing integration.

Nor can one accept as reasonable the fear of lower property values. The weight of evidence is to the contrary. Property values are driven down only when, and after, racists have succeeded in scaring all white residents out of an integrated area and converting it into a ghetto. Then municipal authorities cut down on all necessary services. Landlords stop maintaining buildings. And values ultimately are likely to decline, although even here there is an opposite tendency for ghetto prices and rents to increase because of the seller's market—the excess of Black people needing housing in a limited area.

But when Blacks move into a previously all-white area on a significant scale housing values *increase*. In the first instance, taking advantage of the relative lack of choice on the part of Black buyers, sellers raise prices to them. Then, by the entry of Blacks, the demand-supply balance is shifted towards the advantage of sellers, and towards higher prices. That can be changed only if racist real estate manipulaters can scare enough whites into selling cheaply, so that they can turn around and sell at a huge markup to the Blacks. There are many places in the country where housing prices have declined drastically, and generally these are lily-white areas. The prices declined because plants closed down or military bases were abandoned and the economic foundation of the area was destroyed or diminished. A surplus of housing then appeared, and prices of all homes declined.

Forcing Blacks to live in ghettoes also costs white homeowners taxwise. The decline in values of ghetto housing reduces the tax yield, especially for rental housing, and most Black families are renters. Owing to the concentration of poverty among Black families, and racist policies of housing officials, more and more of the Black population of the cities live in public or publicly subsidized housing, which yields little or no real estate tax. Simultaneously more and more tax exemptions are given to industrial and commercial and financial properties. The result is that an increasing share of the real estate tax burden is placed on the—largely white—small homeowners. Real property taxes have increased more than five fold in the past twenty years, and the rate of increase has been even faster on small homeowners.

Twisting the chain of causality, racists try to mobilize white homeowners against public housing. *However the answer to excessive taxes is not less public housing, but the uniting of Black and white residents to campaign for shifting the tax burden from their backs.* Such a campaign can become effective when the process of housing integration reaches a sufficient stage to make unity among the working people more general than racial separation and suspicion.

The costs to white working people are more apparent in education. For twenty years, since the famous Supreme Court decision of 1954, the battle for desegregating the country's school system has been waged, without decisive result. Legal segregation has been ended in the South. Many Black pupils now go to more or less integrated schools. But the majority of children, white and Black, go to schools which are overwhelmingly of one color, and this phenomenon has actually increased in many northern metropolitan areas.

The movement towards racist private schools has become massive. Social pressures on white families to participate in such racist escapes have become very powerful. The main sufferers from this ''backlash'' are the Black children, who are afflicted with second rate segregated education. But the white population loses also. Most of the segregated private schools provide an inferior brand of education, partly by the very fact of segregation and the immanent racism in the school, but also because teachers are more poorly paid and trained, and because the curricula are below the public education standard. And there is a financial cost, as in Memphis, where schools are desegregating after a decade of racist resistance, but:

Under a federal court order, buses began mixing the races last January, and now almost a fourth of the city's 119,000 school children are being transported to integrated schools.

As a result, every weekday morning in the Rideway section of this city, dozens of lunch-box-toting white youngsters dutifully scramble aboard a bus for the long ride to class.

However, these children "aren't headed for the predominantly Black, inner-city school to which the federal court assigned them. Their buses are owned by churches, and they are bound for the all-white private schools blossoming here in the wake of desegregation."

White public school enrollment in Memphis declined from 69,809 in 1970 to 35,799 in 1973, despite an annexation that added 4,500 white students. Meanwhile, private school enrollment jumped from 13,071 to 33,012.

The annual tuition in one of the schools described in the article is $550 a year. This is a major burden to a working class family, especially when there are two or more children. Of course, one result is that the lowest paid white workers are forced to comply with the desegregation ruling. Besides the tuition paid by their parents, the children in private schools are subjected to reactionary, clerical-oriented schools "where prayer, bible-reading and discipline are in and slovenliness and sex education are out."

Wealthy patrons provide liberal endowments to these "segregation academies," while the public school system loses revenues, based on per capita attendance, is approaching a financial crises, and is already being forced to cut back on staff and educational activities.[14]

Thus segregated housing patterns and school systems, discriminatory employment patterns, are becoming an increasing burden on all the working people of the country. *The costs of semi-Apartheid are mounting.* Inflammable social tensions reached the flash point more than once during the 1960s. It would be naive indeed to think that much more serious racial clashes and ghetto uprising can be avoided while segregation in living and education continues and even worsens.

The condition is wholly incompatible with the requirements of a modern, highly industrialized society in the epoch of the internationalization of economic and cultural life, the period of the striving for a peaceful solution of international problems, of the scientific-technical revolution.

White people not only are losers from discrimination. They not only will gain from helping to end it. *But they must do so on pain of being themselves the victims of a continued and accelerated decline in the quality of life in the United States, on pain of the loss of democratic rights, of being victimized by fascist demagogues, of being involved in bloody racial conflicts, of being defenseless because of the social divisions against monopoly robbery, against plots of the military-industrial complex to subject them to devastating wars.*

White people *must* take a stand for equality. In certain ways more and more are doing so. But the majority have not yet moved. *In what direction? Where is the solution?* These questions will be discussed in the following chapters.

... letting a few of our capitalists share with whites in the exploitation of our masses will never be a solution ...

W.E.B. DuBois

11. Black Capitalism

During the frightful post-reconstruction decades of Jim Crow and Lynch Law, a Black educator, Booker T. Washington, rose to prominence. Backed by white captalists, he founded Tuskegee Institute, in Alabama, to teach Black youth craft skills and some business methods. He urged Black people to accomodate to oppression, not to resist it, to be good workmen, and for some to seek advancement in the business world. Towards that end he organized the National Negro Business League in Boston. Washington became the Establishment-appointed spokesman for the Black people, and his institute was granted $600,000 by steel magnate Andrew Carnegie. Early in the twentieth century he acted as go-between in the appointment of Blacks to federal jobs.

In the 1920s Marcus Garvey preached liberation with his plan for the Afro-American masses to go back to Africa and set up businesses there. He raised millions of dollars from among the Black people to set up a steamship line to carry travelers to Africa. It went bankrupt, and Garvey was imprisoned, then deported to his native Jamaica.

Washington and Garvey, however misguided, reflected the aspirations of Black people for *a means of escape* from their oppression. More recently, the theme has been revived by the biggest white capitalists, as *a means of maintaining* that oppression.

In 1969 the Nixon Administration and heads of the leading corporations joined in a campaign of "Black capitalism," promising advancement to the Black people through becoming capitalists in their own ghettoes, and through entering the bureaucracies of the great corporations.

All three of these movements had a common theme, and all three aimed to divert the Black people from mass struggle against their oppressors, to the futile effort of striving to obtain improvements through some of their number being admitted to the capitalist class.

W.E.B. Du Bois, the most advanced prominent leader of the Black people over a span of many decades, while not always free of similar illusions, was basically oriented to a program of mass struggle. He clashed with Washington and Garvey, and later, when he came to orient himself on the working class and socialism, wrote:

I saw clearly . . . that the solution of letting a few of our capitalists share with whites in the exploitation of our masses, would never be a solution of our problem, but the forging of eternal chains.[1]

If Washington and Garvey started movements on their own initiative, which in the case of Washington was adopted by the ruling white Establishment, the recent Black capitalism campaign was hatched in the board rooms of U.S. corporations and in the political power center. It came into being at a time of upsurge of the Black liberation struggle. The leaders of business and government made a major propaganda campaign for it, and the government appropriated hundreds of millions of dollars to support it. Leaders of a number of the petty bourgeois radical Black organizations were won over to it, and took on jobs within its framework—the Black Panthers and CORE are examples. Other Black-led organizations, such as the Reverand Jesse Jackson's PUSH, attempt to combine mass actions for jobs and other gains of the working people with a focus on winning financial support for various aspects of Black capitalism.

By 1974 many of the illusions about Black capitalism had been shed. The failure of major Black enterprises to develop, the bankruptcies among existing small enterprises of Black capitalists, the revelation of mass corruption in the Nixon administration bureaucracy carried on in the name of promotion of "Black capitalism," the use of "Black capitalists" as political pawns by the Administration—all foreshadowed the early demise of this fad, as of so many other formulas for the salvation of capitalism.

But undoubtedly a residue of such propaganda would remain, and similar illusions would continue to be fostered. While the Nixon years saw a decline in the relative overall economic position of the Black population, it saw the appointment of Black individuals to the boards of directors of some tens of the most prominent U.S. corporations, and the appointment of token Black executives within many corporate bureaucracies. These, together with a highly publicized handful of successful Black capitalists, would provide the "models" which the ruling establishment would set before the Black masses to emulate, and would be a group to be promoted as political and ideological leaders of the Black population.

Extent of Black Capitalism

A Census of Minority-Owned Business conducted for 1969 reported 163,000 Black-owned firms, with total receipts of $4,474 million. The majority of the Black firms were one-man or one-woman operations of self-employed artisans or merchants. Only 38,000 employed workers, and therefore could be considered capitalist enterprises, if small ones, in the proper sense of the word. The total number of employees was 152,000. In both sales and employment, *the Black firms accounted for only one quarter of one percent of all businesses in the country.*[2]

The Black people were even weaker, as capitalists, than the "Spanish speaking" and "other" (Native American and Asian combined) groups. Accounting for two-thirds of the minority population, Blacks accounted for only two-fifths of minority business receipts.[3]

Black capitalism was overwhelmingly concentrated in subsidiary, dependent fields. Of total receipts of Black-owned firms, 63.1% were in retail trade, services, and miscellaneous industries. The corresponding proportion for all firms was 27.5%. On the other hand, only 6.8% of the receipts of Black firms were in manufacturing, as against 39.3% of the receipts of all firms. This means, in effect, that Black capitalists owned less than one tenth of one percent of the industrial means of production.

It is interesting that 10.4% of the receipts of Black-owned firms were in the construction industry, as compared with 6.1% of the receipts of all firms. This reflected mainly the racist exclusionary practices of key craft construction unions, forcing Black craftsmen to set up as self-employed artisans or small contractors, with an average of only 5 employees.

Of the 12,306 employees of Black-owned manufacturing firms, 3,345 were in logging camps and sawmills, most of the rest in light industry, and a mere 2,694 in all durable goods industries combined. No Black-owned mining enterprises were listed.

A few figures illustrate the triviality of Black business.

There are 18 companies in the United States each of which had more sales then all Black capitalists put together.

There were only 347 Black-owned firms with sales of a million dollars or more, and their combined total sales, $877 million, and combined total number of employees, 17,687, equal the customary total for a single medium-sized U.S. corporation.

Whereas in U.S. business as a whole, corporations accounted for 81% of all receipts, in the case of Black firms, only 29% of receipts were by corporations. Black business is concentrated in the ghettoes. More than 80% of the business of Black firms in Massachusetts, Illinois, New York, Michigan, and Louisiana, for example, is done by firms in the metropolitan areas of Boston, Chicago, New York City, Detroit and New Orleans, respectively, where the Black population of the states is concentrated.[4]

There was some growth in Black business during the early 1970s, partly stimulated by the Black capitalism propaganda campaign and special credit programs.

Even so, the scale of Black business remained trifling by 1973.

The 100 largest Black-owned non-financial businesses had combined total sales of only $601 million, or $6 million per firm, representing an increase over the previous year only comparable to that of large white firms. The largest, Motown Industries, grossed $46 million in the entertainment business. Second was Johnson Publishing Co., publisher of Ebony and Jet magazines, the former devoted largely to advertising the successes and promotions of Black capitalists and executives. The other three with sales of $20 million or more were a supermarket company, a cosmetics manufacturer, and a record producer.

Most of the companies had fewer than 100 employees. Only one had more than 500, and this was a franchising company which apparently included its franchised dealers with employees.

The Black banks listed separately were all dwarf-sized, the largest,

Independence Bank of Chicago, with assets of $56 million, and the largest Black savings and loan association, the Carver Federal of NY, with $61 million. All the Black banks and savings and loan associations combined had deposits of less then a billion dollars. The two largest Black-owned companies are two insurance companies dating back to the turn of the century, North Carolina Mutual and Atlanta Life, each with over 1,000 employees, and with $136 million and $84 million in assets, respectively. Able to survive because of the traditional refusal of white insurance companies to insure Blacks, they still remain dwarfs in comparison with the big white-owned companies. The largest white-owned life insurance company had 157 times the assets of the largest Black owned life insurance company, and the fiftieth largest white-owned life insurance company had more assets then all 41 Black owned life insurance companies put together.[5]

Failure of the Black Capitalism Campaign

After a brief period stories of the failure of Black capitalism became increasingly frequent. A National Industrial Conference Board study of 30 minority enterprises established with the aid of government funds and credits concluded:

"To date these efforts have had little overall impact. New ghetto enterprises have provided relatively few jobs; and most have not been successful in terms of conventional business criteria of productive efficiency and profit. Furthermore, one type of undertaking, direct investment by outside capital in fully controlled installations (i.e., fully controlled by Blacks and other minorities) virtually ceased after 1968."

The enterprises were "severely affected by the general business recession since 1968, or cutbacks in government defense and aerospace spending, or both." Following the rule of "last hired, first fired" against Black workers, by 1971 employment in these enterprises was down an average of more than 25% from their peak. The capitalists who talked freely about helping Black business in general, continued to discriminate against them in practice:

"Established businesses have not been as ready as had been expected to become customers of certain new ghetto ventures."

Government agencies did not provide promised support and assistance.[6]

Black businesses striving to break out of the ghetto bind face innumerable handicaps. The Cheatham and Smith Company of Ossining, New

York, a retail fuel oil distributor, for many years competed with a number of white-owned enterprises in northern Westchester County, New York. However, at the first hint of a company-organized shortage of fuel oil, this Black capitalist enterprise was discriminated against by its supplier, the Mobil Oil Co., and was compelled to sell out to a white-owned company which had the primary access to Mobil supplies.[7]

In October, 1970 the Nixon administration announced a program to encourage corporations to deposit $100 million in new deposits in the nation's 35 minority banks. One year later, with much fanfare, deposits of $30 million had been announced. Obviously, the whole program, involving less than $3 million per bank, was a "peanut" operation.

But in 1971, 11 of the 26 Black banks reported losses, and the largest Black bank, the Freedom National of Harlem—which, incidentally, had majority white stockholdings when inaugurated—had the largest loss, $704,530, reducing its capital funds by one-third to $1.3 million.

Ironically, bankers commented, the Nixon administration program for increasing the banks' deposits had increased their problems. Their capital failed to grow in proportion, and their capital coverage—or lack of it—had reached the "critical" stage in many cases.

In a rescue operation the American Bankers Association asked member banks to contribute capital investment to the minority-owned banks. But 600 banks combined contributed a miserly $4.5 million. According to Federal Reserve Board Governor Andrew F. Brimmer, the Black banks have "limited outlets for funds in the Black community," and hence are forced to make their loans and investments in outside areas, where, of course, they have relatively little contact and basis to decide which are safe loans, and little access to the more lucrative operations.[8]

Oakley Hunter, president of the Federal National Mortgage Agency, (Fannie Mae), "conceded . . . that a three-year-old effort to start and help Black mortgage banking companies had been an almost complete failure."

Conceding that worsened conditions in the industry and intense competition were factors, Hunter placed the essential blame on the Black capitalists for "lack of business know-how," and on the Black people in general for lack of "confidence" as the cause of their poverty.

For this racist, it was impossible to acknowledge that the fundamental problem was and is the specially intense racism that permeates the mortgage banking industry, and the entire real estate industry, and the lack of capital of potential Black capitalists, resulting from the whole history of the oppression of a people.

Under his leadership, Fannie Mae rejected the government appeal made to all corporations to put some of their deposits in these banks, "because . . . these banks . . . were not using their deposits to better their communities."[9]

Needless to say, Hunter does not examine white-owned banks to determine their batting average in "community betterment" as a condition for depositing in them. His refusal to make deposits in Black-owned banks is an admission of the more open racism than that of most corporate heads, who satisfy the Administration's propaganda objectives by making a token deposit in a Black-owned bank.

And it's necessary to consider the repercussions of such an attitude on the part of an agency, which while now nominally private, was initiated by and is still regarded as a federally sponsored agency, whose $22 billion of outstanding debentures and notes are regarded as governmental rather than private debt. This agency holds $24 billion of rediscounted mortgages. It plays a vital role in the new housing market, and is in a position to determine where housing can go up and for what kinds of residents.

Is it any wonder that, like other federal housing agencies, this one supports the segregationist, grossly discriminatory housing policies of the private real estate and banking industry?

Is there any doubt that Hunter's attack represents a propaganda attack on existing Black banks, and tends to discourage potential customers and investors from dealing with them?

Business Week reports that "Philadelphia's Carver Loan & Investment Co., Inc., which went bankrupt last year after serving as a symbol of Black business success for a generation, has received a second chance." When this consumer finance company filed for bankruptcy the 1,800 Black people, mostly poor people, who had bought $3 million of bonds in the bank, were almost wholly wiped out. In the reorganized institution, they will get less than $½ million of speculative common stock in exchange for their bonds. Control will be in the hands of "venture capitalists" presumably big ones, who will put up $2 million in a reorganization scheme sponsored by the Sun Oil Company and supported by leading Philadelphia banks. The Girard and Fidelity Banks will "lend" the reorganized banks Black vice presidents, and the new

president is a 28-year old Harvard Business School graduate heading the
Sun Oil Company's minority business subsidiary.

The failure of the finance company is blamed in the article on the
policies of the previous president, who committed suicide. But would it
not be more accurate to blame its failure on the poverty of the Black
population, their subjection to first to be fired rules, the discriminatory
prices charged them, and their consequent inability to keep up payments
on many consumer loans? Is there any way that "counselors" from the
billionaire banks can overcome these handicaps, so long as the Carver
Loan & Investment Co. is essentially limited to serving on a profit-
seeking basis the grossly discriminated-against Black community of
Philadelphia?[10]

Metalworking News describes the tribulations of a Black capitalist
trying to make it in a capital goods industry:

"Can a minority-owned metalworking firm succeed in business
—even when trying? Alpha Machine Works, Inc., was formed last
January, specializing in the grinding of metal cutting tools. Ten months
later—and with a tremendous infusion of money and of manpower from
the Small Business Administration, a minority bank, the Black
economic union Job Corps, and Urban League—Alpha's plight is
'desperate' according to Maurice E. Sims, general manager."

Two large firms, Western Electric and Bendix "had a hand in the
company's formation" and "are Alpha's two best customers." But
evidently they limited their "benefactions," as did other firms contacted throughout the Kansas City area which gave "a favorable response" but hardly any actual business.[11]

A relatively large Black contractor, Winston A. Burnett, got into a
joint venture with a big conglomerate, Boise-Cascade, in order to get
necessary capital and bonding for his projects. However, the enterprise
collapsed in a few years, amidst mutual recriminations. Burnett wrote:

> I felt I had located a void in the construction industry and I was attempting to
> fill it. The same as you tool up a plant, we attempted to gear up the huge
> untapped Black labor resource that exists in this country to build housing. . . .
> That void still exists. The corporation or institution that has the $100-million to
> fill it, a high price tag for most but negligible for gaining a substantial slice of
> the $100 billion construction industry—will reap the benefit, not just in money,
> but would make a lasting contribution to this society.

Giving up on Black capitalism in the United States, Burnett turned to
contracting in the Bahamas and Nigeria.[12]

As other scandals erupted around the Nixon administration, its minority business program was not exempt. The Office of Minority Business Enterprise was accused of shaking down minority capitalists seeking loans and contract renewals. More than half the federally aided minority businesses studied in a General Accounting Office survey were "either failures or near failures." The Nixon administration converted the whole operation into an appendage of its electoral politics.

A New York Times survey concluded:

> The Nixon administration's program to provide funds and other aid to minority businessmen was turned in 1972 into the vehicle by which the president's re-election effort sought nonwhite support. Not only were minority businessmen under intense pressure from the White House and the president's campaign staff to support him . . . but few minorities were awarded contracts last year without at least an attempted political quid pro quo.
>
> Minority capitalism was the centerpiece of Mr. Nixon's civil rights program in 1968. The idea was to replace the Democrats' antipoverty programs of the sixties, which provided direct aid to the poor, with a program that would generate jobs through minority business opportunities. . . . But a great number of those businesses were small, and the impact on the economy of the minority community was considered minimal.
>
> Beside political misuse of the program, there were instances of money set aside for minorities ending up with whites. . .

Political angling of the operations continued after the election. Bureaucratic positions were filled almost wholly by former campaign workers. In 1973 the Agency shifted contract awards and jobs from Blacks to Spanish speaking minorities, because "Republicans concluded it was futile to go after the Black vote . . . of the 36 contracts dropped so far this year . . . 28 were held by Blacks."[13]

Dr. Thomas W. Matthew, an early advocate of Black capitalism, became an ardent Nixon supporter, and was pardoned by the latter from an income tax conviction. Later, however, Dr. Matthew was sentenced for misappropriation of medicaid funds.[14]

It must not be thought that the government programs supposed to aid minority business do indeed constitute some sort of special favor. The total of such aid, including loans, loan guarantees, and Federal procurement, claimed for fiscal year 1973 came to about $942 million. In the same year the net credit advanced to private industry under federal auspices came to $26.1 billion, government "investment-type outlays," the main type of procurement from private firms, came to $63.5 billion. Additional billions went to purchase current supplies and as subsidies of various kinds to private companies. The total in all comparable categories certainly exceeded $100 billion. The "minority aid," therefore, came to less than one percent of all federal funds paid out to business, and less than one half of one percent went to Black business.[15]

Far from representing a special benefit to minority business, the much-touted federal expenditures on their behalf cover up a continuation of gross discrimination against them. Even in order to bring the share of the minorities up to their share in the population, the amount of federal orders, loans, and grants going to such enterprises would have to be multiplied 20 times. Even more would be needed to start to overcome the discrimination within the private capitalist world, to include actual "special assistance" for minority business.

Reasons for Failure of Black Capitalism

With the economic dominance of huge financial-industrial conglomerations—whether organized in single corporations or connected groups of corporations—a fresh entry into the ranks of really large-scale business becomes exceedingly rare. Personal capital ownership is correspondingly concentrated. Individual companies rise and fall, but the men who own the dominant shares in them are generally inheritors of substantial capital, rather than "self-made" men rising from the ranks of petty enterprisers, and even more rarely workers.

U.S. capitalism remains overwhelmingly, even among whites, in the hands of members of those ethnic groups which originally dominated it—mainly the Anglo-Saxon stock deriving from the British Isles and Germany. To a limited extent, in big business, these are supplemented by Jewish and Irish capital.

The various "ethnic groups" which have "made it" in terms of achieving average wage levels—Italians, Poles, and others, remain limited primarily to small and medium capital. The majority of names appearing on lists of the wealthiest families, and even more of those with the greatest control of industries and banks, are names of English, Scottish and Welsh origin. Such people constitute an estimated 14.4% of the population.[16]

If such large population groups as Italian, Irish, French, and Polish had to depend on "their own" capitalists for jobs the majority would become unemployed. Most work for large corporate employers with their predominantly Anglo-Saxon ownership. U.S. capitalism is in a phase of rapidly increasing monopolization in which the possibility of *any* new grouping making a major dent has become trivial. *So, even in the absence of racist discrimination, the chances of Black capitalism getting far would be slight.*

But, even more important, the same types of discrimination which keep Blacks out of vast housing areas and major job categories operate with *triple effect* to keep them out of control of industry and finance. To be "successful" in business requires not some generalized type of talent, nor a degree in business administration. It requires first of all ownership of capital and access on favorable terms to credit, supplies of materials, equipment, and markets. The access, however, is provided primarily through social and family connections. Socially and geographically isolated from the ruling white families, the would-be Black capitalist cannot get advantageous terms. The residential enclaves of the very rich are the most lily-white, with Blacks limited to the role of live-in servants. The private clubs of the rich are the last holdout of court-approved exclusion of Blacks, and many politicians and capitalists who boast of their "Civil Rights" records, stubbornly maintain membership in such clubs, because the value of the contacts exceeds the political cost of exposure of membership in a club that refuses to accept Black members.

Consider the position of the Black man who wishes to become a financial capitalist via the route of stock brokerage and investment banking. In terms of customers, he would be largely limited to Blacks who, except for a handful, lack the capital to go beyond trivial investments. He could hardly expect to be more than a retailer of stocks, rather than an investment syndicator. Even more important, he would likely lack the social and business contacts which provide the inside information essential for success in stock market operation. Similar problems beset the pitiful handful of Black auto dealers.

Fallacy of the Ghetto Enterprise Concept

The Black capitalism propaganda campaign followed the eruption of uprisings in Black ghettoes by desperate masses seeing no way out of poverty, discrimination, and unemployment. A capitalist project was to install Black-owned enterprises in these ghettoes that would employ the idle youth and thereby dissipate discontent. The earliest and most publi-

cized enterprise of this type was a small subcontracting outfit in the
Watts area of Los Angeles, where one of the most serious uprisings had
occurred in 1965, Representatives of the white ruling establishment
actively recruited certain Black organizational leaders as sponsors of the
idea of ghetto industry.

Thus Louis Kelso, a white San Francisco lawyer and propagandist for
capitalism and against socialism—he is co-author of a right-wing
paperback, "The Capitalist Manifesto"—switched to progandizing
Black capitalism, and organized companies to cash in on this program.
Attempts were made to sell stock in such companies in the Black communities and former Black activists were enlisted as salesmen.

Roy Innis, national director of the Congress of Racial Equality
(CORE) became associated with Kelso and emerged as a leading advocate of ghetto capitalism, under the rubric of "community self-
determination." He claimed that Black people could obtain effective
rule of their inner-city enclaves, including "managerial control" of
enterprises operating there . These would provide employment and have
a guaranteed market in the ghettoes.

The main fallacies in this approach include:

• The inadequate base for industry within the ghettoes. These are
geographically tiny areas, overcrowded, heavily built up, already
over-polluted. It would be quite impossible to build any substantial
industrial enterprises within them, and even for small-scale enterprises,
the tendency is to move outside of central cities to suburbs and rural
locations.

• The inadequate employment base within the ghettoes. In practice,
employment possibilities within the ghettoes are limited to trade and
service enterprises, and government establishments. Even if all white
employees in the ghettoes were replaced with Blacks, this would
amount to but a fraction of the total number of Blacks who are employed, and would fall far short of those remaining jobless.

• The overwhelming majority of Black workers will continue to work
outside of the ghettoes. As a matter of fact, of course, most workers
have their place of employment in nonresidential areas—either industrial of commercial. What Black workers need, among other things, is
not a hopeless attempt to move industry and finance to the ghettoes, but
rather the opening up of all residential areas to them, so that they can
live within ready traveling distance of job locations.

White and Black sponsors of Black capitalism have different specific interests in this line of propaganda, which merge in their impact on the Black community as a whole.

White capitalists wish to create a layer of favored Blacks, who will obtain political and ideological leadership in the Black community, and dissuade the Black people from a militant struggle for equality and against segregation. Thereby they hope to maintain and extend their derivation of superprofits from the inequality and segregation of the vast majority of Blacks.

Black sponsors wish to obtain a larger share of the trade and service business of the ghettoes, and to profit from hiring segregated Black workers at low wages. Thus they support separatist ideology and oppose the unity of Black and white workers. This explains how Roy Innis could acclaim the racist decision of the Supreme Court in the Detroit school integration case as "a major victory against the civil rights aristocracy."[16a]

The futility of Black capitalism as a means of solving the unemployment problem among Blacks is indicated by the following figures:

Total employees of Black capitalists, 1969 152,000
Black employees, all employers, 1973 9,000,000
Black unemployed, 1973 (official figures) 900,000
Black unemployed, 1973 (realistic minimum). . . . . .1,800,000[17]

One would have to multiply employment by Black capitalists 13 times to provide jobs for the unemployed Blacks, and 60 times to make a self-contained Black economic community. The impossibilty of this is evident from the above discussion.

Henry Winston writes:

. . . the first "natural sociological units" in which Blacks lived in this country were the slave quarters . . . The contemporary "natural sociological units" in which most Black people live are the ghettos—and they are kept there by power descended from the slave owners to state monopoly capital.

Just as the inhabitants of the slave quarters could exist only through their labor in the plantation economy controlled by the slave owners, their descendants . . . can exist only through labor within the country's total economy. And just as freedom from chattel slavery could not be won within the slave quarters, but demanded a national struggle to break the power of the slavocracy, liberation from racist oppression—the survival of slavery—can be won only through a broad people's struggle to break the power of the monopolists.[18]

Black Executives and Directors

While the campaign for more Black-controlled enterprises appears to have little lasting results, definite changes are underway in the corporate bureaucracy. Controlling interests of the giant corporations have decided to create a layer of Black capitalists under their control and loyal to them. These Black men and women become symbols of progress towards equality. If a Black man or woman has been blocked from obtaining employment appropriate to his or her potential, he may look up to the Black face now shown in the annual report picture of boards of directors.

And thus the Rev. Leon H. Sullivan is now one of the 28 directors of General Motors, and attorney Patricia R. Harris one of the 24 directors of IBM, and has also been placed on the Board of the Chase Manhattan Corporation.

Neither of these people are on any of the operating committees of the boards of directors. Nor is it likely that they represent significant stockholdings. But they are important assets to the companies. Sullivan is a prominent person in the Black community, with a record of striving for better employment opportunities. Ms. Harris is a prominent figure in the Democratic Party, who acted as chairperson of its 1972 convention. Jerome H. Holland, Black sociologist and former executive of the Sun Shipbuilding Co., and more recently Ambassador to Sweden, has been appointed director of several corporations, including the Manufacturers Hanover Trust and the American Telephone & Telegraph Company. His appointment preceded by several months the historic court finding of major discrimination by AT&T against Blacks and women. George E. Johnson, president of Johnson Products, is a director of Commonwealth Edison and Metropolitan Life. So far the appointment of Black directors has been mainly limited to top corporations, and these have consisted primarily of public figures. There is some analogy to the appointment of university presidents to some corporate boards, *but the appointment of Blacks is even more clearly part of a public relations campaign,* and was so concentrated in time as to suggest a program agreed in advance by the top men of the leading corporations.

On the operating side, corporations are making more openings for Blacks at the lower and middle management level. In 1973 a Black man was appointed general manager of one of the Chrysler Corporation's 81 United States plants. But an appointment at this level is most exceptional. Many corporations have personnel men, usually Black, whose task is to seek out out promising Black college graduates for positions in the corporate bureaucracy. In sections of auto plants where there are heavy concentrations of Black workers, the management finds it expedient to hire or promote Black foremen and other lower level supervisors.

Yet, in general, Blacks are kept from positions of operating control, and in the lower and lower middle management and professional ranks. A Labor Department sponsored study of 500 Black professional persons hired by corporations found that they soon reached limits of promotion, and generally obtained no advancement after 9 years of employment.

"The data do suggest . . . that there is an effective ceiling on Black advancement in business, together with a limit on the kinds of jobs for which they are accepted."

The great majority "were in staff rather than line (command) positions and few had supervisory or managerial responsibilities. About three fourths were technical specialists. Only 23 per cent were supervisors and even fewer, 4 per cent, were employed at higher managerial levels. . ."

One Black person interviewed said:

Blacks are not in the mainstream of management. We do meaningful work to aid the over-all operations of the company, but we are in few, if any, decision-making positions. Blacks are mainly collectors and organizers of information. The concept of working your way up is futile for Blacks.[19]

It would not be correct to dismiss the increased employment of Blacks in the corporate bureaucracy as mere tokenism. But this tendency has its limits, as indicated above, in degree, and its specific features which fit the political strategy of monopoly capital, without abandoning its overall racist discrimination. It is building up a more significant Black bourgeoisie than existed formerly, and to that extent increasing the class differentiation within the Black population. It is not a substitute for, or even a partial substitute, for the achievement of real equality in employment for the entire working population among the 28 million Black people. But it can be used as a distraction from the struggle for equality in employment.

Politically, the Black members of the corporate bureaucracy are already appearing as leadership forces in Black people's organization and political action groups of various kinds. Regardless of the intentions of individual Black executives, this stratum on the whole is bound to reflect corporate interests within the movements they join, bound to weigh against an anti-monopoly orientation in the struggle for Black equality.

Dr. Andrew Brimmer told an NAACP audience in 1971 he was "afraid of a schism developing" between "a handful of Black people" who are "doing a hell of a lot better than any of us thought they would do," and the "vast proportion of Black people" who "still do not have marketable skills." He was "particularly distressed" by the declining emphasis on job opportunities, in contrast to a rising demand for expanded opportunities for Blacks to own and manage their own businesses.[20]

Legitimacy of Demands for Equality for Black Business

In his speech, just cited, Brimmer went on to say:

"I must hasten to add that, while I personally have serious reservations about many of the numerous programs aimed, hopefully, at increasing business ownership by Blacks, I believe that those Black men and women who are convinced that they can succeed in business should have a chance to try their luck."[21]

This combined approach of the Black former Federal Reserve Board member is justified. To see the fallacy of Black capitalism as the solution for Black inequality and oppression is one thing. But to condemn and belittle the demand for the *right* of Blacks to own businesses and to obtain high positions in the corporate and governmental bureaucracy, is something else again.

Part of the entire democratic struggle in the country requires that Black capitalists and would-be capitalists have all of the necessary access to credits, supplies, government subsidies and loans, technical aids, etc., that are necessary for their success. Given the historical pattern of discrimination and exclusion from business opportunity, this requirement means much more than the elimination of existing gross discrimination against Black business. It requires real, as distinguished from token, special government assistance and guarantees, on a very large scale, to provide the possibility of Black capitalists making definite headway in overcoming their past virtual exclusion from industry and finance, and from controlling positions generally in the national economy.

At a symposium of Black economists Professor Richard F. America proposed the allotment of $2 to $5 billion, presumably by the federal government, for the formation of major Black-owned business concerns.[22] The amount is not unreasonable, in relation to the many times larger government subsidies going to white-owned businesses, and the existing lack of substantial Black-owned enterprises, because of the long history of discrimination.

But such a demand cannot be a substitute for, nor can it replace in primacy, the struggle for the economic equality of the masses of Black working people. Moreover, it can only be to the disadvantage of the majority of Blacks if it is used to distract the Black people and their white allies from the main, really forward looking economic struggles.

Capital or Labor? Which Side to Take?

Bayard Rustin, veteran Black socialist and executive director of the A. Philip Randolph Institute, writes:

Since the end of slavery Black leaders have argued over how to end discrimination and poverty, but the most fundamental debate has centered on the question of which social force—capital or labor—blacks should align themselves with . . . Black capitalism, whether it consists of buying shares in a ship company or operating a corner grocery store, can at best lead to the economic uplift of a very marginal segment of the Black community. It cannot reach the masses of working people or impoverished families that comprise the vast majority of the Black populace.

The only institution capable of transforming the conditions of working people—Black and white—is the labor movement. . . History has taught us that progress is gained only through a strategy which seeks the economic and social elevation of great masses of people. And that strategy is best embodied in the programs and ideals of the American labor movement.[23]

Unfortunately, Mr. Rustin identifies the American labor movement with the reactionary, racist, top leadership of the AFL-CIO, with which he actively collaborates, to the detriment of workers in general, and Black workers in particular. But the general sentiment he expresses is central—the Black people to obtain their liberation must align themselves with the social class of their own overwhelming majority, the working class. Even more, the entire working class must align itself with the Black people's struggle for equality, or it cannot achieve its goals. This relationship is discussed in the next chapter.

12. Labor Union Influences

Unions represent the collective power of workers in dealings with their employers. They inevitably have an impact on all employer practices, including discrimination on account of race. There are two extremes in the appraisal of this impact. Bayard Rustin, as quoted in the previous chapter, sees Black aspirations as wholly encompassed in the "programs and ideals of the American labor movement," by which he means the AFL-CIO. Black separatist and largely white "New Left" radical groups tend to an opposite view, regarding unions as components of an overall system of discrimination and their white members as "middle class" beneficiaries of that discrimination.

Both extremes are wrong. The reality is much more complex. Labor unions, representing the economic interests, and within limits the political interests of workers, to that extent represent those of Black workers also. Operating under the general slogan of "an injury to one is an injury to all," "unity of all workers regardless of race or creed," etc., the unions have a moderately egalitarian philosophy, which favors improving the conditions of the most exploited workers.

However, U.S. unions, by and large, do not carry on an active struggle to overcome the discrimination against Blacks, nor do their leaders understand the need for such a struggle. Moreover, a number of unions actively discriminate against Blacks, and a degree of racism is reflected in the policies of virtually all of them.

Trade unionists, for the most part, find themselves opposed to capitalists locally, and with respect to national economic issues. But the AFL-CIO leadership upholds the system of capitalism, and supports

197

many of the policies of the capitalist class. It is very much imfluenced by capitalist ideology, including capitalist racism.

Yet, on the whole, the unions are a positive force in the struggle for equality. Without them, there would be no perspective for victory in the struggle. In order to achieve victory, it will be necessary to overcome some of the weaknesses of the unions, to transform them into more consistent instruments of class struggle, to convince their members, especially their white members, that an active struggle against racism is in their interests.

The general program of the trade union movement is in the interests of the Black working people. But in addition the Black people must have their own liberation program, to meet their special needs, to end their special extra exploitation, to achieve equality. What is needed is an alliance of the whole working class with the Black people around the overall program of labor and the special program of the Black people.

Inevitably, such an alliance will be on a clear labor versus capital basis. It cannot be created without participation of the trade union movement, which, for all its weaknesses, is the best organized section, and a decisive section, of the American working class. And it cannot be created without renewing the leadership, and broadening the perspective of the trade union movement, in which the recognition of the need for Black leadership and placing a high priority on a special program for Black equality have a prominent part.

Today the dominant leaders of the trade unions align themselves with the capitalists on vital issues. They not only uphold the system of capitalism, but they believe in collaboration with capitalists in foreign policy, in anti-Communism, in raising labor productivity—they believe in the fundamental harmony of the interests of labor and capital. As such, their actions and policies are not in the interests of Black or any other workers. And as such, they also are aligned with the racist policies of capitalism. Thus AFL-CIO President George Meany, who boasts of never having been on a picket line, also is the chosen representative of the construction craft union leaders, notorious for their racism.

Historical Development

For over a century U.S. labor unions have been a battle ground of two ideologies—a narrow guild ideology of winning favors for a selected small group of workers by exclusion of others, and even at their expense; and a one-for-all, all-for-one ideology of unity of the entire working class against employers. Racism has been a main ingredient of the former ideology, and along with it political capitulation to employers on all general issues concerning the people. The latter trend has been associated with a better record and must ultimately prevail.

Black-white relations have been a major theme in the history of U.S. unionism, with ups and downs associated with this ideological struggle. The main development of trade unionism dates from the end of the Civil War, and in the first decades the overall trend was positive. The National Labor Union, emerging in the late 1860s, favored unity of Black and white workers, but lacked a specific program to that end. It was paralleled by a cooperating Colored National Labor Union. The Marxist-led International Workingmen's Association had a more conscious policy. The Knights of Labor reached its peak in the 1890s as the largest labor organization in the world, with 600,000 members, including 10-15% Blacks. It represented a high point of an approach to industrial unionism and of Black-white labor unity.

However, it was replaced by the American Federation of Labor, which came to the fore late in the century as a federation of craft organizations, with a practical approach of winning relative security for some white workers by removing Blacks from traditional areas of work. Many AFL unions formally excluded Backs. By 1902 only 3% of its more than a million members were Black.

The Industrial Workers of the World (IWW) challenged the AFL early in the twentieth century. Blacks were prominent in its leadership, and it organized Blacks and whites jointly, even in the Jim Crow South. But the IWW did not understand the need for special demands to end discrimination against Blacks in industry, incorrectly believing that there was "no race problem . . . only a class problem. The economic interests of all workers, be they white, Black, Brown or Yellow are identical, and all are included in the program of the I.W.W."[1]

The southern Brotherhood of Timber Workers extended this tradition in several years of militant struggle against the open-shop employers and the entire weight of the National Association of Manufacturers. This union, moreover, organized by Socialists, maintained Black-white unity against open attempts of the employers to use race divisions to break the union.

During World War I Blacks obtained industrial jobs in substantial numbers. The first really successful organizing drive conducted on an industrial basis, was that of the packinghouse workers, led by left-wing leaders of the Chicago Federation of Labor, William Z. Foster and Jack Johnstone. About 20,000 of the 200,000 organized packinghouse workers were Black, and Black-white unity played a major factor in the wartime victories of this union.

The founding of the Communist Party in 1919 brought into the labor movement, for the first time, a political grouping which made a major issue of the fight for equality of the Black people in every sphere of life, and against all forms of racist practices and ideology. Following the expulsion of Communists from unions during the 1920s, the left forces formed the Trade Union Unity League, in 1929, as a grouping of small left-led unions in previously unorganized industries. At its convention 64 of the 690 delegates were Black, an unprecedented proportion for a national trade union gathering.[2]

All during the 1930s the Communists and other left-wing forces contributed substantially to the rapidly growing strength of Black workers in the trade union movement. This was particularly important in the industrial unions of the Congress of Industrial Organizations established during the period 1934-1941 in basic industries, including auto, steel, chemical, rubber, electrical and other machinery, and most other major industries.

Black membership in labor unions increased from about 60,000 in 1930 to more than 700,000 in 1945, and from a little more than 2% of total membership to 5% of total membership. The number and proportion of Blacks was higher in the CIO than in the older, craft-oriented AFL, although some of the AFL unions were organized on an industrial basis and were more like the CIO unions in policy.[3]

The new industrial unions set up fair employment committees, and were instrumental in establishment of the government Fair Employment Practices Committee in World War II, after Black trade union leader A. Philip Randolph organized a march of 50,000 Blacks on Washington to protest employment discrimination. The Communists and other left elements led the fight for hiring of Blacks in the burgeoning aircraft, shipyard, textile, and other industries primarily serving or greatly stimulated by wartime demands.

At the end of World War II, the Communists raised the demand for special measures to preserve the jobs of Black workers, in order to prevent the operation of the customary first-to-be-fired rule as postwar layoffs took place. However, during this period of cold war and McCarthyism, the Communists and other left-wingers were driven out of leading positions, and thousands were driven out of the unions and industry altogether. For a decade there was virtually no progress against discrimination in the unions and discrimination in industry increased, with a resulting marked deterioration in the relative economic position of the Black people (Chapter 4).

The civil rights struggles emerging in the mid-1950s were accompanied by a revival of action for equal employment within the unions. This affected the terms of the merger of the two labor federations into the AFL-CIO in 1956. A Civil Rights Department was set up, and strong statements were put into the merged federation's constitution, but there was little practical implementation.

Randolph and other Black unionists organized the Negro-American Labor Council, to exert pressure on the AFL-CIO and to combat its organizational discrimination. The continued growth of Black union membership and of the general democratic struggle of the Black people forced a gradual ending of the most blatant racist practices of some old craft unions, such as formal exclusion of Blacks and separate locals.

Under the impact of the broad civil rights movement and corresponding legislation, the Vietnam War boom in industry, and the revival of progressive currents within the labor movement, Black membership in trade unions expanded to about 2 million in 1970, out of a total membership of 20 million. Thus Black labor union membership approached the proportion of Blacks in the labor force.

Role of Unofficial Labor Groups and Progressive Peoples Organizations

In the late 1960s and 1970s there emerged within a number of key unions Black caucuses devoted to overcoming the discrimination against Black workers by employers and union officials. In 1972 a Coalition of Black Trade Unionists was organized on a national scale. This group was formed in a sharp break with AFL-CIO President George Meany, for his failure to oppose the racist President Nixon in the 1972 election. It focussed on national political action, as well as questions of discrimination in unions and by employers. Some 1,200 delegates attended its third annual convention in Detroit in 1974, and chose as president, William Lucy, secretary-treasurer of the 500,000 member American Federation of State, County, and Municipal Workers. [3a]

Broader rank and file caucuses, involving white and Black workers, gave major attention to this issue as a central part of a campaign for invigorating the trade unions and changing them from class collaborationist to class struggle policies. One of the most successful of these was the Miners for Democracy movement, which succeeded in winning control of the United Mineworkers of America from the corrupt, criminal Boyle machine. While the Miners for Democracy are not as conscious as some other rank and file groups of the priority of the struggle against discrimination, the new, democratic manner of the union's operation inevitably helps in that direction.

A group in the steel industry, the National Steelworkers Rank and File Committee, has obtained a substantial following and gives much prominence to the struggle for Black equality. Another important national group, the Ad Hoc Committee of Concerned Steelworkers is in the field and regularly unites with the National Steelworkers Rank and File Committee in a common front against racism. There are a number of similar local groups in the UAW and other unions.

The National Coordinating Committee for Trade Union Action and Democracy, centered in Chicago, and with Black and white leadership, plays a certain role in stimulating and unifying movements of this type. It also features the struggle against racism.

These groups have a very great potential, because of their base among white as well as Black workers. Ultimately, white workers must play a major part in a victorious struggle for Black equality. Similar groups played an important role in setting the stage for the organization of the masses of basic industry workers in the 1930s, and the rank and file groups today are much more conscious than their predecessors of the centrality of the fight against racism in the labor movement and in industry.

Communists are prominent in this new rank and file movement, as they were in similar movements, and especially in earlier struggles against discrimination. The special, positive role of Communists in the struggle for Black equality is generally conceded, even by those opposed to their general policy, and those who attribute ulterior motives to the Communist participation in this struggle. Professor Ray Marshall writes:

"The CIO's equalitarian racial policies stemmed directly from the ideological positions held by many of its leaders, who were young, idealistic people with broad social outlooks. Some of them were Communists, a group which has almost always adopted equalitarian racial postions. Although many doubted the sincerity of the Communists' racial policies, there can be little question that, by emphasizing the race issue to get Negro support, the Communists forced white union leaders into paying more attention to racial matters."[4]

The NAACP, the largest non-religious membership organization of Black people, has a long history of legal struggle for equal employment. With the present more favorable legal framework, and its legal actions, increasingly successful, the NAACP has won substantial gains. These victories have prodded the federal government to improve enforcement activities. The National Urban League also plays a positive role, although in a less activist fashion. Corresponding groups among Puerto Rican and Chicano people are becoming more active. The National Organization of Women carries out law suits and other forms of struggle for equality of employment for women. The struggles of women and Blacks for equal employment and other economic gains are mutually reinforcing.

What is yet missing, but vitally important, is a new, broad, national political organization, of Black and white people, that will include the struggle for equality as a *major* item in its overall program, along with other positions of an anti-monopoly and pro-peace character.

Economic Effect of Unionism on Black Workers Conditions

In 1970, according to a Census Bureau study, among trade union members, Black males earned 83% as much as white males, while among non-members of unions, Black males earned only 62% as much as white males. Considering female workers, Black trade unionists earned 91% as much as white trade unionists, but Black non-members earned only 82% as much as white non-members.[5]

This is a strong indication of the substantial overall positive contribution of the unions to the struggle for equality of the Black working people. At the same time, it makes clear that the unions *still have a long way to go*. To understand this process more deeply, its limitations and its future potentials, we must consider differences among the unions in policy and practice.

Professor Herbert R. Northrup writes:

In general—although not always—older industries like railroads, printing, and building construction, are ones unionized on a craft basis with its concomitant jobs scarcity consciousness and antiminority group bias. A community of feeling between craftsmen and employers on racial employment matters exists in such industries. The interaction tends to strengthen discrimination. Moreover, the fragmentation of unions adds additional barriers which must be overcome if existing discriminatory patterns are to be modified.[6]

Also, it should be added, fragmentation of employers, even where there is a single industrial union, can fit into a system of collaboration between unions and employers on the basis of a small number of favored workers in each establishment, including relatives of the employer, hiring by personal connections, etc.

These conditions do not *necessarily* result in racist practices. Unions such as District 65 of the Distributive Workers in New York, and Local 1199 of the Drug and Hospital Workers Union, dealing with numerous small establishments, have a generally superior record in race relations, and take an active part in combating racist practices of employers. But these exceptions are generally the newer unions, coming into the picture during the advanced period of trade union activity of the late 1930s.

The building trades unions provide the crudest example of racist policies, involving full collaboration with employers in exclusion of Blacks from better jobs. Superficially, this collaboration pays off in the receipt of high wages by the closed circle of related workers admitted into a number of skilled crafts of the building trades. But these racist practices are used by the construction employers, in the long run, to worsen the conditions of all building trades workers, and to undermine the advantages gained by a minority of the white skilled trades workers. For one thing, partly offsetting their high wage rates are irregular employment, lack of paid vacations and other fringe benefits won by unionized factory workers. Then there is the system of favoritism, whereby a few workers have regular employment at very high wages —and these are publicized as the models of "middle class" workers; while many—and in some crafts the majority, do no better than ordinary-assembly line workers.

Finally, as the unions restrict membership, more and more employers get around them by hiring non-union workers, including Blacks, at much lower wages. By the 1970s most residential construction was done by non-union labor. In the Miami area, it was reported, 78% of apartment house construction was non-union. In a Cleveland suburb, a bomb wrecked a car agency building being erected partly by non-union subcontractors.[7]

However, sabotage and violence cannot protect the unions' position, so long as they refuse to organize Black workers, and fight for the equal rights of Black workers to all jobs and all conditions of work, throughout the industry.

In 1969 the mean earnings of male construction craftsmen came to $8,478, not much different from the mean earnings of $8,618 of male motor vehicle production operatives. But the fringe benefit advantages of the latter, in vacations, SUB benefits, paid holidays, etc., made the real average of the motor vehicle operatives considerably higher than that of construction craftsmen as a whole, and perhaps higher than that of any of the major single construction crafts. But the differentiation among motor vehicle operatives was much less than among construction craftsmen. Only 1½% of the former earned more than $15,000, while 5% of the latter did. On the other hand, 14% of the motor vehicle operatives earned less than $5,000, while 25% of the construction craftsmen earned less than $5,000.[8] The top earning fraction of the construction craftsmen form the power base of the reactionary trade union bureaucrats running these unions, as well as being carriers of the racist, exclusive ideology which is part of the armor protecting their favored place.

In the summer of 1974, as housing and public construction declined sharply under the impact of inflation and budgetary stringencies, 30,000 New Jersey construction workers stopped work and rallied to a demonstration at the state capitol in Trenton against a 20% unemployment rate and the impoundment of state funds for construction projects.[8a] Yet, undoubtedly many of these same construction workers supported racist politicians who have all but cut off mass public housing construction nationally, and neo-fascists like Anthony Imperiale of Newark, who leads the struggle against housing for Black workers.

At the same time William Slidell, president of the International Carpenters Union, called for nationalization of the housing industry to remove it from the restrictions of the private bankers and reduce the 12% unemployment rate among the union's 800,000 members.[8b]

Only by changing their discriminatory, and often exclusionary policy against Black workers, only by supporting the demand of the Black people for equal access to housing everywhere, and for the mass construction of housing that Black and white workers can afford—will the construction workers win more steady, relatively full employment.

The Teamsters Union is an old union, which has transferred many of the negative features of narrow craft unions to the modern motor trucking industry. The largest union in the country, in point of membership, the Teamsters has collaborated with employers' racist hiring practices against Blacks and Spanish speaking drivers, as it has collaborated with California agribusiness against the largely Chicano Farm Workers Union. Owing to this collaboration, Black workers seeking over-the -road drivers' jobs are forced to go to employers who have not been organized by the union, pay considerably lower wages, and provide inferior working conditions. J. Stanley Pottinger, assistant attorney general for civil rights, filed suits against 349 trucking companies, their trade association, and the Teamsters Union, for their racist employment practices, in 1973.

In March 1974, seven large trucking firms and the Department of Justice filed a consent decree under which one-third to one-half of all new hires would be Blacks and Spanish surnamed persons, the exact percentage depending on the density of Blacks and Spanish surnamed persons in the population. In regions where they are numerous, Indians and Asian Americans will be covered. Apparently this includes the better paying over-the-road driver jobs from which Blacks have been traditionally excluded, and employers are required to train the workers when necessary.[9]

The Teamsters Union was expected to accede to the consent decree. While it is a strong decree, and appears to have fewer loopholes than most, the whole history of racism in industry makes it clear that automatic action cannot be expected. So long as racists remain in control of the Teamsters Union, and employers remain what they are, and the government is dominated by racists, organized pressure by progressive workers in the industry and in the communities where trucking firms are headquartered can provide the only guarantee of enforcement.

The situation remains better in the industrial unions formed in the 1930s and 1940s with left leadership, based on the principles of Black and white unity and the striving for equality. Despite expulsion of left leaderships from most of these unions, enough of the older tradition of equality remains to make a substantial difference from the situation in the old craft unions.

Yet serious discrimination persists against Black workers in the basic industries where these newer unions operate. The union leaders do little to counter the continued exclusion of Blacks from the highest paying skilled jobs, and their concentration in the lowest paying, most unhealthy jobs. They tend to exclude Blacks from top leadership positions.

The United Automobile Workers has a relatively good record. Its Fair Practices and Anti-Discrimination Department carries on significant educational activity. Its contracts provide a basis for grievance action against the many cases of discrimination in the plants. And yet, discrimination has been sufficiently severe to bring about the self-organization of Blacks into special caucuses, and Blacks are leaders in the militant rank-and-file groups developing in this—as in other unions. Blacks have been elected presidents of many locals in the Detroit area, and are prominent in local leadership generally.

Table 28 shows that the relative wages of Black workers to those of white workers are considerably better in industries where powerful industrial unions with a militant tradition embrace the majority of production workers, than in industries where craft unions, or weak industrial unions, or no unions at all prevail.

TABLE 28

PERCENTAGE OF MEDIAN EARNINGS OF BLACK MALE WORKERS TO
MEDIAN EARNINGS OF ALL MALE WORKERS, SELECTED INDUSTRIES 1969

	%
Strong Industrial Unions	
Automobile (UAW)	84
Iron & Steel (USWA)	83
Primary nonferrous metals	
(Mine Mill &Smelter Workers—	
now part of USWA)·	82
Rubber products (URWA)	78
All Manufacturing	71
Craft Unions, Weak Unions,	
or Largely Unorganized	
Furniture and fixtures	69
Yarn, thread, and fabric mills	75
Printing & Publishing	68
Professional and photographic equipment	67

SOURCE:US-D-240

A negative example of an industrial union organized in the 1930s is the Communications Workers of America. It was organized under right-wing leadership, in opposition to the left-led, equality-striving American Communications Association. With government and company help, the CWA defeated the ACA. Moreover, the CWA has lacked the power of industrial unions in auto, steel, etc. Because the companies could maintain operations through the use of unorganized supervisory employees, CWA strikes have never succeeded in actually stopping telephone service.

The leadership of the CWA played a racist role in the case of the hearings and consent decree compelling the AT&T to pay $15 million in back wages to women and Blacks, in partial compensation for past discrimination, and to take corrective measures for the future. During more than two years of court hearings and negotiations, the union officials rejected repeated invitations to participate in the proceedings. But when a settlement was about to be reached, they sought to delay implementation on the grounds that the ruling infringed on the union's rights as sole bargainer for 600,000 telephone company employees. Federal District Judge A. Leon Higginbotham denied this petition.

Actually, the legal action became necessary precisely because the union had abdicated its responsibility as collective bargainer, and had instead collaborated with the giant racist employer, in order to preserve the fleeting privileges of a minority of white male craft workers, and the monopoly of union officer positions enjoyed by a clique, dependent for political support on this narrow group of workers.

Similarly, the national leadership of the United Steelworkers, and the local leadership at the giant Bethlehem Steel Sparrows Point plant, have collaborated with employers in opposing court actions seeking the ending of seniority systems which keep Black workers out of better jobs. However, there are significant forces within that union seeking to end the racism of the present officialdom as they are simultaneously striving to end the no-strike, collaboration with employer policies of the leadership of the union, headed by I. W. Abel. Progressives within the union won a big victory in 1974 with the election of Ed Sadlowski as president of the largest district, in the Indiana-Illinois area, by a nearly two-to-one margin over the Abel machine candidate. Black workers comprise nearly one-third of the blue collar steel workers in the district. Black and white rank and filers provided the forces for Sadlowski's election, and he indicated continued reliance on them, and a break with Abel's racist policies, after his election.

Aside from the big unions, a positive contribution has been made by some of the smaller, left-led unions, in fighting for equality. Thus, the left-led International Longshoremen's and Warehousemen's Union is the leading trade union force in the San Francisco Bay Area and on Hawaii. It not only established practices minimizing discrimination among its members on account of race, but has influenced the entire labor situation in this respect. The minimal income differentials between whites and Asians in Hawaii is one result. Another is the success of the Hawaiian agricultural workers, organized by the ILWU. in winning relatively decent wages and working conditions. The accomplishments of this union were won in battles not only with employers, but against a 20-year long attempt of the federal government to deport or imprison its outstanding leader, Harry Bridges. Local 1199 of the Drug and Hospital Workers Union has helped tens of thousands of Black and other minority workers to win decent working and wage conditions, in bitter combat against the managers and owners of hospitals, and state governments which helped the employers with injunctions and jailings and fines of the union leaders. District 65 of the National Distributive Workers (AFL-CIO), the United Electical Workers (UE-IND), and the Transport Workers Union (TWA-IND), are other unions with a background of continuing progressive leadership which have made significant overall contributions to reducing discrimination and combating racism in industry. Rand and file movements, and individual locals of major unions have a similarly good record. And yet, even the better unions have fallen short of doing all that is necessary to combat racism.

While the balance is far from satisfactory, one must conclude that the net, overall effect of trade unions has been to reduce inequality, and that where union leaderships have conspired with employers or failed to fight against discrimination, it is not the unions which are in the controlling position, but the employers. Indeed, often the racist union leaders have obtained their positions with the help of the employers and the government.

A decisive victory over economic inequality will require a transformation of the trade unions into militant fighters against discrimination and for positive measures to bring about real equality for Black and Brown workers.

Political Role of the Trade Unions.

As the civil rights struggle developed during the 1950s and 1960s, the political front became increasingly important in the struggle of the Black people for social and economic equality. In no other area was the clear overall differentiation in position of the working class and the capitalist class more clear. The civil rights organizations and the trade union centers formed a united front on most legislative and electoral issues, on a national level and in a number of states. Major unions gave active support in personnel and funds to the civil rights campaigns in the South. A white woman worker of the United Automobile Workers was killed by racist deputies in a famous Alabama civil rights march. In turn, the civil rights struggles proved a stimulant to trade union organization, of white as well as Black workers, and helped overcome repression against trade union organizers.

The trade union pressure was very important in winning enactment of the key civil rights legislation of the mid-1960s. An NAACP legislative leader said: "organized labor gave unfailing, consistent and massive support where it counted most" in the drive for this legislation. At the same time, the civil rights organizations supported trade union legislative objectives.[10]

The unions provided the main political force behind the enactment of periodical improvement and broadened coverage of minimum wage legislation. Precisely because of the traditional consignment of Blacks to the worst paid jobs, such legislation is of particular importance to Black workers. At the same time, the opposition to this legislation always comes from employer groups. Regardless of the racist ideology and racist practices of many union officials in their own unions, when the class interests of the workers force them into conflict with employers, as in the case of labor legislation, Black workers gain, not only as workers in general, but tend to especially gain in the sense of reducing the prevailing economic discrimination against them.

The new federal minimum wage law enacted in 1974 for the first time extends coverage to some 7 million workers, including household workers, low-paid government employees, and others previously excluded. It also calls for ending, in a few years, the large differential against agricultural workers in minimum wage legislation. These improvements are of special importance to Black, Chicano, Puerto Rican, Asian and Native American workers.

The trade unions have been the major force behind public housing legislation, and again Black working people, who have lacked and still lack decent housing to the greatest extent, have proportionally benefitted most from the low-cost public housing that has been built, inadequate as it has been in scale. Here too, the trade unions as well as the Black people's organizations have been in combat with the private housing and banking industry, racist to the core.

Similar considerations apply to many other types of welfare and labor legislation. Moreover a comparable alignment of forces has operated in the state and municipal political arena. In states with strong unions, minimum wage legislation, unemployment insurance benefits, workmen's compensation laws, and other labor and social welfare legislation, is considerably superior to the federal standard—and again, this is of particular value to Black workers.

Trade unions have an uneven record in relation to the campaigns of the growing number of Black elected officials. But more often than not, when a Black candidate has run against a racist white candidate, the trade union influence has been mainly on the side of the Black, while the business establishment has been mainly on the side of the white racist.

The overwhelming majority of Black officials have been elected on the Democratic Party ticket, which has the support of most trade unions. The big business establishment, while having a dominant influence in both major parties, throws its main support to the Republicans. The shift of the Black vote from the Republicans to the Democrats in the 1930s coincided with the emergence of the new, militant, industrial trade unions and the allegiance of these unions to the Democratic Party.

At the same time, the trade unions have been significant in opposing ultra-right and fascist tendencies in politics. Thus the AFL-CIO opposed the racist George Wallace candidacy in 1968, and despite the foot-dragging of the Meany leadership, launched a strong propaganda drive against Wallace in the closing stages of the campaign.

Black Contribution to Labor

If the Black struggle for equality has gained, on balance, from the activities and policies of the organized labor movement, the working class as a whole and the trade union movement in particular have gained even more from the struggles of the Black working people.

The Black caucus in Congress has emerged as *the most progressive grouping,* by far, and one which, by virtue of this, is indispensable to the legislative causes of the workers. Earlier, the late Adam Clayton

Powell, for decades the representative of Harlem in Congress and for long one of the two sole Black members, attained the chairmanship of the House Labor Committee.

In that capacity he conducted a militant pro-labor policy, and achieved more in the interests of the working class and the trade union movement than any of his predecessors or successors. The reactionary forces in Congress, obedient to anti-labor big business groups, launched a clearly discriminatory impeachment campaign against Powell, and succeeded in driving him out of the chairmanship, then out of Congress and out of the country. To his everlasting dishonor, AFL-CIO chief George Meany was prominent in the campaign to "get" Powell. The Black congressman's personal weaknesses and petty political corruption, of a type and scale characteristic of American politicians, gave the reactionaries the opening they sought, but not the justification for the racist, anti-labor campaign against Powell.

In recent years, Black judges have played a progressive role on a national and local level.

Black voters have supported pro-labor candidates for office by a wider majority than any other sector of the population.

The contribution of Blacks to the entire U.S. working class has been felt even more distinctly in the shops and factories and picket lines. Black workers, to an extent beyond their proportion numerically, have participated actively and with special militancy in organizing campaigns, strike struggles, and day-to-day lesser conflicts of labor and management. Currently Black workers are especially prominent among rank and file forces striving to remedy the conservatism and class collaboration tendencies of some key industrial union leaderships.

Historically, employers have banked heavily on being able to use Black workers as strikebreakers, calculating on their desperate need for employment, and the possibility of bringing in Black workers, ignorant of the situation, from distant parts of the country. But this has rarely succeeded. Black workers have usually been among the most steadfast in strike situations, despite the fact that they feel the economic pinch of a strike more because of their lower incomes and lack of accumulated savings.

Establishment propagandists, and some progressive writers, who come out against racism, convey the impression of Black strikebreaking as a general phenomenon, and of a widespread hostility of Blacks to unions as 'such. the actual situation was quite different. In the last century Blacks strove continually to get into unions. Foster wrote:

Unfortunately, however, there were white chauvinist prejudices among the white workers and their leaders to bar the Negro from the unions to keep him out of the skilled trades, and to force him into the role of strikebreaker if he wanted to work in industry—all of which errors dovetailed neatly with the employers' plans for the Negro in industry.Early American labor history is replete with the tragic experience of white workers striking to bar Negroes from skilled jobs and unions. Wesley lists 50 such strikes against Negro workers between 1882 and 1900. On more than one ocasion white workers also broke the strikes of Negro workers. . .

By their anti-Black policies, the AFL leaders "drove a wedge between the labor movement and the Negro people." This "tended to force Negro workers. .to the conclusion that if they wanted. .work in industry, their only way to get it was by acting as strikebreakers, as the employers wanted them to do. And in fact, this sometimes happened. . . the matter of Negro strikebreaking, however, has been grossly overstated. The fact is that for every Negro who took a striker's job there were dozens of white strikebreakers."[11]

Thus, the number of Blacks among strikebreakers has been disproportionately small—and, in recent labor history, almost non-existent.

The historical development of the Black role in labor unions is governed, in the final analysis, by the objective community of interests of Black and white workers. Within that overriding community of interests, the Blacks have special interests—the need to overcome age-old discrimination and extra exploitation. To the extent that white workers and their leaders are guided by racism, and do not recognize these special needs, the community of interests of Black and white workers is disrupted.

It is in the self-interest of white workers to recognize that their general needs as workers can only be met with any degree of sufficiency and security to the extent that the special needs of Black workers are met simultaneously. Evidence of this self-interest is provided in Chapter 10.

The U.S. trade union movement has been in a phase of relative decline in influence and in the proportion of all workers who are members. Union membership declined from 35.5% of the total of nonagricultural employees in 1945 to 27.4% in 1970.[12] The 20 million members do not have a single direct representative in the Congress of the

United States, and no trade union leader or member has ever been elected President of the United States. In no other large industrialized country is the influence of the labor union movement so weak.

One of the keys to the revival and strengthening of labor, the majority of the population, to achieving its proper weight in the affairs of the country, is the recognition by its membership, of *the centrality* of the fight for full equality for Black workers within the general objectives of the working class as a whole. It also needs to elect a leadership which will see and act on this central struggle in a similar manner.

13. Government Influences

The federal government is controlled, in all of its three fundamental branches, by representatives of capital, and very big capital at that. Considering all the publicity of recent years about campaign contributions, it is scarcely necessary to argue the point that in most cases, ownership of millions of dollars, or favorable access to those who own millions, is a precondition for election to Congress; that the minimum fee, so to speak, goes up to the tens of millions for the U.S. Senate, and to the hundreds of millions for the presidency. More, one cannot solve this problem merely by having access to some off-beat multi-millionaire—and such do exist. Considering the intricate relationship of party machines, conventions, electoral campaigns, publicity media, it is necessary to have the approval and support of a sizeable section of the controlling interests of major corporations. The presidency, in fact, invariably involves the direct participation of corporations—(and often illegally)—or by proxy through executives, with assets running into the hundreds of billions of dollars.

It is also clear that those who pay the election bills expect a return on investment in the form of favorable government regulations, contracts,

215

appointments,etc.—and a rate of return inconceivable in private business, which might be justified in business terms by reference to the risk involved of losing the entire investment.

Thus, the executive and legislative branches of the government, through the terms of their election, and the judicial branch, through appointment, are closely linked with and have incurred obligations to the dominant corporations of the country. This determines the main course of policy with respect to all issues

In the most fundamental sense, the regime of racism and discrimination could not be maintained except through enforcement by the government. This concept may be difficult to grasp in view of the common picture of the government as at least a potential force against discrimination. But it becomes clear if we examine the matter historically. The system of slavery was maintained only through the crudest application of the military and police power of government, at state and national levels, with support by all three branches of government. Following the Civil War and a brief period of indecision, the power of the federal government came down hard in support of the former slave owners against the Black population of the South.

A whole network of state and local law was created to deepen and enforce discrimination against Blacks in all areas of life. A number of federal laws were in the same direction. Moreover, throughout the country, regardless of law, the whole weight of government was directed towards "keeping the Negro in his place".

If it is true that the government, dominated by capitalists, operates *above all* to maintain and increase the exploitation of labor by capital, and to enforce the corresponding social system—and this is true, and capitalist domination could not continue without it; if it is true that the government, despite the anti-trust laws, has operated to promote and subsidize monopolies in a thousand different ways at the expense of weaker business and farmers—and this is true; then it is equally true that the government, despite constitutional guarantees and laws to the contrary, is the essential protector and enforcer of the entire system of discrimination and superexploitation of Blacks in the United States. This fundamental role of the government of monopoly capitalism *is moderated by the course of political struggle,* in relation to economic discrimination as with other specific issues.

Private business profits from discrimination against Blacks, and manipulates it to aggravate divisions among working people. The top

people in government often come from a milieu of the wealthy aristocracy, with an ideology of extreme racism, living in exclusive estate
areas, belonging to private clubs which exclude Black people, and
reflecting the ideology of caste and race superiority.

Government departments, often administered by big business executives *temporarily* on the government payroll, strive to duplicate the
labor relations of private industry. There is an expressed attempt to
avoid overpaying any group of workers, so as to avoid increasing the
bargaining power of workers in private industry. There is a similar
tendency to duplicate the channeling of groups of workers—white and
Black, male and female, into occupational slots found most profitable
by private industry. And, in the increasingly pervasive and intricate web
of governmental regulations of private business, there is the tendency to
support the segregationist, discriminatory practices of private employers, mortgage bankers, and local school authorities. And this includes, where necessary, the use of the police powers of the government
to repress mass actions of Black people which threaten a stable status
quo.

However, the above case must not be over-simplified. The government executives and legislators *are also subject to the pressures of a
democratic legal structure,* limited and hemmed in as the democratic
rights of the public may be. Those running for office strive to straddle
between the private commitments to their wealthy backers, on the one
hand, and the need to make public commitments to the voters for
reforms and improvements which may interfere with the profits of the
wealthy backers. The same conflicts have their impact on those in
office, who wish to stay there or move on to higher positions.

Here the climate of public opinion among the white poulation is
especially important. The basic capitalist strategy is to maintain racist
prejudices among the white population. Since crude racism can no
longer be preached with political success, the propaganda of racism
takes disguised forms, although the disguise may be rather flimsy.
Thus, the campaigner for segregated schools is "against forced busing;" the campaigner for repression of the ghetto community is
"against crime in the streets;" and the campaigner for discrimination in
employment is against "reverse discrimination through employment
quotas."

However, the practical reduction of segregation in important aspects
of life, the increased political and social activity of the Black people,

the sweep of world events, have created a broad trend towards the reduction of racism among the white working population, towards support for measures in the direction of equality. Office seekers and office holders must take this into account, as they must take into account a growing body of law upholding the principles of equality and integration.

The international collaboration of government and business is increasingly important to the most powerful multinational industrial and financial corporations. Their rapidly rising profits from overseas investments are contingent on the political status of the United States in the countries where they operate, on the ability of the U.S. armed forces to have bases and maintain alliances and provide military "aid" to reactionary ruling groups, on the maintenance of a capitalist social system in these countries. In this global striving, U.S. capital is up against the class conscious working class movement of many capitalist countries, the national liberation movement in the Third World, and the ideological influence of the socialist system and its practice. Domestic racism is an increasingly serious handicap to U.S. big business in the propaganda war with Communist and other anti-imperialist movements. Hence it becomes desirable to make certain concessions to the demands of Blacks and other oppressed peoples at home. These are then widely publicized, even if they are more cosmetic than substantive, even if there is no intention to significantly implement the announced reforms.

The most direct and powerful influence has been the outstanding increase in the scope, mass participation, and effectiveness of the Black people's struggles for equality. Features of this have been the mounting of mass civil rights struggles in the South and of less structured mass actions in Northern cities; the developing electoral organization and successes of the Black people and their white supporters as measured by the rapidly increasing number of Black elected officials at all levels; the growing numbers, militancy, and organizational activity of Black industrial and service workers; the increasing impact of Black legal service and propaganda agencies.

Aside from political influences, government executives are not subject to the pressure to report a maximum profit from the operations under their jurisdiction. They do not feel the need to maintain, to the same extent as in private industry, historical employment patterns which meant higher profits from the employment of Blacks, women, and others in segregated, lower paying jobs. The corporate executive moving to a corresponding government slot retains his racist prejudices, but he will be less adamant in indulging it, because of the lack of profit pressure as well as the counteracting political pressures which are felt throughout the government apparatus, appointed as well as elective. In addition, prominent positions in the government are occupied by professional people, who are somewhat less restricted in their freedom of action in a governmental environment than they would be in a corporate post.

Under the combined weight of these pressures, the general tendency over the past several decades has been for the federal government to "tilt" in the direction of concessions to the Black people. The positive balance remains small in relation to the scope of the problem. The tri-centered legislative, executive, and judicial system of "checks and balances" is used all too often *to delay and obstruct* any gain, to "check" and "balance" down to zero a gain won through one branch of government by the opposite action of another. Similar sabotage is achieved by passing the buck between federal, state, and municipal levels. There are constant attempts by the most racist and reactionary circles to halt and reverse whatever progress is being made towards equalization, and at times these attempts are successful.

Thus, the government is a major arena of the struggle for equality, and one of increasing importance as the power and scope of government intervention in the economy expands. To the extent that political forces in the country exert pressure against discrimination, for equality, the more possibilities arise for winning government concessions, and limited governmental assistance in reducing discrimination, the less easy it will be for the government to act as a buttress of racism.

Federal Activities Concerning Equal Employment

Governmental intervention on behalf of fair employment for Black people dates back to 1941, when President Roosevelt created by executive order a Fair Employment Practices Committee (FEPC). Limited in scope, and under fierce attack by southern racists, it accomplished little. Gains in Black employment during World War II were realized through the struggles of masses of workers under progressive leadership, but the existence of an FEPC and the moral authority of the principle on which it was based assisted these struggles.

Later presidents set up various agencies required to police companies holding federal contracts for non-discriminatory employment practices.

Most northern states and some cities set up fair employment practices or human rights commissions. However, these have mainly been concerned with arbitrating individual complaints, and have had little impact on the overall situation.

The first major congressional action on behalf of equal employment was the inclusion of Title VII in the Civil Rights Act of 1964. This went beyond the scope of earlier executive actions, by covering most employers with more than 100 workers, and not only government contractors. It made it an unlawful practice to discriminate in hiring, discharging, classifying, or otherwise dealing with workers on account of race, color, religion, sex or national origin. Similar strictures were placed on employment agencies, labor unions, and governmental employers. An Equal Employment Opportunity Commission (EEOC) was established, with powers to investigate complaints of discrimination, and, either in response to complaints or on its own initiative, seek to persuade the offending employer to mend his ways.

Obviously, this was *a toothless power*. However, the attorney general was given power to launch civil actions, and obtain injunctions, restraining orders, or other relief. By coordinating actions of the Equal Employment Opportunity Commision and the Justice Department, the administration under this act, should have gone to court to enforce compliance. *In fact, however, this was not done*. For eight years, under Democratic and Republican presidents, very little was done under Title VII.

Lack of action by the federal government, in the past, has been rationalized on the basis of a narrow definition of its responsibility to see to it that the employer does not engage in a clearly provable act of discrimination on account of race—such as advertising "whites only" or channeling all Blacks without exception into particular jobs, and excluding them totally from others.

So long as this approach remained dominant, "affirmative action programs" negotiated by government agencies with particular employers or unions setting goals for hiring or promotion of Blacks were weakly formulated, never seriously followed up or enforced, and sometimes cancelled by "higher authority." Thus President Nixon insisted on the abrogation of such an agreement with the Grumman Aircraft Corporation, a prime military contractor.

But the limited phrasing of authorizing legislation, or of executive orders, was never more than an excuse. The government *always* had ample power to enforce equal employment, if the men running it had the will and desire to do so. There have been innumerable cases of swift and decisive government action on the basis of much more tenuous, or without any, legal foundation, when the top officials and the social forces they represented wanted to take action. Undeclared wars, government strikebreaking and crushing of demonstrations, including those of Black people, are cases in point.

Moreover, the power to cancel government contracts on account of discrimination goes back decades. If utilized, this alone would cover virtually all major corporations, as almost all of them have some federal contracts. However, in order to make enforcement administratively difficult, responsibility has been divided among a dozen government agencies. And every administration has made certain that these agencies would understand that no significant contracts, especially military contracts, would be cancelled or withheld from signature because of discrimination in employment.

There has never been a single important contract cancelled. Military contractors, knowing they have nothing to fear in this respect, have continued to be especially bad in discrimination against Blacks. As of 1968, the aerospace industry had only 1.7% Black representation in white collar jobs, in an industry where the majority of employees are in the white collar categories.[1]

The law was strengthened, and amended into the Equal Employment Opportunity Act of 1972, which removed all doubt of the *power* of the federal government to bring about equality in employment, rapidly and decisively. It added the key provision that the EEOC is now "empowered. . to prevent any person from engaging in any unlawful employment practice", the commission may, after attempts to conciliate fail, go to court in a civil action, and the judge may "order affirmative action. .which may include, but is not limited to, reinstating or hiring of employees, with or without back pay. . ." The power of the Attorney General to initiate suits is maintained, and only the Attorney General may do so in the case the accused is a government agency.

The law has serious weaknesses. It specifically permits discrimination against Communists. While this has not been tested yet, and may be thrown out in court, as similar provisions have been in maritime employment, it remains a "sleeper" which may be used against militant workers, and provides ammunition to right-wing labor officials, in their attempt to retain power in the unions. Considering the history of Communist efforts on behalf of equal employment, this discrimination against them weakens the announced intent of the Act, and of course, it overtly discriminates against Black Communists. It also permits refusal to hire "security risks" in designated places. In the establishment view, Blacks are more apt to be regarded as "security risks" than whites.

Educational institutions are excluded from the provisions of the act, as are policy-making or elected government employees.

Another provision bars requiring an employer to grant preferential treatment to minorities to correct existing imbalances. If literally followed, this would cancel out the "affirmative action" provision of the Act.

Finally, there are no criminal penalties against those who discriminate.[2]

Despite these weaknesses, the 1972 act has taken away any shred of excuse that there are no enforcement powers.

Moreover, recent court rulings have provided a firmer basis for positive action programs, and most recent decisions and consent decrees have included specific hiring requirements. This is the key advance, in principle. A mere requirement to stop discriminating is subject to continual argument as to whether or not the offending party is still guilty. But a requirement to hire a specified number of Black people in specified jobs within a specified time period *is unequivocal*.

Moreover, Congress has gradually increased appropriations for enforcement of civil rights laws. By now there are more than a score of federal agencies and sections of agencies having specific responsibility in the civil rights field, and most of these with respect to employment. The federal budget provides for an increase in spending for civil rights enforcement from $313 million in fiscal 1973 to $604 million in fiscal 1975, of which $250 million relates to employment, and a slightly larger amount to education.[3]

Certainly, in any proper scaling of values within the overall $300 billion federal budget, a spending of more than two tenths of one percent of that for solving the worst domestic evil—racist discrimination—would be in order. But money can not now be regarded as a decisive obstacle to rapid progress. The difficulties, and they are serious, are political.

The agency with primary responsibility for fair employment action is the EEOC. Even at best, it has shown the typical weaknesses of a capitalist government bureaucracy supposed to be of service to working people. Cases have taken years to be handled, and the overwhelming majority have led to no action.

In the fiscal year 1972, 51,969 new charges were received or set for action after additional information was obtained. Of these, 28,337 were recommended for investigation. On all of the tens of thousands of charges handled, successful settlements were negotiated or won in only 726 cases. In 3,068 cases, there were "unsuccessful settlements," meaning, presumably, that there was agreement to let an employer get away with his discriminatory practices.[4]

But meanwhile, a number of private court cases were finally won, requiring employers to pay millions in back pay and to hire or promote thousands of Black workers. The NAACP was prominent in a number of these, and other organizations were active in the field. Some suits were simply carried out by private individuals.

These private actions began to build up a record; they "built a fire," so to speak, under the stagnant government bureaucracy and, combined with the 1972 act, stimulated increased activity.

The Record Through 1972

Regardless of the legal basis, the actual record of the federal government with respect to discrimination in employment has been among the weakest in the whole area of civil rights, and the overall record has been hardly any better. The U.S. Commission on Civil Rights is part of the Washington bureaucracy without any operative function, responsible for reporting on progress or regress in the area of civil rights. Its January 1973 report came to a devastating conclusion:

"Our findings are dismayingly similar to those in our earlier reports. The basic finding of our initial report, issued in October 1970, was that executive branch enforcement of civil rights mandates was so inadequate as to render the laws practically meaningless . . .

"This deplorable situation did not develop accidentally. . . . The enforcement failure was the result, to a large extent, of placing the responsibility . . . upon a massive federal bureaucracy which for years had been an integral part of a discriminatory system. Not only did the bureaucrats resist civil rights goals; they often viewed any meaningful effort to pursue them to be against their particular program's self-interest . . .

"In this, our most recent assessment, we have found that the inertia of agencies in the area of civil rights has persisted. In no agency did we find enforcement being accorded the priority and high-level commitment that is essential if civil rights programs are to become fully effective."

The commission expressed confidence that this situation could be changed, but only "if our presidents and their agency heads and sub-cabinet level appointees had persisted in making clear that the civil rights laws were to be strictly enforced, and had disciplined those who did not follow directives and praised those who did . . ."[4a] However, in practice, all presidents since passage of the Civil Rights Act of 1964 have operated to severely limit enforcement.

This critique stresses what the government failed to do to reduce discrimination. The other side of the coin is what the government did to encourage discrimination, and even to reward it.

Here we refer not just to the general operation of the police, the courts, the bureaucracies at all levels, but to specific measures which in effect *subsidize* racist discrimination on a vast scale.

Herbert Hill of the NAACP charges that the "United States govermement directly subsidizes racial discrimination in many areas of American life—especially in employment," and that such "duplicity" reached an all-time high during the Nixon administration. One should add state and local governments to the list of subsidizers of racism. The most glaring examples include:

● In education, the school taxing and districting system grossly favors the nearly all-white suburban districts over the largely Black inner city districts.

● In housing, the federal government provides tens of billions annually in loans and guarantees for private housing which segregates and largely excludes Blacks from occupancy.

● "The State Extension Service of the Department of Agriculture provides vital services to farmers across the country. The department has never terminated any funds for this program, although it is well known that the program in southern states, and elsewhere, is operated in flagrant violation of Title VII of the Civil Rights Act."

But one can go further than this: the multibillion dollar programs of the Agriculture Department have essentially financed the mass expulsion of Blacks from southern agriculture.

However, it is through government contracts that Washington most clearly subsidizes racial discrimination, and this is in the area of employment. It is useful to quote Hill at length on this:

During the last fiscal year, the federal government spent more than $100 billion through contracts awarded to private corporations for a vast variety of goods and services. It has been estimated that approximately 40 percent of the total civilian work force of the nation is employed by companies that operate with federal government contracts. These corporations are usually the huge multi-plant employers that establish racial patterns for entire industries.

The Fifth and Fourteenth Amendments to the Constitution prohibit the use of public funds to discriminate against a class of citizens and since President Franklin D. Roosevelt issued Executive Order 8802 in the summer of 1941, there has been an anti-discrimination provision in all government contracts. Futhermore, the courts have repeatedly sustained the legal validity of contract compliance efforts. . . . Under the Nixon administration, federal contract compliance has become a shameful travesty.

Here's how it works. As required by law, a federal agency makes a compliance review of a government contractor and finds discriminatory employment practices. In due course formal notification is sent to the company indicating the requirements of the Executive Order and requesting that the company submit an affirmative action program. The company replies by denying that it discriminates, but under protest submits a proposal for an affirmative action program, which is then accepted by the government. A whole year goes by and absolutely nothing changes . . . another review is made, another formal notification is sent, the company responds in exactly the same way and it all goes on and on and on. This is the reality. 4b

And there are many other forms of government subsidy, to government contractors and others—shipbuilding and shipping subsidies, tax subsidies to oil companies, banks, manufacturing companies setting up new plants in particular states, bailouts to armament manufacturers, credit to exporters, etc. etc., and the same characteristic of permitting and objectively encouraging the perpetuation of gross discrimination in employment applies to all of them.

The 1973 Cases–Breakthrough or Flash-in-the-Pan?

Following the 1972 act there was a spurt of major actions launched by the EEOC and the Justice Department, with more far-reaching potential than any previously taken by the federal government. They stimulated action by other federal agencies, by some state bodies, by unions and peoples organizations.

The first big victory was in the case against the American Telephone and Telegraph Company, settled in January 1973, after more than two years of court hearings. Under the consent agreement 13,000 women and 2,000 Black males received a total of $15 million in back pay, as well as raises in future pay. The company agreed to hire specified percentages of minorities and women for the better jobs, and to eliminate segregated women's jobs.

This case showed the fallaciousness of the "lack of powers" excuse. The EEOC had launched it originally in 1970, by intervening to block a rate increase called for by the telephone company.

Following Labor Department actions against Bethlehem Steel, a far-reaching federal court ruling in the summer of 1973 ordered the U.S. Steel Corporation to expand job opportunities for 3,800 Blacks among 13,000 workers at its Fairfield, Alabama plant. This ruling called for ending the discriminatory departmental seniority system which had blocked Black promotion to better jobs. It required equal hiring of Black and white apprentices, Black and white clerical and technical employees, until Blacks held 25% and 20% respectively of all positions in these categories, and the hiring of one out of three Blacks among supervisory personnel until the 20% mark was reached. Implementation was entrusted to a three-man committee consisting of a company and a union representative and a Black worker appointed by the court, and with the overall agreement to be monitored by the Civil Rights Division of the Justice Department.

Soon thereafter the Detroit Edison Company was fined $4 million in punitive damages for discrimination against Black employees, and a local of the Utility Workers of America was fined $250,000. The Judge, a Black man, ordered the company to raise its proportion of Black employees from 8% to 30%—which is more in line with the Black proportion of the population—and set hiring requirements for the better jobs similar to those in the Fairfield case.

The suit, in this case, had been filed by a Black caucus of Edison workers, after the locals of the Utility Workers of America and the International Brotherhood of Electrical Workers had refused to file their grievances. The worker-initiated suit was later joined by the Justice Department and the relief was ordered only after several years of court proceedings.

In September 1973 the EEOC notified four giant corporations, General Motors, Ford, General Electric, and Sears Roebuck, that it was launching investigations of charges of discrimination involving these corporations and unions of their workers.

These are only the most outstanding of numerous actions taken by the EEOC, by the Civil Rights Division of the Justice Department under

Assistant Attorney General Stanley Pottinger, by trade unions and by groups of workers, and civil rights organizations. The initiation of these actions, and the first major victories, have prompted a flood of complaints to the EEOC. The EEOC planned to investigate 33,000 complaints in fiscal year 1975, nearly double the fiscal 1974 rate, and to reach 15,000 settlements, up from 3,500 projected in fiscal 1974. Even the Contract Compliance Division of the Labor Department was stimulated to action, and offered hopes of 500,000 new hires and promotions of minority workers and women on the part of employers holding federal contracts.[5]

The Equal Employment Opportunity Commission issued a 158 page guide to employers on requirements for fair employment. The key paragraph warns:

"If a statistical survey shows that minorities and females are not participating in your work force *at all levels* in reasonable relation to their presence in the population and the labor force, the burden of proof is on you to show that this is not the result of discrimination, however inadvertent."[5a]

This expresses the advanced positive approach to equal employment, that it is not enough to avoid obvious methods of discrimination, it is necessary to achieve the result of eliminating it in practice. Wary of large financial penalties, and loss of goodwill resulting from government and organizational law suits against discrimination, large corporations have set up and given scope to equal employment offices within their bureaucracies, and retained specialized consultant firms. The aim is to satisfy these criteria sufficiently to avoid losses, and it necessarily involves practical concessions.

There is some tendency for preventive actions of this type to be concentrated in the executive-administrative departments of corporate headquarters, and to move to reduce discrimination against women —mainly white women—more than against Blacks. From the viewpoint of corporate advertisers, women are a larger bloc of potential customers who should not be alienated. And it is easier for capitalists to overcome their prejudices against women—which are of a non-hostile, patronizing variety—than their racism, which is hostile and fearful.

Yet, if enforcement is pressed sufficiently by the workers and their organizations, the concessions resulting from these revisions in corporate hiring promotion practices can be substantial.

But there was no guarantee that these dramatic events would initiate a mass breakthrough in Black employment at better jobs, leading to a rapid reduction in the scale and severity of discrimination. Each process, under the existing laws and procedures, takes years. Court orders, in turn, take years to be executed to the full. There is no real enforcement machinery. There are no punitive provisions, involving imprisonment or individual fines of executives and union officials guilty of discrimination.

A decisive political balance in favor of equality is needed to bring these decisions to full fruition, and to generalize them in the economy as a whole. Such a political balance does not exist at present.

Indeed, how could such cases be brought, and carried through to victory, by government officials in the administration of the most racist President (Nixon) in a generation? The positive activity of honest personnel in federal agencies was in direct contradiction to the positions of the president. How was that possible? Mr. Nixon, beleaguered by the threat of impeachment, found his control over the various agencies of government seriously weakened. As one correspondent put it:

> With White House officials busy defending the president and themselves against mounting Watergate and related scandals, lower-echelon officials were left to their own devices, and they thereby gave the Administration a stronger pro-civil rights record than it might have desired.
>
> Lately these lower officials have come down hard on suspected violators of federal antidiscrimination laws, often taking them to court. This is the direct opposite of the White House's softer approach, which has caused black leaders to accuse the Nixon administration of being antiblack.[6]

But soon enough centralized power was reestablished to permit the resumption of a hard racist line by the federal government. President Nixon, who had consistently supported segregation and discrimination, tried to stop enforcement of the 1972 law by firing the most active officials and pressuring others. Earlier the Reverend Theodore M. Hesburgh, president of Notre Dame, had been forced out as chairman of the Commission on Civil Rights after taking a strong position. Late in 1973 William H. Brown 3rd, the EEOC chairman who had converted it into an activist agency, was removed and replaced by John H. Powell, Jr. a man with a reputation of not actively combating discrimination.

Detroit Edison and other companies appealed decisions to higher courts. Corporate, union, and government officials conspired to frustrate the Fairchild decision on the steel industry. This culminated in a court-approved consent agreement covering the United Steelworkers of America and nine major steel companies, in April 1974, under which:

• Some of the Black, Hispanic and women workers discriminated against would be given small payments in compensation.

• Blacks would be permitted to apply for jobs in previously all-white seniority lines without financial loss.

The press headlined the estimated $30 million in back pay that it was claimed would be awarded to 50,000 workers. But this was very deceptive. Even if the payments reach $30 million, that would amount to but 4 days profits before taxes of the nine companies, at the 1974 second quarter rate. But historically, and to this date, superexploitation of Black and other minority workers has accounted for a substantial proportion of the total profits of these steel companies. The amount offered to most workers, a few hundred dollars each, would account for but a small fraction of the thousands each has lost through prolonged discrimination. There is no provision for interest, nor added compensation for depreciation of the dollar, nor for punitive damages against the steel companies for their many years' violation of the law. Payments would be made only to workers hired before 1968, thereby excluding most minority workers. And to get the paltry sums, the workers would have to agree not to sue the companies further. The Justice Department will intervene on the side of the companies and the union leadership against any workers suing for more back pay than offered. The NAACP, lacking the vast resources of the government, has won much larger settlements from the steel companies for individuals and groups of workers, settlements running up into millions of dollars.

The consent decree fails to provide for plant-wide seniority, or for effective notification of Blacks and equality of access to jobs opening up in previously all-white sections. Nor does it specify minimum numbers of Blacks and other minority workers and women to be employed in better jobs, thereby in effect repealing the most vital operative part of the Fairchild decision.

Furthermore, the consent decree was negotiated without the participation or consent of Black workers, and there is no provision for Black or other minority representation on the company-union-government commission set up to oversee the execution of the consent decree.

Accordingly, the NAACP, the National Organization of Women, and the National Steelworkers Rank and File Committee sued to overturn the consent decree, but without immediate success. Hill of the NAACP charged that: "Should this agreement become the pattern for other industry wide agreements, it will have the effect of nullifying, of gutting, Title VII."[7]

The reference is to Title VII of the Civil Rights Act of 1964.

And the Supreme Court, now dominated by right-wing racists appointed by President Nixon, is casting a very long shadow over the economic and employment situation of Blacks. Its racist decision against integrated education is an invitation to employers, landlords, and all who profit from racism to defy civil rights laws, while relying on ultimate vindication at the highest judicial level.

The law suits being waged *against* equal opportunity, such as the De Funis case, and those attacking employment quotas for minorities, aim ultimately to obtain a Supreme Court decision *outlawing* the principle of employer responsibility to provide roughly proportional employment of minorities and women at all levels. And short of the Supreme Court, there are judges at lower levels who will not hesitate to water down and vitiate this principle, as well as the entire thrust of the Equal Employment Opportunity Act of 1972.

A year after announcement of the EEOC investigations of four giant companies, mentioned above, no results had been announced or action taken, Meanwhile, employers were increasing their discrimination against Blacks as part of their response to the economic crisis. In October 1974 General Motors announced indefinite layoffs at four assembly plants. The method was unusual, by eliminating the second shift—40-50% of all the workers—at three of the four assembly plants. But, as a result of past discrimination, the great majority of Black workers were concentrated on the second shift. Few second shift workers had enough seniority to "bump" first shift workers when the layoffs occurred. Thus, in Tarrytown, where a substantial majority of the second shift workers were Black and Puerto Rican, the effect was to decimate overall employment of Black workers, and deal a serious blow to the overall level of Black industrial employment in the area.

Nor was this an unfortunate side-result of the operation of racially neutral economic laws. Second shift workers, mainly under Black leadership, had spearheaded militant struggles for all the Tarrytown workers. In the 1973 negotiations, the company threatened the union with closing down the second shift if the local adopted a militant stance. The local leadership did not press its demands strongly. But the company foresaw a time when the militant spririt of the second shift workers would predominate, and used the economic crisis to try to forestall that contingency.

With a racist administration firmly reestablished in Washington, the civil rights bureacracy sank back into its erstwhile lethargy. The multiplied appropriations did not lead to multiplied action. The increased number of complaints simply meant increased delays. By September 1974 there was a backlog of 100,000 cases before the EEOC, and the average time for processing a complaint had increased to 2½ years. By then: "it is often too late to correct the injustice . . . 45 percent of the persons who had charges pending more than two years wanted their cases closed when contacted."[7a] . These setbacks do not reduce the meaning of the positive actions of 1973-74 to zero.

There were tangible gains, and, even more, the AT&T decision, and others like it, provide a more advanced position from which those struggling for employment activity can now campaign. But the already evident racist counteroffensive makes it clear that this struggle still has a long way to go, and requires a very great broadening of active forces behind it, if the gains made are to be extended and generalized, and a reversal of trend avoided.

Major corporations engage in conspicuous advertising of programs of increasing Black employment, including at higher levels. Partly this is an attempt to ward off legal actions. These advertised programs include a considerable degree of ballyhoo. For example, "women and minorities" are sometimes lumped together in statistics in ways that can conceal a lack of really meaningful action. It is not to be expected that giant corporations will readily give up the advantages accruing to their owners from discriminatory employment practices, unless and until the public pressures of Black and white people are so strong that the losses from defying this public threaten to exceed the gains from discrimination.

And this development of public opinion and public action will finally determine the consistency and effectiveness of federal enforcement of civil rights laws.

An example of the kind of action that can bring about a turn was provided by the 7,000 member Local 1104 of the USWA, at the U.S. Steel plant at Lorain Ohio. Learning that the USWA leadership was conspiring with the company to turn the consent decree around and use it to hamper promotions of all workers, white as well as Black, while freezing Blacks into inferior positions, local officials sponsored resolutions passed by the membership against these devices, and calling for a union-wide membership referendum on plant-wide seniority.[7b]   This is the local of George Edwards, co-chairman of the National Steelworkers Rank and File Committee, and has been influenced by the militant and anti-racist policies of progressive steelworkers.

This action is by workers at the point of production. It involves the unity of white and Black workers, it brings out the interest of white workers in supporting demands for Black equality, and it directly opposes an autocratic union leadership that has collaborated with the employers to an exceptional extent, at the expense of the living standards and working conditions of the entire membership.

Above all, it shows that white and Black unity in the struggle against racism can be established, especially among the industrial workers of the country.

The Government as Employer

Gains in the campaign for equal employment policies have been much more definite within the government bodies than in private industry. Government agencies continue to discriminate seriously against Blacks, especially many state and local governments, and branches of the federal government. But the degree of discrimination is now less, and in some respects dramatically less, than in the case of private employers.

And this is doubly important. It serves as an example and a standard. If government agencies can function with less discrimination against Blacks, so can private companies. More, if Blacks can get better jobs in government, it improves their bargaining power in private industry. With more than one out of five wage and salary jobs in government employment, this is no minor matter.

In 1970 Blacks held 9.6% of all private wage and salary jobs,·as contrasted with 12.7% of all government jobs, including 16.1% of federal jobs, 10.1% of state jobs, and 12.0% of local jobs.[8]

Thus the "penetration rate" of Blacks was somewhat higher in government, especially the federal government, than in private industry. One result, with the growing importance of government employment, was that this provided a degree of freedom for many Blacks from the special insecurity of employment suffered by Blacks in the private economy. By 1970, 28% of all employed Blacks had government jobs, in many cases—far from all—enjoying the stability of employment, leave provisions, pension schemes, etc., that pertain to government employment. True, a disproportionate number of Black government employees are consigned to categories that do not enjoy these advantages, or have merely part-time and temporary employment. But the general gain is real.

Much more important than this is the superior penetration rate of Blacks into the better, higher paying jobs in government. Blacks accounted for 3.6% of private employment as professional and technical workers (including self-employed), and 8.3% of the professional and technical jobs in government. Similarly, Blacks held only 2.2% of the private managerial and administrative jobs, but 5.6% of such jobs in government. Approximately 60% of all Black professional workers were employed by governmental bodies. The contrast between the situation in government and in manufacturing, dominated by large corporations, is even more striking. Blacks held only 2.0% of the professional jobs, and 1.0% of the managerial and administrative jobs in manufacturing.[9]

Amongst all the industries of the country, the highest ratio of median Black male earnings to median earnings of all males was in the street railways and bus lines, where the ratio was 99%. Most subway and bus line workers are employed by municipalities, school districts, public authorities of one kind or another. In public administration generally the ratio was 83%, and in the postal service 93%. In governmental educational services the ratio of Black to total median earnings of males was 75%, while in private educational services it was 68%.[10]

If better than in private industry, the federal record is far from good. And some of the statistics have to be viewed with reserve. Thus of the 8.3% "professional and technical" jobs held by Blacks, almost all are technical, and the supervisory jobs are generally at the lowest foreman or office supervisor level, rather than in so-called "policy-making" positions.

Examining data of the Civil Service Commission, the United States Commission on Civil Rights concluded that "These data show modest improvement in employment practices of federal departments and agencies. Nevertheless the overall picture is still one of pronounced disparate treatment . . . While 28.4% of the Wage System jobs are held by minorities, only 15.2% of the more lucrative General Schedule positions are held by minorities . . . Forty-one percent of the minority General Schedule work force is at grades 1-4 (the lowest—VP), while the percentage of nonminority workers at those levels is almost one-half that percentage (22.2%).

"At the other end of the scale, by contrast, there are continuing signs of significant underutilization of minority potential. Minorities at the highest policy levels (GS-16-18) remain below 3%. Many agencies, including CSC (Civil Service Commission) have no minorities in such positions. None of the regulatory agencies have any minorities among their 418 GS 16-18 positions. Less than 1% of the 982 such positions in the Department of Defense are held by minorities. The Atomic Energy Commission and the National Aeronautics and Space Administration each have one minority person at the GS 16-18 level, out of 640 such positions . . ."[11]

Moreover, it is notable that the agencies mentioned are those staffed at the top most decisively by direct representatives of the companies they regulate, and hence people who will tend most to adapt the racist employment policies of the companies which formerly hired them.

In other agencies, such as the Labor Department and the Census Bureau, there is more of a leavening of academic research personnel, and less operative functioning. It is these less powerful agencies which, by and large, have a less discriminatory hiring policy. The quotation refers to all minorities. Recent figures for Blacks separately are available. About half of all federal civilian workers are those in white collar, mainly civil service jobs, under the so-called General Schedule. As of May 1973 Blacks held 12.2% of these jobs. But they held 21.9% of the lowest level jobs, 16.2% of those in the next lowest group of grades, 6.5% of the moderately high grade jobs, 3.3% of the high grade and 2.5% of the highest grade jobs.

Black workers held 22.1% of the nonsupervisory blue collar wage system jobs. Here again 38.4% of the lowest grade jobs were held by Blacks, 19.5% of the next lowest grade jobs, and only 7.7% of the higher grade and 2.7% of the highest grade jobs.

Blacks held 21.4% of the supervisory jobs including 34.3% of the really low level supervisory jobs, and only 5.9%, 1.4%, and 0.3%, respectively, of the jobs in the high, higher and highest groups of supervisory grades.

The discrimination in the postal field service was also significant, although not so sharp.

The statistics showed a modest improvement in comparison with 1970, but it was evident that genuine equality for Blacks in the Federal service was not in sight.[11a]

The vindictiveness of some top government officials towards those who attempt to enforce the law concerning equal employment within their own agency is indicated by a recent example in the space agency. In 1973 Ruth Bates Harris, the deputy assistant administrator for Equal Opportunity of the National Aeronautics and Space Agency, was dismissed after submitting a report pointing out the failure of the agency to adhere to equal employment standards.

The Harris report charged that "during the first 10 years of NASA's existence, the total attention of the agency was focused on meeting the direct challenge of space flights to the exclusion of such other crucial priorities as providing employment opportunity on a nondiscriminatory basis," and there was little improvement later. NASA's minority employees increased from 4.1% in 1966 only to 5.2% in 1972, and then dropped to 5.1% in 1973. Even more than in other agencies, Blacks were completely excluded from the top jobs. *There has never been a Black astronaut, nor a woman astronaut.*

One can amend the statement in the report, to say that during its entire existence, NASA officials have not been so engrossed in the priority of getting to the moon as to be distracted from their enforcement of rigid racist patterns, and, in fact, even narrower limitation of hiring for key positions to certain narrow ethnic and other types of backgrounds.

When Mrs. Harris and several of her aides prepared the report and called for a meeting with the Administrator, James C. Fletcher, he fired them.[12]

To top off the record of official discrimination, it was revealed that at least 19 Representatives and 1 Senator had specified "whites only" or "no minorities" in submitting job specifications to a government hiring agency.[12a]   Included were a number of legislators who had voted for equal employment legislation.

In some cities, where Blacks have been elected to top offices, the employment situation of Blacks in local government has improved. But in general, racism in employment remains much more brazen among state and local government bodies than in the federal government. There has been little or no change from the traditional crudely racist policies in places where Blacks have not yet organized their forces, and won allies, sufficiently to influence the local political picture.

Particularly disgraceful has been the practice of many school boards, which, when forced to adopt integration procedures, got their revenge by discharging large numbers of Black teachers and administrators who had taught in the segregated Black schools.

The federal government, and private parties, have gone to court to try to remedy some of the most blatant cases of state and local governmental discrimination.

Thus in recent years the Justice Department has filed suits against rampant exclusion of Blacks from fire departments in Boston, Los Angeles, and Montgomery, Alabama. This, in fact, is a special characteristic of fire and police departments throughout the country. The Alabama NAACP filed in Federal Court seeking a criminal contempt order against Governor George C. Wallace, for frustrating attempts of the director of state troopers to comply with a court order requiring the hiring of substantial numbers of Black state troopers.[13]

The Justice Department carried out prolonged negotiations with the city of Jackson, Mississippi, after Attorney General William B. Saxbe charged in a suit that "Jackson's employment policies perpetuate a former job segregation system by which virtually all Blacks are assigned low-paying, laborer jobs."[14]

This led to a sweeping agreement in March 1974. Cash payments of up to $1,000 each will be made to Black employees previously never given the chance at better jobs. The city agreed to hire two Black firemen for every white fireman until 40% of all firemen are Black —instead of 2% as at present. In all other departments, including the Police Department, the city agreed to hire one Black for every white until 40% of those on the payroll are Black. It agreed to eliminate discriminatory employment tests, and to seek out Black job applicants.

If implemented—and it will take at least 5 years for the goals to be approached—this may make the city government of the deep South city of Jackson, with its history of extreme racism, the site of a city employment pattern better than any now in existence in the United States.

This agreement was reached by the Mayor of Jackson and his aides under pressure of a series of anti-discrimination decisions by the Fifth

Circuit of the U.S. Court of Appeals, which moved in the same direction, and made it expedient to avoid a losing law suit. Also, in March 1974, this Circuit Court ordered the State Government of Mississippi to give preferential hiring to Black state troopers until they approach a reasonable proportion of those employed instead of the mere one percent now on the force.

If decisions and agreements like this are enforced and carried out in Mississippi, it will be a big stimulus for a drive for the universal application of similar methods throughout private industry and governmental employment. But the drive has to be made. It cannot be left to the spontaneous goodwill of government officials and corporate employers. Fundamentally, future achievements on the way to Black equality in government needs the mobilized pressure of Black and white working people, including government employees themselves; just as these pressures are needed for progress in the private sector.

A REAL AFFIRMATIVE ACTION LAW

POWER TO NATIONALIZE OFFENDERS

A PEOPLE'S POLITICAL PARTY

14. To Be Equal— a Program to Get There

To be equal—for years this has been a slogan of the Black peoples' movement. Decades of struggle by the politically active section of the Black population has made progress towards that goal. But by any standard of measurement, quantitative and qualitative, the progress has been small.

No matter where one looks, most of the battle, and in some respects nine-tenths or more of the battle, is still to be won. This applies, for example, to housing, to the exercise of power in national politics, to control of police forces. In the most generalized economic indicator, income, as we have seen, less than 10% of the gap has been closed in the last 30 years. Progress in access to better jobs has been only a little better.

Gains in some areas have been partly nullified by losses in others. Gains in kinds of employment open to Blacks have been counteracted by increases in the special burden of unemployment on Blacks. Gains in formal school integration have been largely, and in many areas more than completely cancelled by the setting up of all-white private school systems and by intensified segregated housing patterns.

Gains made earlier are under almost constant attack, and there have been serious losses of ground in various areas. A number of presidents of the United States and top business officials have proclaimed generalized goals of equal rights or equal opportunity, but there remain open or barely covert racists, segregationists, persons who obviously favor discrimination against Blacks, in high responsible positions, including today some of the highest in the land. Moreover, there has never been an official program aiming at full equality, and what is more important, containing the operative means to achieve it.

What is required for such a program? Part must consist of special items oriented to the special requirements of Black people (and other minorities), and part must consist of items directly beneficial to all working people, but especially to Black people.

Priorities and Target Requirements for Blacks

When we speak of programs meeting the special requirements of Black people we mean those which specify priority of benefit to Blacks, with quantitative and time targets for achieving equality in the given sector. Not that these and programs for all the people are mutually exclusive. Usually the special priorities for Blacks (and other minorities) will be parts of program directly beneficial to all working people. But some will not, although it is our contention that all programs moving towards equality are objectively beneficial to all working people.

Experience has proven conclusively that the absence of direct discrimination, and the provision of formal equality of opportunity, is quite insufficient. It is just as inadequate for Blacks, as the Declaration of Independence statement of the equality of all people, and their right to "life, liberty and the pursuit of happiness" is inadequate for the realization of these goals for the population at large.

Generalized strictures against discrimination are of minimal significance. Such measures assume that discrimination and segregation is a deviation from some norm of behavior. On the contrary, it is the norm of behavior of those who control the country's economic life, a norm which, for reasons developed in Chapter 9, they wish to maintain.

We may see the financial motivation by analogy with employers' tax strategy. Scarcely any capitalist pays a penny more than his accountant says he is absolutely required to pay, and the details of the law, and of its execution by officials part of, or beholden to, the capitalist class permit huge and rapidly increasing avoidance of tens of billions of dollars of taxes.

But tens of billions are also involved in the preservation of discrimination in employment, wages, housing, etc. Capitalists are not going to give that up any more willingly than they will pay taxes presently avoided. There has long been a billion dollar business of accountants, lawyers, and tax consultant firms serving capitalists in attempts to reduce their tax payments. Undoubtedly the now burgeoning equal employment consultant firms will strive to similarly serve their clients—that is, by advising them how to minimize the degree of compliance, the degree of reduction in discrimination.

Thus, the ending of discrimination requires concretely defined preferential treatment of Blacks in admission, employment, etc. Minimum numbers and percentages of Blacks and maximum time limits must be specified. Machinery for systematic checkup and penalties must be provided, sufficiently severe to deter non-compliance. Most employers, admission officials, and others are involved in greater or lesser degree in racist attitudes and profiteering from underpaid Black labor. Without the necessary pressures, they will "drag their feet" or clearly sabotage required measures.

The setting of quantitative goals to be achieved, and time limits for their realization, has aroused a furious reaction from the foes of equality. The ideological issues raised are comprised in denunciation of quotas and charges of "reverse discrimination." Numerical quotas for the advancement of Blacks are equated with discriminatory numerical quotas for the limitation of other groups, and the ending of discrimination against Blacks is claimed to automatically involve discrimination against whites in general, or particular ethnic groups among the white population.

American universities historically used quotas to limit the entry of Jewish students, regardless of academic qualifications. Because of the Jewish national tradition of study, and specific factors in their geographical and occupational distribution, the proportion of Jewish youth qualifying for college admission exceeded their proportion in the population. These quotas exercised a real discrimination against Jews, based on anti-Semitism, and comparable to the racism directed against

Blacks—who were actually subject to much more restrictive quotas, far below their proportion in the population or the numbers of academically qualified Blacks. While anti-Jewish quotas are less important than a generation ago, undoubtedly some of them still exist. Under such a system, for example, a Jewish youth to qualify for admission might require a mark of 90 in a college entrance exam, while a non-Jewish youth would require only 80.

But now, let's turn that around. And suppose, as a technique for bringing Black college attendance up to 15% of the total—corresponding to the Black proportion of the population of college age—Blacks are admitted with a mark of 70, whereas whites require a mark of 80. An exact counterpart in industry might be a requirement for Blacks to get a mark of 70 instead of a standard 80 in a plumber's exam.

Let's note that in present practice, priorities for college admission are much more far-reaching, and are granted to particular social classes and racial-ethnic groups. Harvard, one of the most prestigious colleges in the country, formally gives priority of admission to children of alumni, and to certain other specified groups. All private colleges give priority of admission to offsprings of substantial contributors of endowments. A son of an alumnus, or of a donor of $100,000, is almost guaranteed admission, regardless of academic or other past record. And admission to Harvard and other Ivy League colleges is virtually a ticket to employment in the upper corporate or government bureaucracy, in major law firms, and other such juicy slots, for students with the "right" social status.

This is a priority for the capitalist class, and in particular for the upper layers of the capitalist class. It is a priority for the Anglo-Saxon-Germanic origin section of the capitalist class, who historically comprised the overwhelming majority of students and others connected with the Ivy League colleges.

Clearly, by any standard of justice and equality, this kind of favorable discrimination, involving crude nepotism and ethnic/religious exclusiveness, should be abolished. But those groups denouncing priorities and targets for Blacks are silent about it. And it is the opposite in its real content to priorities for Blacks. Similarly, quotas limiting the admission of Jews are opposite to quotas guaranteeing the admission of Blacks.

The limiting quotas aim to and do bring about discrimination. So does the system of favoritism for members of the capitalist class, their relatives, etc. But positive quotas for Blacks aim to and do reduce discrimination, and can finally end it, if sufficiently generalized.

Does a positive quota for Blacks act as a limiting quota for whites? Technically perhaps, but to a trivial extent. Thus, an increase in Black admissions to law school from 5% to 15%—using hypothetical figures—represents an increase of 200%, while the corresponding reduction in admission of whites, from 95% to 85% of the total, represents a decline of only a little more than 10%. However, certainly after a brief interval, whites will suffer no decline in admissions, and total admissions will be increased to adjust for the increased number of Black law students. This is so because currently the Black people as a whole simply lack access to legal services of any quality. The large-scale training of Black lawyers will do much to correct this situation, rather than taking business away from white lawyers. But more fundamentally, the decline in the percentage of admissions accruing to whites will not be in any sense discrimination against whites, but merely the correction of historical discrimination in favor of whites.

The perspective is clearer when we discuss doctors and medical schools, employment of skilled workers and professional and specialized technical personnel in occupations suffering from a shortage of personnel. The preferential training and hiring of Blacks will not slow up the training and hiring of whites at all, but can be a spur to the establishment of sorely needed additional schools and other training facilities.

In a case expected to set a precedent, De Funis, a white applicant for admission to a law school, complained that he was not admitted, while Black applicants with lower marks were admitted under a program designed to ease the shortage of Black attorneys. De Funis did *not* attack the simultaneous admission of a number of whites with lower marks than himself, based on a variety of criteria. The Supreme Court ducked the issue by dismissing the case on a technicality. The propaganda battle continues.

The Chamber of Commerce, the National Association of Manufacturers, the AFL-CIO, and a number of Jewish organizations oppose preferential admissions. The United Automobile Workers, the National Council of Jewish Women, the NAACP Legal and Educational Fund, and Harvard College are among groups which support preferential admission of Blacks. In this as in other issues, the position taken by the ultra-reactionary, dictatorial official leadership of the AFL-CIO cannot be taken as representative of the views of the majority of its member-ship. The UAW position, supported by a number of other unions in and out of the AFL-CIO, has at least as much support from union members.

It is tragic, and in a sense ironic, that Jewish and Italian organizations have been particularly vociferous in supporting the racist position on this issue. Both of these groups, not so long ago, were subject to especially severe social and economic discrimination. Indeed, while some Jewish groups campaigned against Black equality, others fought for equality for Jewish people. Thus, in 1974 the American Jewish Committee extracted an agreement from AT&T to make special efforts to recruit Jews for its management positions, from which they have been largely excluded.[1] As indicated by the position of the National Council of Jewish Women, not all members of these ethnic groups support the racist position. The Jewish people, in particular, have an outstanding record of participation in earlier stages of the modern civil rights struggles, as in the historic Abolitionist movement. It is important that the decent and progressive majority of Jewish and Italian working people—as of other white ethnic groups, organize and raise their voices against the racists who misuse their identities.

In connection with the De Funis case, prominent civil liberties attor-ney, John Abt, eloquently argued the basic issues and added the impor-tant point that preferential training and employment are due Blacks as compensation for the handicap imposed upon them by generations of discrimination:

The briefs of De Funis and his supporters . . . rely on expressions by the Court in desegregation cases to the effect that classifications based on race are "suspect" under the equal protection clause. Of course they are when used, as they have been for three centuries, to oppress racial minorities. But to label measures designed to remedy existing inequalities as "suspect" and strike them down as such is to stand the equal protection clause on its head.

No one would deny, for example, that Hitler's decree requiring certain per-sons to wear yellow armbands was "suspect" because the requirement was confined to Jews. But are German reparations for Hitler's bestiality "suspect" because the beneficiaries are likewise Jewish? The AFL-CIO and the Jewish organizations which support De Funis would be among the first to denounce such an assertion as anti-Semitic.

The position of these organizations is no less racist. How else can their failure. to oppose the preferential treatment accorded the 16 white students who had lower scores than De Funis be explained? Or their support of preference to veterans in advanced education and employment? If the latter are entitled to be compensated for their service to the nation, why are not the victims of racist oppression entitled to compensation for the nation's disservice to them? [1a]

Towards Equal Employment

Under the 1964 Civil Rights Act capitalists could not advertise jobs "for whites only," or anything else that would *openly* and more or less directly discriminate against Blacks. Court cases gradually—and tentatively—widened the bounds of what employers could *not* do. Examinations for positions that covered grounds not needed for the job, and which were worded so as to induce lower marks by most Blacks could be defeated, sometimes. Failing to inform Black workers of promotional opportunities made known to whites could be adjudged discriminatory.

But outside of such cases, employers could use any criteria they wished for hiring, and for assigning newly hired employees to tasks. They were not beholden to show any results in the hiring or placement of Blacks. Essentially, they were no more required to hire workers of another race than to marry partners of another race or choose friends of another race.

Where selection of personnel is on a highly individual basis, as with executives, it is possible to exclude Blacks without openly formulating any criterion. Requirements for professional, technical and skilled labor jobs can be formulated in a seemingly objective way and yet discriminate against Blacks. The simplest case is that of the IQ test, which relies on a body of information without relevance to most jobs, but more generally obtained by whites than by Blacks. The different pattern of information obtained in ghetto communities often includes knowledge and experience especially valuable for many skilled jobs, but not covered in the IQ test. The marking of more specialized examinations, and the personal interviews required for many positions, are liable to be influenced by the subjective bias of the examiner or interviewer.

On a different level, there are no controls formulated over the assignment of one stenographer to a top executive's secretarial post, and another to a typing pool; no controls over a mine boss assigning one worker to a surface job, another to go underground; and an auto plant supervisor assigning one worker to the final assembly line, another to the foundry. Historically, and to this day, these selections are made *against* Black workers in the overwhelming majority of cases. There are no generally applicable specific rules governing the selection of clerical and operative personnel for supervisory positions. Here again, the selections are overwhelmingly against the Blacks.

So long as civil rights laws operated on the principle of limiting the forms of discrimination, they accomplished little toward reducing the actuality of discrimination. Progress was made only where economic pressures on employers—that is, labor shortages—forced it, or where mass struggles or particular legal battles forced concessions.

But the logic of the situation compelled recognition that any real concession must include the positive step of employing Blacks in certain numbers and at certain levels. Thus, voluntary "affirmative action programs" were adopted in a number of cases, with Black employment goals, but without firm legal foundation and without enforcement provisions. These had little or no impact, especially in the building trades, where they were widely applied in response to Black picket lines, demonstrations, and court cases.

At the new stage of struggle, following the 1972 law and 1973 court decisions, these have become much more definite, more far-reaching, and with explicit time goals or their equivalent in requiring given percentages of all hires or promotions to be of Black workers. However, as stressed in Chapter 13, these programs still cover only a small fraction of the labor force, and are very much liable to court or congressional reversal.

What would be required to really approach equality of employment? First, there must be a sufficient basis of organized public support, especially from workers, to convert any law into living reality. But a strengthened law itself is also necessary. It has to be a *compulsory* affirmative action law formulated with sufficient precision to make evasion technically difficult. Contrary to the provision Sec. 703 j of the present law, which forbids preferential treatment to correct existing imbalances, an improved law must *require* preferential treatment in employment for Blacks and other minorities previously discriminated against, in order to correct imbalances.

The law must be enforced by a well-financed, strongly-empowered agency manned by enthusiasts for the program, and backed by millions of working people, who would act as civilian assistants and enforcement monitors.

Where national trade unions or trade union locals have a sufficient level of understanding of the centrality of the struggle against racism, they can win the insertion of such concrete, enforceable affirmative action programs for the hiring and promotion of Blacks into union contracts with employers.

A spreading of such contracts, and especially their adoption by large national unions, can go far to defeat employer and government foot-dragging, sabotage, and attempts to reverse equal employment tendencies.

There could be various exact formulas. The most direct and effective would require in each labor market area the hiring of Blacks in every substantial establishment *at every level of employment*, at least in proportion to their numbers in the population. Time limits would be assigned linked to labor turnover rates, and requisite training periods. For all but the most technically advanced occupations, the time required for training would not exceed a year. Historical turnover rates would be taken into account, so that employment of Blacks would not require the laying off of whites. Employers would bear the responsibility of finding actually or potentially qualified Blacks, and of organizing whatever training might be necessary, paying the trainees regular wages during the training period.

It's also necessary to preserve the employment gains of Black workers once they are hired. While the main emphasis should be on full employment programs, as discussed below, realism requires recognition of the built-in instability of employment under capitalism. Seniority systems, designed to provide a kind of equity in layoffs, work out poorly for Black workers because they were usually the last hired and hence have the lowest seniority. Therefore a significant part of the gains in Black employment in every recovery cycle are wiped out in the next recession. Until real employment equality is achieved, Blacks—and other minorities—should be accorded special seniority rights, involving at least proportional retention of jobs in the event of layoffs.

Lawsuits have won corresponding rulings in some cases. However, it is necessary to have this principle codified on a national level. It is also important for union officials to stop opposing the demands of Blacks, women and other groups of workers who have been discriminated against in this regard. Otherwise, there is the danger that seniority systems, originally established as worker protection against arbitrary discrimination by employers, can be used as instruments of systematic discrimination against Black and other minority workers.

Enforcement powers would have to be more decisive than any now in effect, and not be limited to the fines and action orders now sometimes imposed through judicial procedures.

The enforcement agency should have the power, after suitable warning, to take over, nationalize and operate offending establishments, and to carry out the requirements of the law under conditions of government ownership. Only the threat of such an extreme sanction will provide sufficient inducement to many employers to feel bound to really strive to carry out the provisions of the law.

It is interesting to note that the Communist candidates for President and Vice President in the 1972 elections, Gus Hall and Jarvis Tyner, included such a method of overcoming economic discrimination as a major plank in their program. As "minor party" candidates, their proposal did not become known to the majority of the electorate. This may have been the first time such a specific formula for ending economic discrimination entered into a presidential campaign, even as put forward by a minor party. But the proposal was one whose time had come, and shortly after the November 1972 elections, it came to life in a series of court decisions and out-of-court settlements.

It is true that at the very least, an effective equal employment program will force the employer to change some of his methods of operation, some of the previous characteristics of his labor relations. Undoubtedly, for many occupations from which Blacks have been excluded, or for which very few have received an appropriate educational or training background, the learning period for a new Black employee will tend to be longer than for a new white employee, so that for a period the employer will derive less profits from the new Black worker than he would from a new white worker.

But the whole point is that the principle of equality must take precedence over the convenience and extent of profits of employers. And there must be the degree of compulsion necessary to require employers to accept that inconvenience and interference with maximum profits.

The acceptance of unions and collective bargaining imposed a major inconvenience on accustomed ways of managing things, and did cause the rate of profit to be lower than it would otherwise have been. Employers never accepted this voluntarily. They were forced to by the realized strength of the workers themselves, as buttressed by the legal requirements of the Wagner Act.

The same applies to the achievement of employment equality.

Preferences for Blacks in access to education are also necessary, along comparable lines to those developed above for employment. Indeed, with the increasing educational requirements of work at many levels, this becomes more and more an essential part of a long-range program for equal employment. Equal access to education must include unsegregated education, financial means, assistance to overcome the handicaps of third-rate ghetto miseducation, and other elements outside the scope of this book.

Preferences for Blacks are also needed in income, housing, and other areas. These are discussed in the context of overall programs, beneficial to all working people.

Programs Beneficial to All, and Especially to Blacks

The value of preferential employment and educational programs will be enhanced enormously if accompanied by programs providing for employment, education, and other improvements for all working people.

The latter cannot be a substitute for the former. Building trades union officials, for example, who oppose positive measures to admit Blacks to their own unions, claim that what is needed are vast construction programs, which will make favorable conditions for the hiring of Blacks. But even in conditions of construction booms, they go to great lengths to use overtime and to bring in white workers from other areas, to avoid admission of Blacks to skilled trades.

But the special programs will be greatly handicapped in a period of increasing unemployment and declining overall educational opportunities. The combination of both types of program is the guarantee that whites will gain simultaneously with Blacks, and the basis for overcoming the fears which racists try to instill in whites that equality for Blacks means losses for them. It is the basis for creating the unity of the whole working class and Black people in the political struggle that is necessary to obtain both the preferential measures for Blacks and the measures designed to meet the needs of all working people. These needs relate to employment, income, living conditions and social services.

Full Employment

The object here is to end extra-heavy unemployment among Blacks in part by moving towards ending all unemployment of all workers. The main thing here is that Congress would have to put the *"full"* into what is often inaccurately referred to as the "full" Employment Act of 1946, and provide the necessary means for accomplishing it. A real full employment law would guarantee the right to work to every individual 16 and over wanting and able to work. The guarantee would be implemented by the responsibility of the federal government to organize productive and other useful activities on a sufficient scale to employ all those lacking jobs.

This would call for a number of corollary provisions, of undoubted value in themselves, and at the same time, serving as the objects of labor activity sponsored under this law. For example, a huge network of well-staffed, well-equipped child care facilities would be required to make real the possibility of work to millions and millions of mothers who want to work, but are now barred from it for lack of such facilities. And, special provisions would have to be made for the health needs of those millions with health problems currently barred from employment because employers refuse the necessary adjustments and facilities.

A full employment principle was proclaimed in the Hawkins Bill, which won much support in and out of Congress in 1974-5. Unfortunately the bill did not provide adequate direct implementation, placing reliance mainly on "private enterprise," with the federal government having only a residual responsibility.

A very major and important part of the program would concern employment of youth, and in part, provide services and facilities of particular interest to youth. The problem of unemployment is most serious, and most damaging, among the youth of the country, and especially among the Black youth. An example of what is needed in this area is provided by the *Jobs for Youth Bill* project sponsored by the Young Workers Liberation League.

Obviously, *a larger percentage* of the Black population than of the white population would benefit from a full employment program, but *a larger absolute number* of white people than Black would benefit. And this would be true of most of the proposals discussed in this chapter. However, owing to the special severity of unemployment among Black people, they would be entitled to a significant degree of priority in employment as the new government and government-sponsored jobs were organized. Wartime experience shows that under conditions of an organized national effort the country can move from large-scale unemployment to virtual full employment, at least in major labor market areas, within about two years. Without the mobilization of millions into the armed forces, a somewhat longer period might be required.

Where would the money come from, to pay wages and salaries to those requiring jobs, *and what work would the people do?*

Basically, from two sources.

First, there should be a real shifting of priorities from military uses and various big business subsidies, to meeting the social needs of working people. The 1976 fiscal year budget provides authorizations of more than $100 billion in direct military spending. Additional billions are for such military-related purposes as foreign aid used to prop up allied military dictatorships, the operations of the CIA, the US Information Agency, and other relics of the cold war. Literally tens of billions go for costs of past wars, including the support of veterans, and especially interest on the national debt, almost all of which accumulated in wartime.

A change in financial policies could force down the existing very high rate of interest on the short-term debt, which is the main part of the national debt.

Tens of billions are spent to subsidize the profits of mortgage bankers, real estate developers, shipbuilders, shipping line operators, agribusiness enterprises, roadbuilding contractors, and a host of other outfits in the big business category. Another $50-$100 billion per year could be obtained through closing the notorious loopholes through which the very rich and their corporations avoid paying most of the taxes they would pay if these were collected at the stated rates, with no exceptions or deductions, on all direct and indirect, open and hidden, profits and property income.

Altogether, as much as $200 billion per year could be shifted from the military and the rich to the new priorities of meeting the social needs of the people, providing jobs to the unemployed, while ending many aspects of economic discrimination in the process.

The list is simple, elemental, and in its detail, endless. The main necessities are housing, health care, quality education for all, mass transit, cleaning up the environment, providing industrial safety, recreational facilities for the millions, childrens' camps for the inner city kids, cultural services, restoring and broadening scientific and medical research.

The needs in each of these areas are staggering. Operation under government sponsorship and control will cost much less—often by half—than when done through profit-seeking private companies. Basic costs will consist of wages and salaries. The profit elements —dividends, interest, rents, salaries and swindle sheet expenses of corporate insiders—absorb as much again in private industry and will be essentially eliminated. Thus the employment content per dollar will be substantially increased.

If a program of this type is carried out in a serious, comprehensive fashion, it will soon turn out that the limiting factor is not the list of worthwhile projects, but the manpower to carry them out. While of great value to the entire people, all of these projects are of special value to the Black people, whose needs in all of these areas are more than those of whites. Priority for Black people in these projects will be an important contribution toward real equality.

Equalizing Incomes and Ending Poverty

Various groups have proposed payment of cash reparations to the Black people to compensate for past discrimination. Such payments could be justified, but might turn out to mean no more than the token payments to the Indian people for the lands taken from them. And when we try to estimate a complete payment, "make the victim whole" in legal terms, the required financing becomes fantastically large, both from a practical and a political point of view.

Consider the per capita income differential to the disadvantage of Blacks, somewhat short of $1,600 in 1969 (Chapter 3). By 1975, allowing for the depreciation of the dollar and the widening of the relative differential (Chapter 4) the per capita income differential exceeds $2,000. Suppose each Black is compensated for his lifetime losses due to this differential—without attempting to make up for past generations. The mean or average age of Blacks is about 25 years, so reparations would have to average $50,000 per Black person. Multiplied by the estimated 28 million actual Black people in the country (Chapter 2), brings the payment to an incredible total of $1.4 *trillion*—more than the entire national income.

In any case, the main direction of equalizing incomes is to equalize Black people's current income from work. Part of this is accomplished by equalizing employment at all levels, and the remainder by raising wages of all who are working, and nonlabor income of those unable to work, to levels adequate to meet people's basic needs for health and decent living, under modern conditions.

According to the figures of the Labor Department, updated to allow for increases in living costs to 1975, the cost of the *lower* budget—the verge of poverty budget—for a family of four comes to about $8,500, *after deduction of income and social security taxes.* With a full employment program, and the specified collateral measures to make it really effective, relatively few families would be dependent on aid to dependent children, and other "welfare" benefits. However, for those so dependent, the scale of benefits should be raised to reach this amount, for a family of four, and scaled upward or downward for larger or smaller families. Corresponding minimum levels should be provided by social security pensions.

The 1974 revision of the minimum wage law provided most covered workers with a minimum of $2.00, to go up to $2.30 beginning in 1976. Because of the extremely rapid rise in the cost of living, the new minimums are lower in real terms than the old minimum of $1.60 was when it was enacted in 1966. The new law, like the old one, excluded millions of workers who most need the protection of minimum wage laws, and sets lower standards for other millions. In particular, it discriminates grossly against young workers, giving employers very wide authorizations for cutting their wages below the minimum.

The $2.10 in effect in 1975 under this law comes to $4,200 per year, or roughly half of what is necessary to support a family. Even two workers, each making that amount, with two children to support, are doomed to a life of severe poverty, considering tax deductions and the extra living costs absorbed by a two-worker family.

What is needed *right now* to decisively reduce poverty is to double the minimum wage—to well over $4.00 for all workers, and at least $5.00 in manufacturing, construction, mining, utilities and large-scale industry and government generally.

Five dollars per hour is hardly a luxurious wage. By comparison, in 1974, the value added by manufacturing, per production worker man-hour, was $15. Allowing for a normal spread of wages above the minimum, a $5 minimum in manufacturing, all other things being equal, would not increase the total production worker wage bill to more than 40-45% of value added. In recent decades the share received by industrial workers in the values produced has declined precipitately. In

1947 production worker wages came to 40.7% of value added by manufacture. But by 1972 the ratio had fallen to an all-time low of 29.7% of
value added by manufacture.[2] A minimum wage amounting to one-third
of value added per man-hour, would merely restore the relationship for
all workers to that prevailing a quarter of a century ago, if allowance is
made for the expected rise in value added per man-hour between 1972
and 1975.

Of course, along with the doubling of wages at the bottom there
would inevitably be substantial increases in the middle wage levels, and
moderate increases at the upper wage levels—all long overdue to make
up, at least in part, for the losses workers have sustained in the increasingly runaway inflation and part-time wage freeze of the 1970s.

The BLS intermediate budget for a family of four came to $12,626 in
1972, including $10,372 of items other than direct tax deductions.[3]
Allowance for increased living costs brings this to $15,500 in 1975, and
$12,500 after taxes. A $5 minimum wage will not reach that amount,
but would bring in $10,000 per year, before taxes, well above the BLS
lower level, and above the level of serious deprivation and poverty. A
$5 minimum in industry would be consistent with an average wage of
$7.50 per hour, which would come to $15,000 per year, almost up to
the BLS intermediate budget.

In addition to increases in the minimum wages, tax reform, while
increasing taxes on the wealthy, should reduce those on workers, including the complete elimination of direct taxes on workers' families
with incomes below the BLS intermediate budget level.

*The suggested minimum wages should apply to all workers every-
where, without exception, and regardless of age.*

This income program, along with the full employment program,
would radically reduce the income gap between white and Black people
as a whole, and essentially end it, after a few years, so far as white and
Black workers are concerned.

Housing

Improved access to good housing for Black people is a major element
in the achievement of equality. It has long been recognized that the
private housing and real estate industry will not supply decent housing
for lower income people, or for Black people at practically any income
level. The compounded profit goals of bankers, contractors, developers, insurance companies, and real estate agencies inflate prices and

rents far beyond any reasonable relation to actual costs of production. And the historic profitability of segregation has reinforced the racism of the real estate crowd.

Public housing, on a massive scale, is the only way to eliminate the chronic shortage of housing for the lower income third of the population, and for the majority of the Black population. The opposition to public housing is based on the desire to maintain the superprofitable monopoly system of private housing.

Existing public housing programs—as distinguished from various types of subsidies for private or "non-profit" housing—are trivial in quantity, and set up so as to intensify, rather than end, housing segregation. They are often shoddy in quality, and inadequately maintained, as if to emphasize the lower status of the occupants. They are palliatives within a general social and economic environment geared to inequality in every way.

What is needed is a program tied in with an overall social and economic program of ending inequality and segregation. The scale of the program must be at least a million units per year, a figure often cited by advocates of a radical solution to the housing program, and equal to the approximate shortfall of actual housing construction below the target figures which the government says is required.

Public housing under this program would be of good quality, moderate in cost but not skimping on really important matters like durability and those features which provide comfortable living in modern conditions. Rents would be set at not more than 10% of family income. The housing would be located to break up existing patterns of segregation. Through the use of federal power of eminent domain, the vast suburban areas now barred to large-scale public housing would be opened up. Special attention would be given to assisting Black residents to move to places accessible to large industrial units and centers.

Blacks and other minorities would have priority of occupancy, but all projects, whether large apartment dwellings, or garden-type developments, or even separate units, would be rented on an integrated basis. With good quality, good location and low expense, there would be no problem of finding white tenants willing and anxious to move in.

In addition to the major new housing program, much can be accomplished through a supplementary program of rehabilitating existing central city housing. Many of the structures in the "blighted areas" are sound, and architecturally attractive. They can provide the basis for converting these areas into prime residential areas, at much lower cost than new construction.

The federal investment needed for such a program would be approximately $25 billion per year, at present prices. It might well be the largest single element of an overall program of public activities and public enterprises needed to achieve full employment and provide a better life for the working people of the country.

Outlaw Racism

Along with social and economic reforms, it is necessary to make one vital change in the country's legal code. Today various forms of discrimination are illegal, but not felonious. Nobody has ever been imprisoned for discriminating against a Black, for insulting him verbally, for slandering his race; and very few whites have been penalized for assaulting or even murdering Blacks.

Racism, in any form, must be made a crime, for which individuals are punished severely. *In its total impact,* racism is much more serious than such standard crimes as individual murder, robbery, and arson——serious and numerous as these crimes are.

It would be necessary to define evidences of racism. It should include but not be limited to the use of racist epithets, or racial slurs in matter sent through the mails, or physical violence against Blacks and their property by white mobs. Most important of all is economic racism, and our programs for dealing with that have been discussd above.

Racism in housing should be outlawed as a crime. The petty segregationist tricks of real estate and mortgage financing outfits should be swept away, along with the crude spoutings of Ku Klux Klan types. Advocacy of or incitement of segregated schools should also be punishable. The racist evasions of "private clubs" which bar Blacks from restaurants, places of entertainment and sports facilities should also be outlawed. Police forces and courts must be subject to pressures which will put an end to the racial discrimination against Blacks so common in today's law enforcement practices. Police officers who unnecessarily shoot and kill Blacks should be subject to the same penalties as all other murderers.

Medical discrimination against Blacks must be regarded as the most serious of crimes. There are still cases of Blacks dying because they are refused prompt admission to hospitals. A crash priority program of training Black doctors is needed to end this outrageous lack. The geno-cidal practice of forced sterilization of Black women, as well as the application of tranquilizers and other drugs to Black school children, must be stopped and treated as a crime. The list could go on and on, in a society where racism permeates every activity.

It is said that you can't legislate human nature, or compel people to shed their prejudices. It is said that in this racist society no white person is wholly free of racist prejudices. *But you can compel rational people to restrain and contain their racism,* just as the great majority of people are compelled by the power of law to restrain impulses to steal, to assault hostile people, and commit other acts which are legally criminal. It can just as well be said that no person in this society is wholly free of criminal ideas in some form or other, in some degree of intensity. But the great majority have the common sense to repress such tendencies, and they tend to become vestigial aspects of consciousness. Similarly, a legal prohibition against racist actions and expressions will inhibit and repress racist ideology, and help lead to its gradual decline and ultimate disappearance.

Of course, along with an appropriate criminal statute, there must be an official propaganda campaign against racism. And not the mere stamping of occasional slogans, e.g., "An equal opportunity emp-loyer," but everything from revamped school textbooks which actively combat racism and disseminate the culture of the Black people to public interest television programs directed at educating the population, espe-cially the white people.

Political Requirements

To write all the above *and leave it at that* is an exercise in futility, in modern Utopias. In real life things aren't done simply because they are good and just. In a world of conflicting social classes, of exploitation and racism, things that are good and just are done only when those who will benefit from them organize sufficient political power to win them.

Certainly, one cannot rely on a benevolent Congress and administra-tion to confer them on the public on the basis of their merit. There has not been a single government—federal, state, or municipal—that has vigorously and consistently fought against discrimination, enforced anti-discrimination legislation, and striven actively for equality. Even Black mayors have had limited accomplishment, owing, if nothing else, to the limitations of their power within city administrations, and the general limitations of city governmental power within the U.S. political and social system.

Few gains have been consolidated and finalized. The counterattacks of racist reaction are never ceasing. There are continuous attempts —conscious, organized attempts—to resegregate schools, to increase housing segregation, to displace Blacks from jobs and political office, to undermine protective legislation, and even to negate the hard-won right to vote by gerrymandering and other devices.

A prime example was the Nixon administration, which attempted on many fronts to nullify civil rights legislation, and to use the weight of Federal authority and funds to try to block active local programs moving towards economic and social equality. Similar policies were followed by racist city administrations such as that of Mayor Rizzo of Philadelphia, Mayor Yorty of Los Angeles, and the Boston School Board under the influence of Mrs. Louise Hicks. The Governor of Michigan and most of its other leading politicians collaborated with the overt racists in opposing the area-wide integration of Detroit metropolitan area schools, and thereby created the political climate in which the sinister segregationist decision of the Supreme Court could take place. Local racist groups engaging in violent disruptions to prevent access of Blacks to decent schools and housing have gone unpunished in Newark, Brooklyn, Queens, and many other places, and often have won complete or almost complete victories for their segregationist objectives.

From this it follows that *a prime requirement for rapid progress to equality is a change in the political balance in the country*. This can take various forms. But the central requirement is for masses of the white population to join with the Black people in the struggle for equality, and against racism in all its forms.

There are millions of white people who are ready to participate, at some level of activity, in such struggles. But there is the need for an organized base. The most important potential base already in existence is the trade unions. With their formal stand for unity of all workers, with the existence within them of a significant, and potentially very powerful grouping dedicated to that goal, the possibilities here are real. (Chapter 12)

Today there is lacking a really large, broad-based political party dedicated to the struggle against racism, and for equality. Such an instrument is necessary.

Black legislators have formed a Black caucus which exerts pressure on Congress and on the administration in Washington. Two broadly based Black political conventions have been held. So far Black political action has been structured mainly within the Democratic Party. However, that party remains firmly controlled by big business interests, including powerful racist elements. Attempts to "capture" it or decisively change its character by Blacks are likely to have little more success than similar attempts by the more politically active trade union groups.

Nor is a separate Black political party likely to wield enough power—in terms of being able to win elections in the absence of proportional representation systems—to bring about radical gains.

What is necessary is a new party outside of the framework of big business control—one which expresses in political terms the common interests of labor, Black people, and other groups in the community that are exploited, oppressed, or threatened by the increasing monopoly domination of the economy and of the country's political life.

While workers would be the largest group, numerically in such a party, and trade unionists would figure prominently in leadership, this would be somewhat broader in concept and in practice than the British Labor Party or its counterpart in other European countries. In the particular conditions of the United States, Black leadership and membership would have to play a major part, and the special needs of Black people would have to be extremely important in the program of such a party. The same, of course, would apply to other oppressed minorities.

A leading Black daily, *the Chicago Defender,* editorialized:

The prospects for a divorcement from the two major political parties seem brighter today than ever before. In the long history of the struggle to forge a Third National Party, the time has never been more propitious than now.

After discussing specific causes for mass disillusionment with the Republican and Democratic Parties, the editorial continues:

But a more important element in the flight from the two-party system is the growing realization that neither the Republicans nor the Democrats are able or willing to meet fully the people's needs.

The growth of independence in political action is a measure of the awakening of the people's political consciousness. The labor movement can be a powerful force in accelerating the growth of this trend. . . . A coalition of labor and black political leaders could hasten the onset of a Third Party as a major factor in the stream of action.[4]

It is noteworthy that this journal steered clear of a Black nationalist approach, and saw the critical need for a labor-Black coalition as the basis for a third party.

Electoral and legislative activity, the standard arenas of political party operations in the United States, would not be sufficient. Experience shows that at least as important is continuing activity of masses of people in all of the forms which have been developed in the course of generations of people's struggles—demonstrations, marches, strikes, sit-ins, boycotts, and whatever new forms or variations will develop in the course of struggle.

To have sufficient power, the activity must combine the primary interests of all of the groups involved—hence it must fight against racism, against war, against poverty, against pollution, and for a better life, for peace and for equality.

Socialism and Equality

National and racial equality is not a pipe dream. It has been achieved in all its essentials in the Soviet Union, where the construction of a socialist society has been completed, with the establishment of national equality one of its primary goals. The Soviet Atlas shows 87 distinct nationalities. Many of these are various peoples of Asia. Others, while white, speak non-Slavic languages, and in that sense, occupy a position in relation to the Russians similar to that of Spanish speaking people in the United States.

The essential social and economic equality of the Soviet people is visible to all who visit the various union Republics. It is also evident from statistics of retail sales, union republican budgets, and other economic indicators. The tragic lack of Black doctors in the United States contrasts with the situation in Soviet Central Asia. In Uzbekistan, the most populous of the Central Asian republics, there were in 1970 20.1 physicians per 10,000 population, as compared with 15 per 10,000 in England, 19.2 in the United States, and 14.5 in Japan.[5]

Table 29 shows the number of students of various Soviet nationalities enrolled in institutions of higher education, per 10,000 of the population.

TABLE 29

Students in Institutions of Higher Education, USSR
1970/71, by Nationality

	STUDENTS PER 10,000 OF POPULATION
Slavic Nationalities	
Russians	212
Ukrainians	152
Byelorussians	144
Trans-Caucasian Nationalities	
Georgians	271
Azerbaijanians	229
Armenians	196
Central Asian Nationalities	
Uzbeks	164
Kazakhs	189
Tadzhiks	132
Kirghiz	182
Turkmen	144
Siberian Nationalities	
Buryats	356
Yakuts	216
Kalmyks	219

SOURCE: Central Statistical Board of the USSR: Peoples Economy of the USSR, 1922-1972, Statistical Annual Moscow, 1972, (in Russian), pages 32-34, 446.

There are differences, some of which may be due to traditional cultural differences, others to differences in the age composition of the various national populations, others to the choice of nationality designation of the many Soviet citizens of mixed nationality. But the feature that stands out is the absence of special favoritism for the Slavic peoples, or of discrimination against those of non-Slavic and other nationalities. Sixty years ago the peoples of Central Asia were living under almost feudal khanates, or a nomadic existence, within the old Czarist Empire. The Siberian nationalities were hunters, with a past civilization comparable to that of the Indian and Eskimo peoples of North America, and in many cases closely related to these peoples.

Notice that the Buryats, Yakuts and Kalmyks have higher than average ratios of students in universities. This is because the Siberian peoples, by and large, had much more to learn, much more of a burden of illiteracy and poverty and oppression to overcome than other nationalities, so that the Soviet government provided special advantages to these peoples to enable them to obtain their own numerous corps of specialists, while raising the overall cultural and economic level of all of the people of these nationalities. Needless to say, the North American Indians and Eskimos have no such advantages, and are most discriminated against in education.

It is this effective national and racial equality which has made the Soviet system so attractive to the peoples of Asia and Africa, so that today the majority of governments of these continents proclaim socialist goals, even though their leaders have extremely varied concepts of what socialism means and how to get there.

Socialism, by eliminating the possibility of private profit from the labor of others, eliminates the material basis of racism. It doesn't eliminate national differences nor does it eliminate national economic differentials overnight. Nor does it automatically eliminate national and racial prejudices among people. However, the basis exists for the rapid reduction of prejudices, assisted by the whole weight of official propaganda, literature, and the practical integration of peoples. National economic differentials are speedily eliminated because a central plan for the entire country can provide for the development of natural resources and industry at a faster pace in the less developed area, and ensure a faster rise in the living standards of the peoples who live there, while simultaneously benefitting the entire country.

In the Soviet Union the propaganda of national, racial, or anti-Semitic hatred, as well as actions of this type, are regarded as crimes. Thus, if a person is subjected to a racist insult, he may complain to the nearest militiaman, and the culprit is warned, or arrested, depending on the seriousness of the offense.

Of course, the Soviet Union is not a Utopia either, nor is it free of the influence of hatreds and prejudices brought in from outside by airwaves, tourists, students, and others. But the incidence of these throwbacks to the past are trivial compared to the capitalist countries. If somebody in the USSR draws a cartoon character with a long nose, some Western propaganda organs start a major campaign about "anti-Semitism" in the USSR. But such propaganda is forced to nitpick at dubious or marginal cases, to distract attention from the *massive* and *continuous* expressions of anti-Semitism and racism in the United States and other capitalist countries, as well as the racist actions and anti-

Semitic actions—stoning of synagogues etc., which have no counter-part in the USSR.

But more important than the relative absence of national hostility is the predominance of positive evidences of national and racial friendship and cooperation. On April 25, 1966, an earthquake destroyed 2 million square meters of housing in Tashkent, the capital of Uzbekistan, leaving 78,000 families homeless.

Tens of thousands of people came from all over the Soviet Union, from all of the nationalities, bringing their own building materials, equipment, and living supplies, to help rebuild Tashkent. In one year people of Moscow built 230,000 square meters, the Leningraders 100,000 square meters, the Ukrainians 160,000, the Lithuanians, 10,000 etc. Altogether, *in that one year half of the destroyed structures were replaced by people who came from outside of Uzbekistan to help.* By 1971, with the aid of Soviet people of other nationalities, and their own efforts, the people of Tashkent had 1.5 million square meters *more housing* than before the earthquake.[6]

But here in the United States the people have not yet developed the spirit of cooperation, or the social instruments for cooperation, needed for the many times cheaper, and technically easier, job of replacing ghetto housing demolished by Urban Rehabilitation projects, superhighways, and the like.

The economic development of regions in which the oppressed nationalities were concentrated has been truly phenomenal. And liter-ally millions of Russians, Ukrainians, and peoples of other nationalities participated in building the basic industries, the dams for irrigation and hydropower projects, in establishing the institutions of higher education and scientific research institutes, which were *so essential for the achievement of practical equality* of the peoples of these regions.

The social integration of the peoples of the Soviet Union is rapidly increasing, as the relative geographic separation of the nationalities diminishes.

Certainly the establishment of a socialist-oriented society in the United States will be a decisive step in the complete and final elimina-tion of racial inequalities and prejudices in our country.

But the campaign for such elimination is for the *here and now*, in a distinctly capitalist United States, and must be conducted jointly by those who favor continuation of the capitalist social structure and those who see socailism as organically connected with the achievement of the basic equalities of peoples. The important thing is not to permit ideological differences to be used to practically divide the activities of those tens of millions who must strive together to make equality a reality in the United States.

Convention for Reference and Notes and Sources

There are numerous references to the 1970 Census of Population and to the Current Population Reports of the Census Bureau. A short form of notation is used for these.

1970 Population Census volumes are designated according to the preliminary paperbound volumes, e.g. General Social and Economic Characteristics United States Summary PC (1)-C Table 88, is designated as follows: U.S.-C-88.

References to the 1960 Population Census are designated similarly, with the addition of: 1960.

Special subject reports of the 1970 Census of Population are designated by their coding, e.g. the subject report, Persons of Spanish Surname, is designated: PC (2)-1D.

Current Population Reports are designated by series and number, and table number, e.g. The Social and Economic Status of the Black Population of the United States, 1972, Series P-23, No. 46, Special Studies, Table 17, is designated: P-23, No. 46, T. 17.

Reference Notes

Chapter 1.

1. Tilford Gaines, Social Priorities and the Economy, in *Economic Report*, February 1973, of Manufacturers Hanover Trust Co., N.Y.
2. Theodore M. Hesburgh, in *New York Times*, March 17, 1973.
3. *New York Times*, July 26, 1974.
4. Ibid.

Chapter 2.

1. V. Perlo, *Undercounting Black People in the Census*, in *Political Affairs*, April, 1972.
2. U.S.-C-136; P-20, No. 264, T.L.
3. National Urban League, *Estimating the 1970 Census Undercount for State and Local Areas*, July 1973, T. 7.
4. *New York Times*, Dec. 8, 1973.
5. U.S.-B-48.
6. PC(2)-1D. T.1; PC(2)-1E, T. 1.
7. P-25, No. 511, T. 1.
8. *New York Times*.
9. *Special Analyses Budget of the United States Government*, Fiscal Year 1975, pp. 154-155.
10. *New York Times*, Mar. 16, 1974.
11. *Ibid.*, Aug. 1, 1973
12. *Ibid.*, Mar. 25, 1974
13. Anne Braden in *Southern Patriot*, Sept. 1973.
14. Herbert Aptheker, *Sterilization, Experimentation and Imperialism*, in Political Affairs, Jan. 1974.
15. U.S.-C-93 (employees of their own corporations excluded from wage and salary workers).
16. U.S.-D-252.
17. U.S.-C-91.
18. U.S.-C-122, 103.
19. U.S.-D-233, 232.
20. U.S.-C-90.
21. U.S.-C-81.
22. U.S. Dept. of Labor, *Employment and Earnings*, Jan. 1974, p. 153.
23. U.S.-B-48.
24. Statistical Abstract of the U.S., 1973, T. 17, p. 17.

Chapter 3.

    1. U.S. Commerce Dept. Release CB 73-197, Jul. 23, 1973.

    2. P-23, No. 46, T. 13, 14.

    3. P-60, No. 90, T.K.

    4. U.S.-C-94.

       4a. Henry J. Aaron; *Shelter and Subsidies,* Brookings Inst., Washington, 1972, pp.32-34, 55, 74ff, 123.

       4b. Allan R. Talbot in *NY Times,* Aug. 4, 1974, Sec. 8.

       4c. *Wall Street Journal,* April 5, 1974.

    5. C-82.89, 91, 94 for the pertinent states.

    6. S.D.-C-48, 57; PC(2) 1F-9.

    7. N.Y.-C-82, 89, 91, 94, 97, 100.

    8. PC(2)-1F, T. 14.

    9. PC(2)-1G, T. 47, 49.

   10. *Op. Cit.* T. 29.

   11. *Op. Cit.,* T. 7, 22.

   12. U.S.-D-231, 249.

   13. P-60, No. 85, T. 49.

   14. P. 60, No. 90, T. 53.

   15. BLS Special Labor Force Report 163, T. A-2, A-6, A-31.

   16. U.S.-C-90.

   17. U.S. Dept. of Labor, Women's Bureau, *Fact Sheet on the Earnings Gap,* 1970, p. 2.

   18. Barbara Deckard and Howard Sherman, *The Political Economy of Sexism,* unpublished ms.

   19. U.S.-C-95.

   20. *Ibid.*

   21. *Monthly Labor Review,* June 1972.

   22. P. 60, No. 85, T. 19.

   23. BLS, Handbook of Labor Statistics, 1973, T. 137, p. 3 (interpolation by author).

   24. *NY Times,* June 20, 1974; *Daily World,* June 27, 1974.

Chapter 4.

    1. Floyd McKissick, in *New York Amsterdam News,* Sept. 4, 1971.

    2. 1960 U.S.-B-42, 44; 1970 U.S.-B-48. Distribution of rural non-white population between Blacks and other non-whites for 1950 estimated.

    3. BLS. Bulletin No. 1119, T. 23, U.S.-C-94.

    4. U.S.-C-94; PC(2)-1D, T. 12.

Chapter 5.

    1. P-23, No. 42, T. 52.

       1a. Karen De Witt, Black Employment . . . Better but not yet Fair, in *Black Enterprise,* March, 1974.

    2. U.S.-D-223.

       2a. EEOC, *EEOC Report No. 2, Job Patterns for Minorities and Women in Private Industry, 1967* Table 1, p. xxxvii.

       2b. EEOC, *EEO-1 Reports, 1973, Summary for 38,162 Companies, Xerox Sheet.*

    3. U.S.-C-81.

    4. 1960 U.S.-D-209; 1970 U.S.-D-228.

    5. 1960-N.Y.-C, 74, 78; 1960 PC(2) 1D, T. 11; 1970 N.Y.-C-54, 86, 93, 99.

6. U.S. Equal Employment Opportunity Commission *"A Unique Competence": A Study of Employment Opportunity in the Bell System,* in Congressional Record, Feb. 17, 1972, pp. E 1260-E 1261.
7. U.S.-C-81.
8. *N.Y. Times,* Sept. 11, 1973.
   8a. P-23, No. 48, T. 24.
9. *Economic Report of the President,* February 1974, pp. 152-153.
10. P-23, No. 46, T. 40, 41.
11. Employment and Earnings, Jan. 1974, p. 145.
12. *Ekonomicheskaya Gazeta,* Moscow, No. 13, 1973
13. Miss-D-175.
14. N.Y.-D-175.
15. Mich-D-188.
16. *Statistical Abstract of the United States,* 1973, T. 1195, p. 705.
17. *Southern Patriot,* Feb. 1974.
18. P-60, No. 90, T 57.

Chapter 6.

1. *New York Times,* Feb. 16, 1974.
   1a. US BLS Special Labor Force Report 163, *Employment and Unemployment in 1973,* T. A-6.
2. Op. Cit., T. A-3.
3. BLS Report 416, *Unemployment of Black Workers,* p. 2.
4. Leonard Goodwin; *Do the Poor Want to Work,* Brookings Institution, Washington D.C., 1972.
5. U.S.-C-90.
6. BLS Regional Reports No. 22, June 1971, *Working Age Nonparticipants,* T.3.
7. Op. Cit., T. 2.
8. Op. Cit. T. 2, footnote.
9. Op. Cit., p. 2.
10. Op. Cit., pp. 20-21.
11. Op. Cit., pp. 28-29.
12. Op. Cit., pp. 36-37.
13. U.S.-C-78
14. U.S.-C-77.
15. *New York Times,* Oct. 15, 1972.
16. Op. Cit., Jul. 21, 1974.
17. BLS Special Labor Force Report 163, T. A-4
18. U.S.-C-78.
19. Twentieth Century Fund; *Youth Unemployment: Crisis in the Cities,* N.Y., 1971, in Congressional Record, June 18, 1971, p. S 9425.

Chapter 7.

1. William Ryan, *Blaming the Victim,* Pantheon, N.Y. 1971, p. 4.
2. Robert B, Hill, *The Strengths of Black Families,* Emerson Hall Publishers, N.Y. 1971, pp. 38-39.
3. *Economic Report of the President,* 1974, pp. 153-154.
   3a. Ibid. 1975, pp. 112-113.
   3b. Op. Cit.
4. Edward C. Banfield; *The Unheavenly City,* Little Brown, Boston, 1970, p. 73.
5. Op. Cit., pp. 32-33.

6. Op. Cit., pp. 76-77.
7. Op. Cit., pp. 48-54.
8. Op. Cit., p. 266.
9. Op. Cit., p. 69.
10. *Statistical Abstract of the United States,* 1973, T. 17, p. 17.
11. *The Unheavenly City,* p. 68.
12. PC (2)-1D, T. 12.
13. PC (2)-1E, T. 9.
14. *The Unheavenly City,* pp. 68, 69. 71.
15. Mich-D-140.
16. U.S.-D-274.
17. U.S.-D-196.
18. U.S.-C-139, 142; PC(2)-1B, T.9.
19. *The Unheavenly City,* p. 85.
20. Op. Cit., pp. 245-246.

Chapter 8.
1. EEOC, 7th Annual Report, 1972, Appendix A, pp. 51 ff.
   1a. Stanislav Menshikov, *Millionaires and Managers,* Progress Publishers, Moscow, 1969, p. 252.
2. *A Unique Competence,* p. E 1258.
3. Op. Cit., p. E 1260.
4. Op. Cit., p. E 1263.
5. Op. Cit., p. E. 1264.
6. Op. Cit., p. E. 1260.
7. Op. Cit., pp. E. 1260-1261.
8. Op. Cit., p. E. 1259.
9. Op. Cit., pp. E. 1262, 1258.
10. U.S.-D-240.
11. Ibid.
    11a. American Telephone and Telegraph Company, *1973 Annual Report,* p. 9.
    11b. *Wall Street Journal,* Feb. 4, 1975.
12. EEOC, Promise *Performance, A Study of Equal Employment Opportunity in the Nation's Electric and Gas Utilities,* Washington, 1972, p. iii.
13. Op. Cit., p. 5.
14. Op. Cit., T A 1, p. 149.
15. Op. Cit., pp. 24-29.
16. Op. Cit., pp. 15-16.
17. N.Y. Times, Apr. 30, 1973.
18. Ibid.
19. N.Y. Times, Sep. 27, 1973.

Chapter 9.
1. *A Unique Competence,* pp. E-1266-1267.
2. Op. Cit., p. E-1258.
3. Op. Cit., p. E-1258.
4. *Economic Report of the President, 1974,* pp. 151-152.
5. Victor Perlo, *American Imperialism,* International Pubs., N.Y. 1951, pp. 88-89.
6. Union Research and Information Service, *The Economics of Prejudice,* San Francisco, 1952.
7. P-60, No. 90, T. 60.

8. *Economic Report of the President, 1974,* T. C-15, p. 266.
9. *New York Times,* July 7, 1956.
10. P-60, No. 90, T. 44, T. K.

Chapter 10.
1. *Wall Street Journal,* Feb. 28, 1974.
2. *Daily World,* Mar. 7, 1974.
3. Michael Reich, *The Economics of Racism,* in Edwards, Reich, and Weisskopf: *The Capitalist System,* Prentice-Hall, Englewood Cliffs, N.J., 1972, pp. 316, 318.
4. Op. Cit., pp. 317-318.
5. Op. Cit., p. 320.
6. U.S.-D-297.
7. Michael Tanzer: *The Sick Society,* Holt Rinehart Winston, N.Y., 1971, p. 98.
8. U.S.-D-225; *Employment and Earnings,* Jan. 1971, p. 133..
9. U.S. -D-295, 302.
10. BLS Special Labor Force Report 163, T. A-19, A-20.
10a. Thomas Dennis, *Political Affairs,* March, 1974.
11. Statistical Abstract of the U.S., T. 397, p. 250.
12. *New York Times,* May 3, 1973.
13. *The Sick Society,* pp. 104-105.
14. *Wall St. Journal,* Dec. 17, 1973.

Chapter 11.
1. W.E.B. Du Bois: *The Autobiography of W.E.B. Du Bois,* International Publishers, N.Y., 1968, p. 290.
2. U.S. Department of Commerce, *Minority-Owned Businesses:1969,* Washington 1971, T 1, T.B.; Survey of Current Business, July 1972.
3. *Minority-Owned Businesses: 1969,* T. C., p. 3.
4. Op. Cit., T 2, 5, 7, 8, 9.
5. *Black Enterprise,* June 1974; *Fortune,* July 1974, p. 116.
6. *New York Times,* May 24, 1971; Barry Cohen in *Daily World Magazine,* Aug. 19, 1972.
7. Paul H. Smith/Mary L. Mane, Letter to Cheatham and Smith customers, May 1973.
8. *Journal of Commerce,* Oct. 5, 1971; *New York Times,* Aug. 3, 1972.
9. *New York Times,* Aug. 17, 1973.
10. *Business Week,* Oct. 6, 1973.
11. *Metalworking News,* Dec. 6, 1971.
12. *New York Times,* July 30, 1972, Aug. 3, 1972.
13. Op. Cit., Nov. 11, 1973, Nov. 18, 1973.
14. Op. Cit., Dec. 27, 1973.
15. Special Analyses, Budget of the United States Government, Fiscal Year 1975, T. L-1, p. 183; T. E-8, p. 89, T. D-3, p. 63.
16. P-20, No. 249, T. 1.
16a. *The Afro American,* August 3, 1974.
17. *Minority-Owned Businesses, 1969,* T. 1, Part B, p. 16; Special Labor Force Report 163, T. A-1; P. 23, No. 46, T. 39, p. 51.
18. Henry Winston, *A Marxist-Leninist Critique of Roy Innis on Community Self-Determination and Martin Kilson on Education,* New Outlook Publishers, N.Y., 1973, p. 6.

19. *N.Y. Times,* Sept. 11, 1973.
20. *Op. Cit.,* July, 1971.
21. *Ibid.*
22. *Op. Cit.,* June 6, 1974.
23. *Op. Cit.,*Mar.10, 1974, Sec. IV, Advt.

Chapter 12.
1. Philip S. Foner, *History of the Labor Movement in the United States, Vol. 4.* International Publishers, New York, 1965, p. 127.
2. William Z. Foster, *History of the Communist Party,* Intl. Publishers, N.Y. 1952, p. 257.
3. Ray Marshall, *The Negro Worker,* Random House, N.Y., 1967, p. 29.
   3a. *New York Times,* May 6, 1974.
4. Op. Cit., p. 24.
5. P-23, No. 46, T 43.
6. Herbert R. Northrup and associates, *Negro Employment in Basic Industry,* University of Pennsylvania, Philadelphia, 1970, p. 7.
7. *Wall Street Journal,* May 23, 1972.
8. U.S.-D-227.
   8a. *Daily World,* July 30, 1974.
   8b. Ibid., July 31,1974.
9. N.Y. Times, Oct. 31, 1973. Mar. 21, 1974.
10. *The Negro Worker,* pp. 40-41.
11. W.Z. Foster, *The Negro People in American History,* Intl. Publishers, N.Y., 1954, pp. 367, 374.
12. US BLS, *Handbook of Labor Statistics, 1973,* T. 153, p. 345.

Chapter 13.
1. Northrup, *Op.* Cit., T. 20, p. 166.
2. 92nd Congress 2nd Session, *The Equal Employment Opporunity Act of 1972,* Committee Print Washington, 1972.
3. Budget of the United States Government Special Analyses, Fiscal Year 1975, p. 172.
4. EEOC *Annual Report,* Fiscal Year 1972, App. A
   4a. U.S. Commission on Civil Rights, *The Federal Civil Rights Enforcement Effort, a Reassessment,* Washington, Jan. 1973, pp. 25.
   4b. Herbert Hill, Speech, NAACP Convention, New Orleans, July 2, 1974.
5. Wall Street Journal, Feb. 5, 1974; Budget Special Analyses 1975, p. 177.
   5a. Wall Street Journal, Aug. 2, 1974.
6. Paul Delaney in *New York Times,* Jan. 19, 1974.
7. *Daily World,* Apr. 18, May 2, 1974, N.Y. Times, Apr. 14, 1974.
   7a. *Afro-American,*Sept. 21, 1974.
   7b. *Daily World,* Aug. 1, 1974.
8. U.S.-D-238.
9. U.S.-D-235, 232, 233.
10. U.S.-D-240.
11. U.S Commission on Civil Rights, *Op. Cit.,* pp. 42-43.
    11a. P-23, No. 48, T. 42.
12. *N.Y.Times,* Oct. 28, 1973.
    12a. *Ibid.,* Dec. 10, 1973.
13. Ibid., Dec. 10, 1973.

14. *Afro-American,* Mar. 26, 1974.

Chapter 14.
 1. *New York Times,* October 27, 1974.
 1a. *Daily World Magazine,* Mar. 23, 1974.
 2. V. Perlo, *The Unstable Economy,* International Publishers, N.Y., 1973, T. III-1, p. 27; 1972 Census of Manufacturers, Preliminary Report MC72 (P)-1, 1974.p. 2.
 3. *Monthly Labor Review, Aug. 1974, T. 1, p. 57.*
 4. *Chicago Defender,* March 12, 1974.
 5. A. Kudinov in *Pravda Vostoka,* Tashkent, Feb. 9, 1974.
 6. R. Tuzhuhamedov, *How the National Question was Solved in Soviet Central Asia,* Moscow, 1973, in English, pp. 184-185.

Index

By the Same Author

The Negro in Southern Agriculture
The Income 'Revolution'
Militarism and Industry
USA and USSR: The Economic Race
American Imperialism
How the Soviet Economy Works
The Empire of High Finance
The Unstable Economy